PRACTICE
MAKES
PERFECT®

Advanced
French
Grammar

PRACTICE MAKES PERFECT®

Advanced French Grammar

SECOND EDITION

Véronique Mazet, PhD

Mc
Graw
Hill
Education

New York Chicago San Francisco Athens London Madrid
Mexico City Milan New Delhi Singapore Sydney Toronto

1 2 3 4 5 6 7 8 9   LCR   22 21 20 19 18 17

ISBN   978-1-260-01125-8
MHID   1-260-01125-9

e-ISBN 978-1-260-01126-5
e-MHID   1-260-01126-7

Interior design by Village Typographers, Inc.

McGraw-Hill Education products are available at special quantity discounts to use as premiums and sales promotions or for use in corporate training programs. To contact a representative, please visit the Contact Us pages at www.mhprofessional.com

Contents

Introduction

This book is designed for people who have mastered the basics of the French language and wish to hone their skills with more challenging areas of grammar. The book's thorough explanations and expert tips will provide you with a solid basis for building longer and more complex sentences. By helping you better understand the mechanics of the language, instead of just applying sets of rules, it will give you increasing ease and self-confidence in communicating in French.

The book is ordered to reflect sentence construction: the first units are devoted to the verb, then the noun and pronoun, and, finally, to miscellaneous grammatical structures that constitute more challenges. In each unit you will find comprehensive explanations of the grammar, including numerous examples that illustrate and clarify each point. Along the way, sidebars provide further information, or offer tips or guidance on usage. At the end of several units you will find a recap section that can also be used as a quick reference. At the end of each unit, a variety of practice exercises will enable you to review your comprehension of the content covered in the unit. The complete answer key at the back of the book even includes extra explanations for the trickier questions.

I have deliberately chosen simple grammatical terms for reference so that non-experts, as well as those more comfortable with grammatical terms, can feel at ease. And since most learners function first in their native tongue, in this case English, the explanations are compared to English usage, and all the examples are translated into English as well.

The topics in this book have been especially chosen to appeal to high-intermediate and advanced learners.

This book will help you consolidate your knowledge. By the time you have gone through it, your French will be much closer to that of a native speaker.

About *la nouvelle orthographe*

In 1990, a revision of the French orthography was proposed by the government and approved by the **Académie française**. The **Académie** oversees the evolution and preservation of the French language. The goal was to streamline spelling by getting rid of many unnecessary quirks. It affected almost 2,500 words. Although the reform was unpopular at first, it was officially applied in 2016 when all major textbook publishers decided to finally implement it in their publications. In this book, the most common example of **la nouvelle orthographe** (new spelling) is the elimination of certain accent marks that don't change the pronunciation of a word. For example, the word **diner** used to have a circumflex over the 'i' (**dîner**). You can find a detailed list of the changes at https://en.wiktionary.org/wiki/Appendix:French_spelling_reforms_of_1990

Advanced
French
Grammar

Understanding the verb

There are many things you need to know about the verb. Conjugating it correctly is only a first step. To build a good sentence in French, you also need to be aware of usage: can the verb have an object or not (that is, is it transitive or intransitive?); does the verb require a particular preposition (is it transitive direct or indirect?); does it trigger the subjunctive or the indicative when followed by another conjugated verb? Several of these questions can be answered by a dictionary through direct information ("v.t." for *transitive verb* for instance), and through examples. Because French and English usage are different, you should not overlook the examples provided. They will show you the correct word order around the verb and tell you if the verb requires a preposition or not. Let's begin with a question whose answer determines a number of things about your sentence: can the verb have an object?

French transitive and intransitive verbs (verb + noun)

A transitive verb has an object that can be direct (verb + noun) or indirect (verb + preposition + noun). For instance, in French **manger** (*eat*) and **dire** (meaning *say*) are transitive verbs, because you can **manger quelque chose** (*eat something*) and **dire quelque chose** (*say something*). On the other hand, **aller** (*go*) is not transitive because you can't **aller quelque chose**!

English and French don't always have the same transitive and intransitive verbs. An example is the verb *to leave*, which is transitive in English (*I leave the house*, where *the house* is the direct object), but not in French: **partir** (*leave*) cannot take a direct object. As a result the French sentence must have either a different construction (verb + prepositional phrase, first example), or a synonym verb (here, **quitter**) that *is* transitive (second example):

Il est **parti du bureau** à cinq heures du soir.	*He left the office at five P.M.*
Il a **quitté le bureau** à cinq heures due soir.	*He left the office at five P.M.*

1

Some transitive verbs can be used without an object (**je mange**/*I am eating*), while others are not complete without their object expressed: **je donne** (*I give*) is incomplete because in French you need to say *what* it is you give. Still others, such as **fermer** (*close*), **perdre** (*lose*), **sortir** (*go out*), **monter** (*climb up*), **descendre** (*come down*), and **passer** (*pass, stop at*) can be used both ways: transitively (as verbs that can have an object), or intransitively (as verbs that can't have an object).

Now there is one little trick you need to remember with five of these "dual" verbs: when used *intransitively* (with no object) **descendre**, **monter**, **passer**, **rentrer** (*go back home*), and **sortir** take the auxiliary **être** to form a compound tense. However, when used transitively the auxiliary changes to **avoir** (examples 4 and 5; note the highlighted direct objects in the transitive examples).

Intransitive

Cette porte **ne ferme pas**.	*This door does not close.*
Il a joué et il **a perdu**!	*He played and he lost!*
Nous allons **sortir** samedi.	*We're going to go out Saturday.*
Elle **est passée** à la boulangerie.	*She went by the bakery.*
Nous **sommes descendus** dans un hôtel trois étoiles.	*We stayed in a three-star hotel.*

Transitive

Ferme **la porte**.	*Close the door.*
Elle a perdu **ses clés**.	*She lost her keys.*
N'oublie pas de sortir **la poubelle**.	*Don't forget to take the garbage can out.*
Ils **ont** passé **un bon week-end**.	*They had/spent a good weekend.*
As-tu descendu **ta valise**?	*Did you bring your suitcase downstairs?*

Verbs followed by a preposition

As far as the construction of a sentence goes, there is a difference between verb + infinitive and verb + noun. The same verb that requires a preposition before an infinitive may not require one before a noun, as you will see in the following pairs of examples. In this section we will focus mainly on verb + infinitive. For verb + noun, see Unit 10.

Il cherche **à s'enfuir**.	*He is trying to escape.*
Il cherche **la sortie**.	*He is looking for the exit.*
J'ai essayé **de t'appeler**.	*I tried to call you.*
Essayez **ce joli chapeau**.	*Try on this pretty hat.*
Il a choisi **de prendre** ses vacances en mai.	*He chose to take his vacation in May.*
Nous avons choisi **notre déssert**.	*We have chosen/decided on our dessert.*

Vocabulary: English to French

When dealing with these prepositional verbs, the first consideration is one of vocabulary. Does the preposition drastically change the meaning of the verb? In English, knowing if the verb and its preposition are separable or not is important because the verb + preposition often mean something different from the verb taken alone, without the preposition.

In the instance of *to knock* (at the door) and *to knock down* (an object), the preposition *down* is considered "inseparable" from its verb because together they constitute a unit of meaning. You will need to be aware of that when choosing the equivalent French verb. You may know the equivalent of the verb alone, but not necessarily that of the verb + preposition together.

Let's take *to look for* (**chercher**) and *to look like* (**ressembler à**). As you can see, each English verb + preposition has a different translation in French. These do not even include **regarder** (the exact translation of *to look* taken alone). So the next time you look up a verb like *to break up* in the dictionary, be sure to go down the list of entries until you find the exact match. Don't stop at *to break* (**casser** in French) and then add to it the equivalent French preposition (**en haut**), or you'll get an expression that probably does not exist in French. The correct French translation of *to break up* is **rompre**, and it is listed farther down your dictionary page.

The use of "empty prepositions" in French

Prepositional verbs in French have special usage problems. You know by now that you often find a preposition, usually **à** or **de**, between a conjugated verb and the infinitive that follows. In this usage, neither **à** nor **de** has a specific meaning (they don't mean *at* or *to* or *from*) and so we'll call them "empty prepositions." There are no rules to tell you which one to choose, and they have no equivalent in English. How will you know when there should be a preposition between a verb and a following infinitive? This section will help you eliminate some of the guesswork by providing useful guidelines on using these "prepositional verbs." (For conjugated verb + conjugated verb, see Unit 5.)

Verbs *never* followed by a preposition

One thing we can establish right now is that some verbs + infinitive never have a preposition:

- ◆ Modal verbs (**vouloir, devoir, pouvoir**):

Il **veut réussir**.	*He wants to succeed.*
Ils **doivent se lever** tôt.	*They must get up early.*
Tu ne **peux** pas **sortir**.	*You can't go out.*

◆ Several common verbs followed directly by the infinitive:

faire	*to do*
laisser	*to let*
vouloir	*to want*
aimer	*to like/to love*
détester	*to hate*
espérer	*to hope*
savoir	*to know*
falloir	*to be necessary (impersonal)*
valoir mieux	*to be better (impersonal)*
faillir	*to almost (do)*
oser	*to dare*
paraître	*to seem*
sembler	*to seem*

Il n'a pas **osé** lui **dire** un mensonge.	*He did not dare tell him a lie.*
Vous **semblez hésiter.**	*You seem to hesitate.*
Il **espère terminer** son projet à temps.	*He hopes to finish his project on time.*
Ils **aiment faire** la sieste en été.	*They like to nap in the summer.*
La police l'**a laissé passer.**	*The police let him pass.*
Il **faut savoir dire** « non ».	*One must know to say "no."*
Il **a failli tomber** de sa chaise.	*He almost fell off his chair.*
Je **viendrai** te **voir** bientôt.	*I will come to see you soon.*

◆ Verbs followed by the infinitive that express movement, including:

aller	*to go (including as used in the immediate future)*
descendre	*to go down(stairs)*
monter	*to go up(stairs)*
partir	*to leave to*
sortir	*to go out to*
venir	*to come to*

Sortons dîner au restaurant ce soir.	*Let's go eat out tonight.*
Viens dire « bon jour ».	*Come say "hello."*
Il **est parti faire** du jogging.	*He left to go jogging.*
Je **vais monter me coucher** tôt.	*I am going to go upstairs to sleep early.*

Venir de is used to express recent past: *to have just done something.* This expression should not be confused with the regular use of **venir**: *to come.*

◆ Verbs of perception (those involving the senses) such as **regarder** (*look*) and **entendre** (*listen*), followed by the infinitive:

J'ai **senti** mes jambes **faiblir**.	*I felt my legs weaken.*
Nous **écoutons** les oiseaux **chanter**.	*We listen to the birds sing.*
Ils **regardent** toujours le soleil **se coucher**.	*They always watch the sun set.*

Verbs + the preposition à

These common French verbs require the preposition **à** in front of an infinitive:

apprendre à	*to learn to*
arriver à	*to manage to*
avoir à	*must, to have to*
avoir du mal à	*to have difficulties in*
chercher à	*to try to*
commencer à	*to begin to*
continuer à	*to continue to*
hésiter à	*to hesitate to*
parvenir à	*to manage to*
passer son temps à	*to devote one's time to*
réussir à	*to succeed in*
se consacrer à	*to devote oneself to*
s'exercer à	*to practice (-ing)*
s'habituer à	*to get used to*
se mettre à	*to start to, to begin to*
se résigner à	*to give in to*
servir à	*to be used for*
tenir à	*to insist on*

Il **a commencé à pleuvoir** quand je suis sorti.	*It started to rain when I went out.*
Il **s'habituera à vivre** seul.	*He will get used to living alone.*
J'**apprends à skier**.	*I am learning to ski.*
Elle **passe** son temps **à regarder** la télé.	*She spends all her time watching TV.*
J'**hésite à prendre** cette décision.	*I hesitate to/am hesitant to make this decision.*
Ce bouton **sert à appeler** en cas d'urgence.	*This switch is used to call in case of emergency.*

Verbs + the preposition de

These common French verbs require the preposition **de** in front of an infinitive:

accepter de	*to agree to*
arrêter de	*to stop (-ing)*
cesser de	*to stop (-ing)*
choisir de	*to choose to*
craindre de	*to fear to*
décider de	*to decide to*
essayer de	*to try to*
finir de	*to stop (-ing)*
mériter de	*to deserve to*
oublier de	*to forget to*
parler de	*to talk about (-ing)*
proposer de	*to offer to*
refuser de	*to refuse to*
regretter de (+ past infinitive)	*to regret/to be sorry (to have done)*
risquer de	*to risk (-ing), may/might*
s'abstenir de	*to refrain from (-ing)*
se charger de	*to take on, accept (-ing)*
se dépêcher de	*to hurry to*
se souvenir de	*to remember to*
s'excuser de	*to apologize for (-ing); to excuse oneself for (-ing)*
suffire de (impersonal)	*to suffice to, to be enough to*

Il **méritait de recevoir** le premier prix.	*He deserved to receive the first prize.*
Cesse de te plaindre.	*Stop complaining.*
Il **a choisi d'apprendre** le français.	*He chose to learn French.*
Excusez-moi de vous **déranger.**	*Excuse me for bothering you.*
Je **regrette de t'avoir insulté.**	*I am sorry I insulted you.*
Il **risque de pleuvoir**; prends ton parapluie.	*It may rain; take your umbrella.*
J'**ai essayé de** le **suivre** mais il est trop rapide pour moi!	*I tried to follow him but he is too fast for me!*

Sequence of verbs with and without infinitives

In an English sentence such as *he did it because* . . . (**il a fait ça parce que...**); *I will come when* . . . (**je viendrai quand...**); *she'll do it if* . . . (**elle le fera si...**) verbs in each clause must be conjugated because of the linking words: **quand**, **si**, **parce que**. As a result each verb has a subject expressed, whether it is the same for all the verbs in the sentence (first example) or different subjects (second example). See also Unit 5.

| Je **viendrai** quand je **serai** prête. | *I will come when I am ready.* |
| Elle le **fera** si son père **est** d'accord. | *She will do it if her father agrees.* |

When several verbs follow each other without such a link (without **si**, **quand**, **parce que**, etc.), only the first verb is conjugated, and the following verbs must remain in the infinitive. This is when *you want to do something* (**je veux faire...**), or *forget to do something* (**j'oublie de faire...**), or *start doing something* (**je me mets à faire...**), where one subject rules all the verbs. Remember that some verbs require an "empty" preposition before an infinitive (examples 3 to 5).

Elle **voudrait inviter** ses amis.	*She would like to invite her friends.*
Leur fils **semble grandir** rapidement.	*Their son seems to grow up quickly.*
J'**oublie** toujours **de prendre** un parapluie.	*I always forget to take an umbrella.*
L'enfant **s'est mis à pleurer** sans raison.	*The child started to cry for no reason.*
Nous **hésitons à acheter** une nouvelle voiture.	*We hesitate to buy a new car.*

In the previous examples, all the verbs in the sentence have the same subject. Is this always the case? Does a sequence of infinitives always imply the "same subject for all"? Not necessarily. There are several scenarios when it does not. Let's begin with verbs of perception. (For the sequence of conjugated verbs see Unit 5.)

Verbs of perception

With verbs of perception (**regarder**, **entendre**, etc.), even though each verb has a subject of its own, subsequent verb(s) must remain in the infinitive. In the example that follows, **elle** is the subject of **regarde**, but **le bébé** is the subject of **dormir**.

| Elle **regarde le bébé dormir**. | *She watches the baby sleep.* |

If the main verb is in a compound tense with **avoir**, the past participle agrees with the direct object of the main verb as follows: with the direct object pronouns **la** (feminine) and **les** (masculine and feminine plural), as in the following second and fourth lines.

| —Tu as entendu **les enfants**? | *"Did you hear the kids?"* |
| —Je **les** ai entendu**s** rire. | *"I heard them laugh."* |

| —Vous avez vu **la lune** se lever? | *"Did you see the moon rise?"* |
| —Oui, je l'ai vu**e** se lever. | *"Yes, I saw it rise."* |

There are six common verbs of perception in French:

INFINITIVE	PAST PARTICIPLE	
apercevoir	aperçu	*to see (from a distance)*
écouter	écouté	*to listen to*
entendre	entendu	*to hear*
regarder	regardé	*to look at*
sentir	senti	*to feel*
voir	vu	*to see*

A construction with the relative pronoun **qui** + conjugated verb can be used instead of the infinitive after a verb of perception. However, there is a slight difference in meaning when you use that construction. As the English translations with progressive forms indicate (see following), a relative clause + conjugated verb denotes complete simultaneity. The infinitive construction does not necessarily indicate this and is therefore more versatile.

Vous **avez vu** la lune **qui se levait**.	*You saw the moon (that was) rising.*
Tu **as entendu** les enfants **qui riaient**.	*You heard the kids (who were) laughing.*
Elle **regarde** le bébé **qui dort**.	*She watches the baby (who is) sleeping.*
Ils **ont senti** la terre **qui tremblait**.	*They felt the earth (that was) shaking.*

Reported commands and requests

In a sentence of the type *to ask, allow, invite, tell someone to do something*, where the first verb reports an order, a request, an offer, and so on, for someone else to do something, the second verb is in the infinitive, preceded by **à** (after a direct or an indirect object noun or pronoun) or **de** (only after an indirect object). This is how it works: the first verb has a direct or indirect (human) *object* which also functions as the *subject* of the subsequent infinitive. The following examples will clarify this; the human object and the preposition + infinitive are highlighted.

Il faut encourager **les jeunes à voter**.	*It is necessary to encourage young people to vote.*
Ils **m'**ont remercié **de les avoir aidés**.	*They thanked me for helping them.*
Permets-**leur de se coucher** à minuit.	*Allow them to go/Let them go to bed at midnight.*
Le docteur **m'**a conseillé **de faire** le régime.	*The doctor advised me to go on a diet.*
Je **te** défends **de toucher** à ça!	*I forbid you to touch this!*
Elle a invité **sa sœur à passer** les vacances chez elle.	*She invited her sister to spend the vacation with her.*
Elle a dit **aux enfants de dormir**.	*She told the kids to sleep.*

Note that this infinitive construction is used to report commands (*I asked him to help me*), and not for commands addressed directly to the person (*I want you to help me*) which require the subjunctive in French, as follows.

When the main verb does not have an indirect object (which is rare for this type of verb since *you tell "someone" to do something*), an indirect command cannot be expressed using the infinitive construction. In this case you must use a construction with the subjunctive. See Unit 6 for details and a list of such verbs.

Papa **exige que** Sébastien **aille chercher** *Papa demands that Sebastian go get his*
   ses affaires.   *things.*
Elle **souhaite que** les enfants **aillent** *She wishes that the kids would go to bed.*
   au lit.

Infinitive after a direct object: preposition à or de

aider quelqu'un **à** faire	*to help someone to do*
autoriser quelqu'un **à** faire	*to authorize someone to do*
charger quelqu'un **de** faire	*to entrust someone to do*
convaincre quelqu'un **de** faire	*to convince someone to do*
empêcher quelqu'un **de** faire	*to prevent someone from doing*
encourager quelqu'un **à** faire	*to encourage someone to do*
féliciter quelqu'un **de** faire/**d'**avoir fait	*to congratulate someone for*
forcer quelqu'un **à** faire	*to force someone to do*
inviter quelqu'un **à** faire	*to invite someone to do*
obliger quelqu'un **à** faire	*to force someone to do*
persuader quelqu'un **de** faire	*to persuade someone to do*
remercier quelqu'un **d'**avoir fait	*to thank someone for doing*

Infinitive after an indirect object: preposition de

demander **à** quelqu'un **de** faire	*to ask someone to do*
dire **à** quelqu'un **de** faire	*to tell someone to do*
permettre **à** quelqu'un **de** faire	*to allow someone to do*
proposer **à** quelqu'un **de** faire	*to propose to someone to do*
suggérer **à** quelqu'un **de** faire	*to suggest to someone to do*
conseiller **à** quelqu'un **de** faire	*to advise someone to do*
reprocher **à** quelqu'un **de** faire	*to blame someone for doing*
défendre/interdire **à** quelqu'un **de** faire	*to forbid someone to do*

When you are expressing that *you want someone to do something* (**je veux qu'on fasse...**), or *you forget that someone has done something* (**j'ai oublié qu'on a fait...**) in French, each verb is introduced by a linking word and has its own subject. As a result all verbs are conjugated. We will address this issue in Unit 5.

À or de followed by an infinitive?

This pesky issue has an easy fix. If the noun in your sentence is the subject of the conjugated verb (**être** in the examples below), use **à** + infinitive:

C'est difficile **à faire!**	*It is difficult to do.*
Les concombres sont parfois difficiles **à digérer.**	*Cucumbers are sometimes difficult to digest.*
Les petits chats sont amusants **à regarder.**	*Kittens are fun to watch.*

On the contrary, if the noun is the direct object of the infinitive, use **de**:

Il est difficile **de conjuger** le verbe « craindre »!	*It is difficult to conjugate the verb "craindre"!*
Il est parfois difficile **de digérer** les concombres.	*It is sometimes difficult to digest cucumbers.*

Easier yet: when the verb in the infinitive has a direct object, use the construction with **de**.

Il est stressant **de recevoir** des mauvaises notes.	*It is stressful to receive bad grades.*

Conjugating the verb

In this section we do not give a detailed review of specific verb tenses. Only the passive and the imperative will receive this treatment. We will, however, begin with a close look at conjugation patterns with which, once you understand how each pattern functions, you may be spared the annoying task of memorizing each verb conjugation separately.

French verbs are sorted by groups based on their conjugation patterns. There are three groups; the first one is the largest. It includes 90 percent of French verbs—the **-er** verbs. Here are some common examples:

accepter	*to accept, agree*
aider	*to help*
arrêter	*to stop*
autoriser	*to authorize*
décider	*to decide*
demander	*to ask*
empêcher	*to prevent*
encourager	*to encourage*
essayer	*to try*
féliciter	*to congratulate*
inviter	*to invite*
manger	*to eat*
oublier	*to forget*

parler	to talk
persuader	to persuade
proposer	to offer
refuser	to refuse
regretter	to regret
remercier	to thank
se charger	to take on
se dépêcher	to hurry
se rappeler	to remember
s'excuser	to apologize

The second conjugation group contains about 300 **-ir** verbs of the "long" form (with **-iss** before the ending in the plural and the imperfect). If you are not completely familiar with the conjugation of a regular **-ir** verb, there are two little tricks that can help you identify them, as opposed to the "short" form **-ir** verbs (conjugated differently). If the verb has an English translation in *-ish*, it generally belongs to the group of "long" form verbs: **finir** (*finish*), **périr** (*perish*). In addition, if it is derived from an adjective, it belongs to this group: *rouge: rougir, grand: grandir*. They often indicate change: **vieillir** (*grow old*), **jaunir** (*turn yellow*). Other regular **-ir** verbs will have to be learned as vocabulary. Here are some common examples:

avertir	to warn
choisir	to choose
finir	to finish
grandir	to grow
guérir	to heal, cure
obéir	to obey
périr	to perish
réagir	to react
réfléchir	to think
réussir	to succeed
rougir	to blush
vieillir	to grow old

Finally, the third group of verbs includes all those that do not belong to the previous two groups: the "short" form **-ir** verbs, **-re** verbs, **-oir** verbs, and all the other verbs; certain of these groups are called "irregular." This group has about 350 verbs in all. Among them only the "regular" **-re** verbs have a true conjugation pattern. The others follow individual patterns, often with stem changes, such as the verb **venir** (**je viens**, **nous venons**, **elles viennent**). Here are some common examples of verbs of the third group:

accueillir*	to welcome
boire	to drink
devenir	to become

dire	*to tell*
dormir	*to sleep*
obtenir	*to get/obtain*
offrir*	*to offer*
ouvrir*	*to open*
partir	*to leave*
prendre	*to take*
recevoir	*to receive*
rendre	*to return*
sentir.	*to feel*
servir	*to serve*
souffrir*	*to suffer*
tenir	*to hold*
vendre	*to sell*
venir	*to come*
voir	*to see*

*In the present tense, **-ir** verbs marked with an asterisk in the adjoining list are conjugated like **-er** verbs: **J'ouvre**, **nous ouvrons**; **je souffre**, **vous souffrez**, and so on.

Matching the subject and the verb

Beyond the obvious subject-verb agreement, some unusual cases deserve a special mention:

◆ Inversion

Inversion doesn't only occur in a question. Sometimes the real subject follows the verb and you need to look for it.

Dans la forêt se cachaient **des lutins**.	*In the forest, elves were hiding.*
Tout était calme, quand soudain retentit **un grand bruit**.	*All was quiet, when suddenly a loud noise was heard.*

◆ With the relative pronoun **qui**, the verb must agree with the antecedent of **qui**.

C'est **moi qui vais** choisir!	*It is I who will choose.*
C'est **toi qui as** encore gagné.	*It is you who won again.*

◆ When the subjects are linked by **ni** or **ou**, the verb is usually in the singular, but it can be found in the plural as well, if the two subjects are considered to be a group (second example).

| Son père **ou** sa mère **viendra** rencontrer le professeur. | *His father or his mother will come meet with the teacher.* |
| **Ni** la faim, **ni** la soif n'**arrêteront** sa progression. | *Neither hunger nor thirst will stop his progress.* |

◆ When adverbs of quantity are followed by **de** + a noun, the verb will agree with that noun.

Trop de sucre rendra ton café imbuvable.	*Too much sugar will make your coffee undrinkable.*
Peu de gens connaissent cette histoire.	*Few people know that story.*
En vacances, **la plupart du temps se passe** à jouer.	*On vacation, most of the time is spent playing.*

◆ When those adverbs of quantity are used alone (without **de** + noun), the tendency is to put the verb in the plural. This is logical, as the examples will demonstrate.

| J'ai invité mes amis; **la plupart sont venus**. | *I invited my friends; most came.* |

It is clear that **la plupart** refers to **mes amis**, and so the verb **venir** is in the plural.

| Beaucoup de candidats vont se présenter, mais **combien réussiront?** | *Many candidates will apply, but how many will succeed?* |

Here too, **combien** implies **combien de candidats** so it is only logical to conjugate **réussir** in the plural.

◆ The following are always followed by a verb in the singular: **chacun; plus d'un; tout le monde; on; aucun(e); personne; rien; tout.**

| **Personne n'est arrivé** en retard. | *Nobody came late.* |
| Pendant un orage, **chacun s'inquiète**. | *During a storm, everybody worries.* |

◆ Percentages alone are followed by a verb in the plural, unless the number is smaller than 2% (second example, below). Note however, that in English, the singular is typically used.

| Pour sa commission, **20% sont** suffisants. | *For his commission, 20% is ("are") enough.* |
| **1,7% s'est abstenu** de voter. | *1.7% abstained from voting.* |

Simple tenses and compound tenses

Conjugation forms are not equivalent in French and in English. An English compound tense may have a simple tense French equivalent, and vice versa. You will find a useful table at the end of this section.

French simple tenses

A simple tense is a tense that does not require an auxiliary verb (**être** or **avoir** in French) to be conjugated. The forms are marked by the verb endings. In French, the present, **imparfait**, **passé simple**, future, present subjunctive, and present conditional are simple, single-verb forms. See the following first two examples for affirmative, negative, and interrogative sentences. In English, even a simple tense like the present or the preterit, requires an auxiliary in negative and interrogative sentences (last two examples).

Il **fera** ses devoirs plus tard.	*He **will do** his homework later.*
Je **voyagerais** si j'avais le temps.	*I **would travel** if I had the time.*
Il **adore** le jus d'orange.	*He **loves** orange juice.*
Il **n'aime pas** le coca.	*He **does** not **like** Coke.*
Parlez-vous chinois?	***Do** you **speak** Chinese?*

French compound tenses

These are compound or two-verb tenses formed by adding a conjugated auxiliary verb (**être** or **avoir**) to the past participle of the verb. The **passé composé** (following first and second examples), pluperfect (example 3), **futur antérieur** (example 4), past subjunctive (example 5), and past conditional (example 6), are compound tenses. The **passé antérieur** is included in this group, although it is used rarely; it is formed with the **passé simple** of the auxiliary.

Nous **sommes sortis** hier soir.	*We went out last night.*
Ils ne **sont** pas **allés** au cinéma.	*They did not go to the movies.*
Elle n'**avait** jamais **vu** ça.	*She had never seen that.*
Auras-tu **fini** avant le diner?	*Will you be done by dinnertime?*
Je regrette qu'il n'**ait** pas **fait** beau pour la fête.	*I regret that the weather was not nice for the party.*
J'**aurais** déjà **fini** si on ne m'**avait** pas **interrompu!**	*I would have already finished if I had not been interrupted!*

The following table summarizes conjugation patterns. (The English negative and interrogative forms are not given if the English tense is a compound form in the affirmative.)

Présent

Je parle	*I talk*
Je ne parle pas	*I don't talk*
Parles-tu?	*Do you talk?*

Imparfait

Je parlais	*I talked*
Je ne parlais pas	*I did not talk*
Parlais-tu?	*Did you talk?*

Futur

Je parlerai	*I will talk*
Je ne parlerai pas	*I will not talk*
Parleras-tu?	*Will you talk?*

Conditionnel

Je parlerais	*I would talk*

Passé composé

J'ai parlé	*I have spoken (often, "I spoke")*

Plus-que-parfait

J'avais parlé	*I had spoken*

Futur antérieur

J'aurai parlé	*I will have spoken*

Conditionnel passé

J'aurais parlé	*I would have spoken*

The passive form

The passive denotes that the subject receives the action rather than performing it. In the first example below, the mouse does not "eat", and the cat (also called the "agent") is the one doing the action.

La souris est mangée par le chat.	*The mouse is eaten by the cat.*
Le jardin a été inondé par la pluie.	*The yard was inundated with rain.*

In the second example, the direct object of the main verb becomes the apparent subject of the verb in a passive sentence (**le jardin** in the example). The true subject (**la pluie** in the example) is the "agent" and is usually introduced by **par**.

The passive is formed with the auxiliary **être** + past participle, but it is not a past tense unless **être** itself is in a past tense (in example 1 below, **être** is in the **passé composé**). In the passive, the past participle of the main verb, not of **être**, always agrees with the subject of **être**; it is used like an adjective.

La forteresse a été **construite** par les Templiers.	*The fortress was built by the Templars.*
La mariée est **suivie** des demoiselles d'honneur.	*The bride is followed by the bridesmaids.*
Les enfants sont **récompensés** pour leurs bonnes notes.	*The kids are rewarded for their good grades.*
Les nouvelles sont **envoyées** vers 4 heures du matin.	*The news is sent at around 4 A.M.*

A few verbs require **de** instead of **par**, for example: **redouter** (*to dread*); **craindre** (*to fear*); **obéir** (*to obey*); and **suivre** (*to follow*) (second example on the preceding page). But often, as in English, the "agent" is not mentioned (third and fourth examples, on the preceding page).

The passive is formed with the auxiliary **être** + the past participle, but it is not a past tense unless **être** itself is in a past tense (in the first example below, **être** is in the **passé composé**). In the passive, the past participle of the main verb, not of **être**, always agrees with the subject of **être**; it is used like an adjective (examples 2–5). The passive form works almost the same way in French and in English, except for one small yet crucial detail: if in English almost any verb can be put into the passive, in French, only verbs that are transitive direct (that can take a direct object) can.

The direct object of the main verb becomes the apparent subject of the verb in a passive sentence (**le jardin** in example 1). The true subject (**la pluie** in example 1), also called the "agent," is usually introduced by **par**. A few verbs require **de** instead: for example, **redouter** (*dread*), **craindre** (*fear*), **obéir** (*obey*), **suivre** (*follow*). But often, as in English, the "agent" is not mentioned (examples 4 and 5).

Le jardin **a été inondé par** la pluie.	*The yard was inundated/flooded by the rain.*
La mariée **est suivie des** demoiselles d'honneur.	*The bride is followed by the bridesmaids.*
La forteresse **a été construite par** les Templiers.	*The fortress was built by the Knights Templar.*
Les enfants **sont récompensés** pour leurs bonnes notes.	*The kids are rewarded for their good grades.*
Les nouvelles **sont envoyées** vers quatre heures du matin.	*The news is sent at around four A.M.*

Transitive direct verbs only

In French, only verbs that are transitive direct can be put in the passive form. Verbs that only have an indirect object can't have a passive form. In addition, the following verbs cannot be put in the passive form: **avoir** (*to have*), **vouloir** (*to want*), **chercher** (*to look for*) [but not **rechercher** (*to research*)], **porter** (in the sense of *to wear*), **pouvoir** (*to be able to*) and pronominal verbs.

The alternative to the English passive form must be **on** + conjugated verb when no agent is expressed (first and second examples). When the agent is mentioned, it becomes the subject of the active verb (as in the last two examples).

On parle anglais ici.	*English is spoken here.*
On leur **a demandé** de quitter la salle.	*They were asked to leave the room.*
Ses étudiants **se souviendront** de ce prof.	*This prof will be remembered by his students.*
Un Espagnol **porte** le maillot jaune.	*The yellow jersey is worn by a Spaniard.*

Some French verbs can have a double object construction, with a direct object + an indirect object (e.g., **donner quelque chose à quelqu'un**). Since the human object of such verbs (**donner**) is an indirect object, and therefore can't become the subject of a passive verb, French verbs that take both types of objects are rarely, if ever, found in the passive. Here are some examples; note that English naturally uses a passive, whereas the French construction is active:

On a donné une médaille au vainqueur.	*The winner was given a medal.*
On a promis une augmentation aux employés.	*The employees were promised a raise.*
Mes amis me l'**ont dit**.	*I was told by my friends.*

Avoiding the passive form in French

In many cases, and especially when the "agent" is expressed, French tries to avoid the passive. Instead, usage prefers a construction with subject + active verb, when the "agent" is expressed, or, when no specific agent is expressed, **on** + active verb. In some cases, a singular or plural pronominal (reflexive) form with **se** is used (although pronominal verbs themselves are never used in the passive). The following examples show possible alternatives to the passive for each sentence. They also demonstrate the differences between French and English usage; the passive is quite dominant in English. There's no alternative for it when the sentence does not have a true subject expressed! (See following examples 1 and 6.)

La vieille grange **sera démolie** dimanche.	*The old barn will be demolished on Sunday.*
On démolira la vieille grange dimanche.	*The old barn will be demolished on Sunday.*
Ce modèle n'**est** plus **vendu**.	*This model is no longer sold.*
On ne **vend** plus ce modèle.	*This model is no longer sold.*
Ce modèle ne **se vend** plus.	*This model is no longer sold.*
Les plats **sont préparés** à l'avance.	*The dishes are prepared in advance.*
On prépare les plats à l'avance.	*The dishes are prepared in advance.*
Les plats se préparent à l'avance.	*The dishes are prepared in advance.*
Mon portefeuille **a été retrouvé** par un passant.	*My wallet was found by a passerby.*
Un passant a retrouvé mon portefeuille.	*A passerby found my wallet.*

Le matin les volets **sont ouverts** par Papa.			*In the morning, the blinds are opened by Dad.*
Papa ouvre les volets le matin.			*In the morning, Dad opens the blinds.*
Ce débat **est retransmis** en direct.			*This debate is broadcast live.*
On retransmet ce débat en direct.			*This debate is broadcast live.*

The imperative

The imperative (or command form) uses no subject noun or pronoun. It has only three forms; they are all borrowed from the present tense conjugation: second-person singular (corresponding to **tu**); and first- and second-person plural (corresponding respectively to **nous** and **vous**). Exceptions are the verbs **avoir**, **être**, **vouloir**, and **savoir** (*know*) that borrow their command forms from the subjunctive.

The ending therefore becomes the only marker of the subject in the imperative.

AVOIR	ÊTRE	SAVOIR	VOULOIR
aie	sois	sache	—
ayons	soyons	sachons	—
ayez	soyez	sachez	veuillez

Note that **savoir** drops the -i of the **nous** and **vous** subjunctive forms, and that **vouloir** uses only one imperative form.

Verbs that form their present tense second-person singular in **-es** lose the -s when the form is used for commands. This includes the irregular verbs **aller: va; savoir: sache; avoir: aie**; and **-ir** verbs like **ouvrir**, that end in **-es** in the present (as in the following list). The other verbs maintain their -s if they had one in the present tense (two final examples).

ouvrir	Ouvre!	*Open!*
offrir	Offre... !	*Offer . . . !*
souffrir	Souffre!	*Suffer!*
couvrir	Couvre... !	*Cover . . . !*
cueillir	Cueille... !	*Pick . . . ! (a plant, a flower)*

Achète du pain s'il te plaît!	*Buy some bread please!*
Va au lit tout de suite!	*Go to bed immediately!*
Ouvre la porte.	*Open the door.*
Finis ton travail.	*Finish your work.*
Prends ton manteau.	*Take your coat.*

When there is a pronoun in the sentence, whether it is reflexive (examples 1 and 2) or other (examples 3 and 4), it always follows the verb in affirmative commands. In that position, **me** and **te** become **moi** and **toi**.

Couvre-**toi**.	*Cover yourself.*
Reposez-**vous**.	*Rest./Take a rest.*
Regardez-**moi**.	*Look at me.*
Parlons-**lui**.	*Let's talk to him.*

If the pronoun is **y** or **en**, the **tu** forms retain the -**s** that would normally be dropped in the imperative. This is done for ease of pronunciation; thus you must pronounce a *z* sound for the *liaison* between the verb and the pronoun.

Achète du pain s'il te plaît!	*Buy some bread please!*
Achète**s-en**!	*Buy some!*
Va au lit tout de suite!	*Go to bed immediately!*
Vas-**y**!	*Go there!*

Negative commands

The verb form in a negative command is formed the same way as for affirmative commands, and the negative words surround the verb.

N'achète pas le journal aujourd'hui.	*Don't buy the paper today.*
Ne faites pas de bêtises pendant mon absence.	*Don't do anything silly while I'm gone.*

However, negative commands differ from their affirmative counterpart when there is a pronoun (an object pronoun or a reflexive pronoun) in the sentence. In negative commands the pronoun precedes the verb, as in a regular sentence.

Ne te promène pas seul le soir.	*Don't take a walk alone in the evening.*
N'y va pas!	*Don't go there!*
Ne les appelle pas.	*Don't call them.*

The past imperative

This form is rare, but it does exist. Once you are familiar with it, you might even find it useful. The past imperative is a compound tense formed with the usual culprits: an auxiliary (**être** or **avoir**) conjugated in the imperative + the past participle of the verb. Strangely, though, the past imperative expresses an action that must be done by a certain time . . . in the future!

Ayez fini quand je rentre!	*Be done by the time I come home!*
Sois rentrée avant minuit sinon...	*Be home before midnight or else . . .*

There is a more commonly used alternative to this form that uses the verb **tâcher de** (*try to*) + the past infinitive.

Ayez fini quand je rentre!   *Be done by the time I come home!*
or: **Tachez d'avoir fini** quand je rentre!   *Be done by the time I come home!*

Sois rentrée avant minuit sinon...   *Be home before midnight otherwise/or else . . .*

or: **Tache d'être rentrée** avant minuit sinon...   *Be home before midnight otherwise/or else . . .*

EXERCICE

1·1

*Determine if the following verbs are transitive direct or indirect by adding **à** or nothing in the blanks.*

1. Vous rendez visite _____ vos vieux amis.

2. Ils écoutent _____ le prof avec attention.

3. Tu as écrit _____ tes cousins?

4. Allez-vous téléphoner _____ vos grands-parents?

5. Parlez-vous souvent _____ vos voisins?

6. Tu as invité _____ tous tes amis à la fête.

7. Tu dois attendre _____ tes parents.

8. Entends-tu _____ le prof?

9. Tu écoutes parfois _____ de la musique française?

10. Qu'est-ce que tu as dit _____ tes parents?

11. Regarde _____ ces enfants qui jouent!

12. Nous allons appeler _____ le docteur si la fièvre continue.

*Review the lists of verbs that require an "empty" preposition before an infinitive, and complete the sentences with either **à** or **de**.*

1. On m'a chargé _____ vous transmettre un message.

2. Je vous remercie _____ m'avoir aidé.

3. Les enfants me reprochent _____ être absent trop souvent.

4. Personne ne pourra me persuader _____ faire ça.

5. Cette publicité encourage les enfants _____ lire.

6. Le docteur m'a interdit _____ courir à cause de mon genou.

7. Sa mère l'obligeait toujours _____ finir ses légumes.

8. Est-ce que tu m'autorises _____ sortir?

9. Il n'a jamais appris _____ nager.

10. Il m'a invitée _____ dîner, mais il a oublié _____ payer l'addition.

11. Il a commencé _____ pleuvoir au moment où je suis sorti.

12. As-tu réussi _____ trouver le livre rare que tu cherchais?

13. Essayons _____ ouvrir cette vieille porte.

14. Il a cessé _____ pleuvoir: sortons!

15. Il faut éviter _____ manger trop de sucre.

16. Je me chargerai _____ envoyer les invitations.

17. Il risque _____ pleuvoir aujourd'hui.

18. Nous méritons _____ prendre un jour de congé.

19. Malgré son accident il a continué _____ faire de la moto.

20. Attention, tu risques _____ tomber.

21. Cet exercice est trop difficile _____ comprendre.

22. Allons aider les voisins _____ chercher leur chien.

23. N'hésite jamais _____ nous appeler.

24. Après le 1er janvier, il se mettra _____ faire de la gym.

25. Le directeur s'abstient toujours _____ faire des commentaires.

26. Après mes efforts, je crois que je mérite _____ me reposer.

27. L'opération risque _____ pas réussir.

28. L'ouvrier a proposé _____ refaire ce travail raté.

29. Si tu choisis _____ passer par ici, préviens-nous.

30. Elle regrette _____ pas avoir passé son permis de conduire.

EXERCICE

1·3

First, review the section on reported commands and requests, then put the following sentences into French.

1. He told them he was leaving.

   _____

2. The doctor advised me to eat less.

   _____

3. Never blame your parents for pushing you to do better. (**vous**)

   _____

4. Ask Julien to help you. (**tu**)

   _____

5. Who authorized that driver to open the gate?

   _____

6. I propose (to you) to try a new approach. (**tu**)

   _____

7. I thank you for helping us last night. (**vous**)

_____

8. Knowing several languages allows children to understand other cultures.

_____

9. Don't prevent your friends from helping you. (**vous**)

_____

10. She will never convince her husband to eat snails.

_____

11. They made the sick sailor return to port.

_____

12. Try to think about something else. (**tu**)

_____

13. He always entrusts his employees to close.

_____

First, review the compound tenses and the passive form. Then, put the following sentences into French.

1. Will you have arrived by seven? (**tu**)

_____

2. They would take a trip around the world if they could.

_____

3. I had warned you!

_____

4. You would have been late if you had taken the bus. (**tu**)

_____

5. Will you be able to finish in time?

_____

6. An easy solution has been accepted.

_____

7. The results will be posted soon. (**afficher**)

_____

8. Enthusiastic help wanted. (**chercher**)

_____

9. The reason was explained to me by a specialist.

_____

10. Minette was promised a treat.

_____

11. They were allowed to go to bed at midnight.

_____

12. They were given two options.

_____

13. We should have been told that it was canceled.

_____

Focus on vocabulary and verb construction, and put the following sentences into French.

1. This may be difficult to do.

_____

2. Did you learn to swim? (**tu**)

_____

3. I forgot to let the dog out.

_____

4. The president of the federation congratulated the players for winning the match.

_____

5. I would like to hear the birds sing.

_____

6. Do you want to watch the sun set? (**tu**)

_____

7. We almost missed the train.

_____

8. He managed to save enough money for his retirement.

_____

9. You will have difficulties doing this alone. (**tu**) (*don't use* **difficulté**)

_____

10. Don't try to follow me! (**tu**) (*don't use* **essayer**)

_____

11. He chose to come alone.

_____

12. Stop worrying! (**tu**)

_____

13. Do you think they might be late? (**tu**)

_____

14. What is this basket used for?

_____

15. I gave in to keeping my old car a little while longer.

_____

16. I insist on doing this task alone.

_____

*Using the present tense (or the **passé composé** when indicated in parentheses), match the verb to the subject.*

1. Presque tout le monde _____ (préférer) le soleil à la pluie.

2. Peu _____ (être) d'accord avec lui.

3. Chacun _____ (réussir) son projet. *(passé composé)*

4. Sur la rivière _____ (passer) des péniches.

5. C'est toi qui _____ (sortir) la poubelle ce soir.

6. « Quelle heure est-il, s'il vous plaît? » nous _____ (demander) poliment la petite fille. *(passé composé)*

7. C'est toujours nous qui _____ (effacer) le tableau.

8. Ce sont ceux qui _____ (avoir) des vacances en hiver qui _____ (partir) au ski.

9. Un peu de peinture _____ (suffir) à transformer cette pièce. *(passé composé)*

10. Il y avait beaucoup de concurrents au départ, mais plus d'un _____ (abandonner), et très peu _____ (franchir) la ligne d'arrivée. *(passé composé)*

11. Nous nous promenions dans la forêt silencieuse quand tout à coup _____ (retentir) de grands cris. *(passé composé)*

12. C'est toujours moi qui t' _____ (attendre)!

13. La plupart des touristes _____ (apprécier) la cuisine française.

14. Vous êtes les plus grands et c'est vous qui _____ (se plaindre) toujours.

15. Personne ne _____ (entendre) la sonnette. *(passé composé)*

16. La plupart des députés _____ (refuser) de voter. Seulement 1% _____ (voter). *(passé composé)*

17. Trop de chocolat _____ (aller) te rendre malade.

18. En vacances, chacun _____ (faire) ce qui lui plaît.

Compound tenses and agreement of the past participle

In French, all the compound tenses (made up of the auxiliary + past participle) are past tenses, except for the **futur antérieur** and the past imperative (see the previous unit). The **imparfait** and **passé simple** are the only two simple (non-compound) past tenses and won't be considered in this unit. Since all compound tenses are formed similarly, when we say **passé composé** in this unit, we refer to all the compound tenses.

Most verbs form their **passé composé** with the auxiliary **avoir**, including the verbs **être** and **avoir** and impersonal verbs such as **pleuvoir** (*rain*) and **falloir** (*must*). All pronominal verbs and a number of intransitive verbs, most of which refer to movement, use the auxiliary **être**. These verbs are listed here:

aller	*to go*
venir (revenir, devenir, parvenir)	*to come (come back, become, manage to)*
arriver	*to arrive*
partir	*to leave*
accourir	*to come running*
entrer (rentrer)	*to enter (go home)*
sortir (de)	*to go out (of)*
monter	*to go/climb up*
descendre	*to go down*
tomber	*to fall*
rester	*to stay, remain*
retourner	*to return*
passer (à/par/chez)	*to pass (by/at), stop by*
naître	*to be born*
mourir	*to die*

27

Monter, descendre, rentrer, sortir, and **passer** are conjugated with **être** in the **passé composé** when used intransitively (as verbs that can't take an object), as in following examples 1 to 3. When used transitively (with an object), they are conjugated with **avoir** (examples 4 to 6).

Intransitively

Elle **est montée** au premier étage.	*She went upstairs.*
Nous **sommes passés** chez toi à huit heures.	*We came by your house at eight.*
Ils **sont rentrés** tard.	*They came home late.*

Transitively

Il **a monté ma valise.**	*He took my suitcase upstairs.*
J'**ai passé mon livre** à un ami.	*I lent my book to a friend.*
J'**ai rentré les plantes** avant le gel.	*I brought the plants in before the freeze.*

Passé composé with avoir

When the auxiliary of the **passé composé** is **avoir**, the past participle remains invariable: it does not agree with the subject or with the object that follows it.

Ils **ont pris** la navette.	*They took the shuttle.*
Nous **avons regardé** la télé.	*We watched television.*

However, when the direct object (noun or pronoun) precedes **avoir**, the past participle must agree with it. This scenario happens when the direct object is a pronoun that precedes, it also happens in a question (or exclamation) that begins with **quel/quelle/quels/quelles** or **combien**, and in a relative clause introduced by **que**.

Ils l'ont **prise**. (la navette)	*They took it. (the shuttle)*
Nous l'avons **regardée**. (la télé)	*We watched it. (television)*

Agreement with an object pronoun

An object pronoun usually precedes the verb of which it is the object. When the verb is in the **passé composé**, the past participle agrees in number and gender with its *preceding direct object*. This happens with the direct object pronouns **la (l')** (feminine), **les**, **nous**, and **vous** (masculine or feminine plural). There is no agreement of the past participle with other object pronouns (following final two examples).

Ce chien **nous** a **adorés**.	*This dog has loved us.*
Tes lunettes? Je **les** ai **vues** sur la table.	*Your glasses? I saw them on the table.*
La navette? Je l'ai **vue** partir.	*The shuttle? I saw it leave.*

However, agreement of the past participle does not occur with indirect object pronouns, or with the pronouns **y** and **en**.

Je **leur** ai vite répondu.	*I responded to them quickly.*
Il m'a prêté des livres, mais j'**en** avais déjà lu plusieurs.	*He lent me some books, but I had already read some of them.*

Whenever the sentence also has an infinitive, two things can happen. As is often the case, the object of the conjugated verb (the verb in the **passé composé**) doubles as subject of that infinitive and the regular rules of agreement of the past participle apply: the past participle agrees with the object pronoun that is placed before **avoir**. In the first example below, **la navette spatiale** is the object of the verb **avons vu,** as well as the subject of the infinitive **traverser**.

Nous avons vu la navette spatiale traverser le ciel.	*We saw the space shuttle cross the sky.*
Nous **l'**avons vu**e** traverser le ciel.	*We saw it cross the sky.*
J'ai entendu les choristes chanter.	*I heard the choir sing.*
Je **les** ai entendu**s** chanter.	*I heard them sing.*
Elle a regardé sa fille jouer.	*She watched her daughter play.*
Elle **l'**a regardé**e** jouer.	*She watched her play.*

Sometimes though, the direct object does not double as the subject of the infinitive. In such cases, there will not be an agreement of the past participle. In the first example below **la vieille prison** is the object of **voir** but is not the subject of **démolir**.

Nous avons vu démolir la vieille prison.	*We saw the old jail being demolished.*
Nous l'avons vu démolir.	*We saw it being demolished.*
Ils ont regardé leurs châteaux brûler.	*They watched their castles burn down.*
Ils les ont regardé brûler.	*They watched them burn down.*

quel

With the interrogative or exclamatory adjective **quel** (**quels, quelle, quelles**), the past participle agrees with the noun that **quel** modifies, when that noun is the direct object of the verb in the passé composé. This happens with the constructions: **quel(le)(s)**+ noun, and **quel(le) est/quel(le)s sont** + relative clause introduced by **que**, and no other relative pronoun. See the last example in which the relative clause is introduced by **dont**, and no agreement occurs.

Quelle actrice as-tu préférée?	*Which actress did you prefer?*
Quels employés a-t-il licenciés?	*Which employees did he lay off?*

Quelles sont les chaussures que tu as mises samedi soir?	*Which are the shoes that you wore Saturday night?*
Quelle peur j'ai eue!	*How scared I got!*

But:

Quels sont **les sujets dont** il a parlé?	*What are the topics that he talked about?*

Agreement also occurs with the interrogative pronoun **lequel** (**laquelle, lesquels, lesquelles**).

Laquelle de ces **robes** as-tu choisie?	*Which one of those dresses did you choose?*
Lesquels de ces **livres** as-tu lus?	*Which one of those books did you read?*

combien

If **combien** asks *how many?* about the preceding direct object of the **passé composé** with **avoir** (**invitations** in the first example), the past participle must agree with that object.

Combien d'invitations as-tu reçues?	*How many invitations did you receive?*
Combien de vestes a-t-il essayées avant de se décider?	*How many jackets did he try on before making up his mind?*
Combien de cadeaux as-tu offerts aux enfants?	*How many gifts did you give to the children?*

However, if the noun described by **combien** is not the direct object of the verb, no agreement occurs. In the following first example, **fois** is *not* the direct object of **as-tu lu**.

Combien de fois as-tu **lu** ce livre?	*How many times did you read this book?*
Combien d'enfants ont **reçu** des cadeaux?	*How many children got gifts?*

Agreement in a relative clause with que

The past participle agrees with the relative pronoun *que* when its antecedent (highlighted in the following examples) is the direct object of the verb in the passé composé. This is the same rule that applies to the interrogative pronoun *quel(le)(s)* (see earlier discussion).

La tarte que j'ai mangée était délicieuse.	*The pie that I ate was delicious.*
Il a lu tous **les livres qu'**on lui avait prêtés.	*He read all the books that were loaned to him.*
La punition que tu as reçue était sévère.	*The punishment you got was harsh.*
Quelle est **la scène que** tu as préférée?	*Which scene did you prefer?*

The situation changes when the relative clause has an infinitive. When the antecedent of **que** is the direct object of the infinitive (instead of the antecedent of the verb in the passé composé), there is *no* agreement of the past participle. In the following examples, the infinitive and its object are highlighted:

La bague « en or » qu'il a voulu me **vendre** était fausse.	*The "gold" ring that he tried to sell me was fake.*
Je suis au courant **des efforts** qu'il a dû **faire**.	*I know about the efforts that he had to make.*
Où sont **les CDs** que j'avais choisi d'**écouter**?	*Where are the CDs that I had chosen to listen to?*
La composition qu'il a dû **écrire** était difficile.	*The paper he had to write was hard.*

Exceptions

The past participles of the following verbal expressions must remain invariable: **laisser** and **faire** before an infinitive,* impersonal expressions such as **il y a eu** (*there was*), **il a fallu** (*it was necessary*), **il a fait** (in weather expressions), **il a plu** (*it rained*), **il a paru** (*it seemed*), and the fixed expression **l'échapper belle** (*to make a narrow escape*).

Elle l'a **échappé** belle!	*She made a narrow escape!*
J'ai cassé **mes lunettes** parce que je **les** ai **laissé** tomber.	*I broke my glasses because I dropped them.*
Si tu voyais **les dégâts qu'il y a eu**.	*If you could see the damage there was.*
La montre que j'ai **fait** réparer marche bien maintenant.	*The watch I had repaired works well now.*
Tu ne peux pas savoir **les choses qu'**il a **fallu** faire pour amuser ce bébé!	*You have no idea the things we had to do to entertain that baby!*

*This rule follows the French spelling reform of 1990 which is slow to be adopted universally. As a result you will still come across French grammar books that tell you to make **fait** and **laissé** agree with the preceding direct object before an infinitive.

Agreement of the past participle with être: non-pronominal verbs

We will consider non-pronominal verbs first and deal with pronominal verbs separately.

When the auxiliary of a compound tense is **être**, you can consider the past participle as an "adjective." Adjectives are naturally found after **être**. Even though these verbs are active, not passive, the verb **être** will remind you to make the past participle agree with its *subject*, as you would with an adjective.

Elle est parti**e**.	*She left.*
Ils sont arrivé**s** en retard.	*They arrived late.*
Elles sont né**es** en Afrique.	*They were born in Africa.*
Les touristes sont entré**s** dans le musée.	*The tourists entered the museum.*

The passive form in the **passé composé**

In the **passé composé** and other compound tenses, the passive is always formed with the conjugated auxiliary + **été** + past participle. In that construction, **été** remains invariable, but the past participle that follows agrees (as highlighted in the following examples) with the subject of **être**. (See Unit 1 for more on the passive.)

Les enfants ont été **punis**.	*The kids were punished.*
Elle aurait été **avertie** si elle avait gagné.	*She would have been warned if she had won.*
Son opération a été **bâclée**.	*His surgery was botched.*
Les limites de temps n'ont pas été **respectées**.	*The time limitations were not respected.*

Passé composé with être: pronominal verbs

For the agreement of the past participle of a pronominal verb, consider the reflexive pronoun **se** (as well as **me**, **te**, **nous**, and **vous**), keeping in mind that **se** also reflects the subject. If **se** (always preceding the verb) is the *direct object* of the verb, and if it is the only direct object, then the past participle agrees with **se** (and/or the subject it replaces). There are two exceptions to this rule: (1) when **se** is an *indirect object* instead of a direct object, and (2) when there is another more obvious direct object in the sentence.

Ils **se** sont **mariés**.	*They got married.*
Elle **s'est sentie** faiblir et elle **s'est assise**.	*She felt faint and sat down.*
Nous **nous** sommes **levés** tard dimanche.	*We got up late on Sunday.*
Est-ce que vous **vous** êtes bien **amusés**?	*Did you have fun?*

Some pronominal verbs are considered "essentially pronominal" (they are also called "idiomatic"), that is, they do not exist in a non-pronominal form. As a result, you can't determine if the pronoun **se** is a direct object or an indirect object. What to do about the agreement? In general, make the past participle agree with the **se**. Exceptions are: **se rendre compte de** (*realize*) and **se plaire/se complaire** (*enjoy oneself*). The past participles **rendu** and **plu/complu** always remain invariable. The following are common examples of "essentially pronominal" verbs:

s'absenter		to be absent
se disputer avec		to argue with
s'enfuir		to run away
se méfier de		to mistrust
se mettre à		to start (-ing)
se passer		to take place
se réconcilier		to make up (after a quarrel)
se souvenir de		to remember

Après leur dispute, ils **se** sont vite **réconciliés**.	*After their fight, they quickly made up.*
Sa fille **s'est enfuie** avec le plombier!	*His daughter eloped with the plumber!*
Ils ne **se** sont pas **méfiés** du piège.	*They did not heed the trap.*

But:

Nous ne **nous** sommes pas **rendu** compte de l'heure.	*We did not realize what time it was.*

Exceptions: the reflexive pronoun is an indirect object

If the reflexive pronoun represents an indirect object, there is *no* agreement. A good way to determine this is to use the verb in its non-pronominal form—that is, *without* the reflexive pronoun. Take **se parler**, for example. The non-pronominal form **parler** takes an indirect object (**parler à quelqu'un**), so the reflexive pronoun in **se parler** is also an indirect object, and no agreement occurs. Here are some common verbs that take an *indirect object* in their non-reflexive form. Most of these are pronominal verbs with a *reciprocal* meaning (*each other*). Note that their English equivalents do not necessarily take an indirect object:

s'acheter	acheter à	*to buy for*
se dire	dire à	*to tell each other/oneself*
se donner	donner à	*to give (to)*
s'écrire	écrire à	*to write*
se parler	parler à	*to talk to*
se partager	partager avec	*to share between/among*
se promettre	promettre à	*to promise*
se rappeler	rappeler à	*to remind*
se téléphoner	téléphoner à	*to call, phone*

Elle **s'est dit** qu'elle y arriverait.	*She told herself (that) she would make it.*
Nous **nous** sommes **écrit** pendant les vacances.	*We wrote (to) each other during the holidays.*
Ils **se** sont **parlé** longuement.	*They talked (to each other) for a long while.*
Elles **se** sont **donné** rendez-vous.	*They made a date.*

Exceptions: the verb has another direct object

If the pronominal verb has a direct object expressed in the sentence, usually following the verb (such as **les cheveux** in the first example), there is no agreement.

Elle s'est **lavé les cheveux**.	*She washed her hair.*
Elle s'est **fait une tartine**.	*She made a slice of toast for herself.*

However, if the direct object appears as the pronoun **la** (**l'**) or **les** instead of as an object noun, it is placed before the auxiliary **être** (as all object pronouns are). As a result, the past participle must agree with it (in the following examples the pronoun and the past participle are highlighted).

Il s'est cassé la cheville. Il se **l'**est **cassée**.	*He broke his ankle. He broke it.*
Cette salade? Je me **la** suis **préparée**.	*This salad? I prepared it for myself.*
Elle s'est lavé les mains. Elle se **les** est **lavées**.	*She washed her hands. She washed them.*

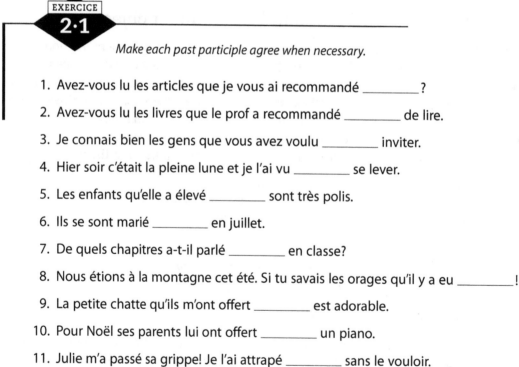

EXERCICE
2·1

Make each past participle agree when necessary.

1. Avez-vous lu les articles que je vous ai recommandé _____ ?

2. Avez-vous lu les livres que le prof a recommandé _____ de lire.

3. Je connais bien les gens que vous avez voulu _____ inviter.

4. Hier soir c'était la pleine lune et je l'ai vu _____ se lever.

5. Les enfants qu'elle a élevé _____ sont très polis.

6. Ils se sont marié _____ en juillet.

7. De quels chapitres a-t-il parlé _____ en classe?

8. Nous étions à la montagne cet été. Si tu savais les orages qu'il y a eu _____ !

9. La petite chatte qu'ils m'ont offert _____ est adorable.

10. Pour Noël ses parents lui ont offert _____ un piano.

11. Julie m'a passé sa grippe! Je l'ai attrapé _____ sans le vouloir.

12. Marie-Antoinette n'est pas né _____ en France.

13. La soirée que nous avons passé _____ chez vous a été formidable.

14. Quelle date avez-vous choisi _____ pour le mariage?

15. Elle s'est brossé _____ les cheveux cinquante fois.

16. J'ai eu un accident avec ma cheville: je me la suis cassé _____.

17. J'ai ouvert la cage aux oiseaux. Je les ai laissé _____ partir.

18. Ils se sont marié _____ en juillet.

19. J'ai acheté des gâteaux que j'ai servi _____ aux invités.

20. L'histoire est une chose à laquelle il s'est toujours intéressé _____.

Write the correct form of the past participle, based on the referent/antecedent of the pronoun (in parentheses).

1. Elle se l'est posé _____. (la question)

2. Tu l'as senti _____ trembler? (la terre)

3. Nous les avons vu _____ appréhender. (les voleurs)

4. Elle se les est brossé _____. (les cheveux)

5. Ils l'ont entendu _____ siffler. (leur chanson préférée)

6. Le chat les a vu _____ se poser sur la fenêtre. (les oiseaux)

7. Il l'a senti _____ monter en lui. (la colère)

8. C'est avec émotion qu'elles l'ont entendu _____ chanter. (la Marseillaise) – *the French national anthem*

Use of the past tenses

English has a multi-tasking past tense, the preterit (*I went, we were*), which can describe various aspects of a past action, whether it is naming a single occurrence (example 1), or describing an action that was happening on a regular basis (example 2).

Hier matin **j'ai lu** le journal.	*Yesterday morning, I **read** the paper.*
L'année dernière, je **lisais** le journal tous les matins.	*Last year, I **read** the paper every morning.*

In French you must distinguish between the various aspects of past actions in order to choose the appropriate past tense. For instance, you have learned that **passé composé** is the past tense for actions, whereas the **imparfait** is the past tense for describing and reminiscing. In this unit we will focus on the trickier uses of the **passé composé** and the **imparfait**.

Uses of the **passé composé**

The task of the **passé composé** is to present an action as past without dwelling on its description or process. That action is considered in its finite aspect, not in its unfolding. And when the **passé composé** is used with verbs that do express a process such as **penser** (*think*), **avoir envie** (*want*), **être** (*be*), it changes their meaning (see "Verbs expressing thoughts").

Single events

When listing (as opposed to describing) past events and past actions, you use the **passé composé**. Such sentences often contain expressions of time that name a single occurrence.

le 2 juillet (*a specific date*)	*on July 2*
tout à coup/soudain	*all of a sudden*
tout de suite	*immediately*
d'abord, ensuite, puis, enfin	*first, then, next, finally*
une fois	*once*

Elle ne **s'est trompée** qu'**une fois** dans son problème.	*She only made a mistake once in her problem.*
D'abord il **a enlevé** son manteau, **puis** il **a enlevé** ses bottes et **enfin** il **s'est assis**.	*First he took off his coat, then he took off his boots, and finally he sat down.*

Completed actions

The **passé composé** is used for naming (as opposed to describing) actions that happened within a defined period of time. The key word here is *within*. You are considering the period of time as a sealed time capsule, and it does not matter how long the period was, a day or a decade, as long as it is finite in the mind of the speaker. In the first example, **il a neigé** does not mean it snowed only once. It states that it snowed last year ("last year" being considered as a finite period of time), as opposed to this year. In the following second example, even though his youth lasted a long time, it is over by now! He is not in his youth anymore but the event of *learning to ski* occurred while he was still in his youth.

Il ne neige jamais ici, mais l'année dernière il **a neigé**.	*It never snows here, but last year, it snowed.*
Quand il était petit, il **a appris** à faire du ski.	*When he was little he learned to ski.*
Aujourd'hui il fait beau, mais hier il **a plu**.	*Today it is nice (out), but yesterday it rained.*

Past actions with ties to the present

Use the **passé composé** to present an action that started in the past but has not ended yet. In the first example, my cat has slept on my bed for as long as I can remember, and still does. Note that in contrast to the previous section (where the **passé composé** represents a completed action), there is no precise expression of time in this case.

Tied to the present

Mon chat **a** toujours **dormi** sur mon lit.	*My cat has always slept on my bed.*

No ties to the present, therefore the imparfait

Quand j'**étais** célibataire, mon chat **dormait** sur mon lit.	*When I was single, my cat used to sleep on my bed.*

Tied to the present

J'**ai** toujours **aimé** sortir le soir.	*I have always liked going out at night.*

No ties to the present, therefore the imparfait

Quand j'**étais** plus jeune, j'**aimais** sortir le soir.	*When I was younger I liked going out at night (understood, but now I don't anymore).*

Verbs more likely in the **passé composé**

Verbs such as **arriver, commencer, comprendre** (*understand*), **décider, dire, entendre, finir, oublier, (se) mettre à, voir**, and so on denote a swift action, as opposed to an event that would unfold over a long period of time. As a result, you are more likely to find these verbs in the **passé composé** than in the **imparfait**. However, in a specific context they could also be found in the **imparfait** as the following fourth example shows:

Est-ce que tu lui **as dit** merci?	*Did you say thank you to him?*
Il **a commencé** à pleuvoir.	*It started to rain.*
Nous **avons décidé** de faire une fête pour ton anniversaire.	*We have decided to throw a party for your birthday.*

But:

Au lycée, il **comprenait** toujours après les autres.	*In high school, he would always understand after the others (students).*

Verbs expressing states of being or thoughts in the passé composé

Use of the **passé composé** can also change the meaning of a verb. This is a rather subtle point of grammar, but we hope you're finding such learning challenges intriguing! The meaning can change when you're dealing with verbs that describe a state of mind or of being, a thought, or an appearance, as opposed to an action. Typically, you can expect to find these verbs in the **imparfait** (see the following table). However, when they are found in the **passé composé**, their meaning changes, and an English translation will need to reflect this. The following verbs describing states of mind are typically used in the **imparfait** (as opposed to the **passé composé**):

aimer	*to like/love*
avoir	*to have*
croire	*to believe*
détester	*to hate*
espérer	*to hope*
être	*to be*
paraître	*to seem/appear*
penser	*to think*
pouvoir	*to be able to*
savoir	*to know*
sembler	*to seem*
trouver	*to find/think*
vouloir	*to want*

"Decisive thoughts"

Verbs expressing a thought or a state of mind conjugated in the **passé composé** instead of the usual and expected **imparfait** reflect a "decisive thought" that is almost equivalent to an action, as is illustrated in the examples that follow. In the first one with the **imparfait**, the outcome of the situation is not clear in French, and ambiguous at best in English. Did they go out or not? In the second example, the use of the **passé composé** in French makes the situation fairly clear: they did not go out because he pretty much said "no." To achieve the same clarity in English, you would have to add something like *so we did not go out*, or change the verb as is showed in the translation (see the highlighted verbs).

Hier soir je voulais que nous sortions mais mon mari **ne voulait pas**.	*Last night I wanted to go out but my husband **did not want to**.*
Hier soir je voulais sortir mais mon mari **n'a pas voulu**.	*Last night I wanted to go out but my husband **declined/said no**.*
Je **n'avais pas besoin** du sac que tu m'as prêté.	*I **did not need** the purse you lent me.*
Je **n'ai pas eu besoin** du sac que tu m'as prêté.	*I **did not use** the purse you lent me.*

The result of an action

A verb describing states of being or appearance can be expressed in the **passé composé** to emphasize the result of the action that precedes it. In the first example, *they were happy* as a result of finding out about their friends' visit, but they were not happy before then. So perhaps a more accurate translation of **ils ont été contents** is *they became happy.*

Quand ils ont appris que leurs amis venaient, ils **ont été** contents.	*When they found out that their friends were coming, they were/became happy.*
Quand Pierre a vu les autres enfants manger une glace, il **a eu envie** d'en manger une aussi.	*When Pierre saw the other kids eating ice cream, he got a craving for one, too.*
Hier soir il a croqué trop de bonbons et il **a eu mal** aux dents toute la nuit.	*Last night he snacked on too many candies and his teeth hurt all night.*
Quand j'ai vu Julie déguisée, **j'ai** tout de suite **su** que c'était une blague.	*When I saw Julie in costume, I knew/saw right away that it was a joke.*

The future in the past

When you need to introduce an idea of the future within a past context, you can't use the future or any other structure used to express the true future in French. Instead, use one of the following two options:

With the conditional

If you are reporting what someone said *they would do* in the future, use the conditional. (For more details see Unit 5 on reported speech.)

Papa **a appelé** pour dire **qu**'il **serait** en retard ce soir.	*Papa called to say that he would be late tonight.*
Le patron **a annoncé qu**'il **n'aurait** plus besoin de nous aujourd'hui.	*The boss said he would not need us anymore today.*
Elle a oublié de nous **dire quand** elle **arriverait**.	*She forgot to tell us when she would arrive.*

With aller + infinitive

As in English, when speaking about the past, you may also use the immediate future form (**aller** + infinitive), but don't forget to conjugate **aller** in the **imparfait**, not in the present.

La chaise n'était pas solide. Il **allait tomber**.	*The chair was not sturdy. He was going to fall.*
Les œufs **allaient éclore** à tout moment.	*The eggs were going to hatch at any moment.*
Nous savions que les oiseaux **allaient revenir** au nid.	*We knew the birds were going to come back to the nest.*

The imparfait

Think of the **imparfait** as the past tense of calm, beauty, and thought: it paints portraits and scenes, thoughts and memories; it does not busy itself with actions. If you were on stage, the **imparfait** would not be the tense of the actors but rather of the stage manager who oversaw the set, the lighting, and everything that prepared the stage for the actors to act. Because the **imparfait** is more straightforward to use than the **passé composé**, this section will be a simple recap of what you already know. Use the **imparfait** when:

+ The English verb is or could be *was/were* + *-ing* (past progressive), without changing the meaning.

Elle **conduisait** prudemment parce qu'il **pleuvait**.	*She drove (was driving) slowly because it was raining.*
Nous **dînions** quand le téléphone a sonné.	*We were having dinner when the phone rang.*

+ The English verb is or is the equivalent of *used to* + infinitive, with the same meaning in both languages.

| Il **mangeait** toujours à Macdo quand il **était** étudiant. | *He always ate (used to eat) at McDonald's when he was a student.* |
| Avant de commencer son régime elle **mangeait** du chocolat tous les jours. | *Before she began her diet she ate (used to eat) chocolate every day.* |

◆ The sentence has a verb that describes (as opposed to listing an action or actions). It can describe the weather, the time and the date (example 1), a setting (how things were, as in example 2), states of mind or of being (examples 1 and 2), and physical characteristics (example 3). Note that a sentence with such a verb can also have another verb in the **passé composé** (examples 4, 5, and 6).

Il **était** midi et nous **avions** faim.	*It was noon and we were hungry.*
Tout **était** calme. Une brise légère **soufflait**, Julie **se sentait** bien.	*All was quiet. A light breeze was blowing, Julie was feeling good.*
Quand il **était** jeune il **avait** les cheveux longs.	*When he was young he had long hair.*
Il a pris un cachet d'aspirine parce qu'il **avait** mal à la tête.	*He took an aspirin because he had a headache.*
Le jour où elle s'est mariée, elle **était** radieuse.	*The day she got married she was radiant.*
Quand j'ai quitté la maison, il **pleuvait**.	*When I left the house it was raining.*

◆ You encounter an expression of time that denotes a habitual past action. See the following list. Expressions that could also be found with the **passé composé** are not included here.

tous les jours/tous les ans/tous les mois...	*every day/year/month . . .*
chaque jour/mois/année	*each day/month/year*
le lundi/mardi...	*on Mondays/Tuesdays . . .*
tout le temps	*all the time*
d'habitude	*usually*
pendant que	*while*
autrefois	*formerly*

Passé composé versus imparfait

When a sentence has several conjugated verbs, it is important to understand how each action relates to the others. Even though you understand that some verbs occur more frequently in the **passé composé** than in the **imparfait**, or vice versa, the scenario may change based on the other verbs in the sentence. Note that parts of this section take up elements of previous sections in this unit.

The relationships between two verbs that you may be the most familiar with are "ongoing versus interrupted" (following first two examples) where the **imparfait** describes the ongoing event that was interrupted by another event, and "description versus action" (last two examples).

Remember that these guidelines are only rules of thumb to help you; there are times when other factors may determine usage of the past tenses.

Quand M. Martin **est rentré** hier soir, sa femme **embrassait** un homme!	*When Mr. Martin came home yesterday evening, his wife was kissing a man!*
Tout **était** silencieux quand l'alarme **s'est** soudain **déclenchée**.	*Everything was silent when the alarm was suddenly triggered.*
Il **portait** un manteau quand il **est sorti**.	*He was wearing a coat when he went out.*
Il **pleuvait** quand je **me suis levé**.	*It was raining when I got up.*

Think also in terms of "cause and result," where the result is expressed in the **passé composé** (highlighted in the following examples), even when the verb expresses a state of mind or a state of being.

Quand il a vu sa note, il **a été** content.	*When he saw his grade, he became happy.*
Je ne me sentais pas bien, mais quand il est arrivé, je **me suis sentie** mieux.	*I was not feeling well, but when he arrived, I felt/got better.*

Finally, let's not forget that all the verbs could be in the same tense, expressing either a series of actions (examples 1 and 2) or all description (examples 3 and 4).

Quand M. Martin **est rentré** hier soir, il **a embrassé** sa femme.	*When Mr. Martin came home yesterday evening, he kissed his wife.*
Il **a pris** ses clés et il **est sorti**.	*He took his keys and left.*
Autrefois, quand M. Martin **rentrait** chez lui, sa femme **l'attendait**.	*Formerly, when Mr. Martin would come home, his wife was waiting for him.*
Il **faisait** beau et nous **avions** envie de faire une promenade.	*The weather was nice and we wanted to go for a walk.*

The pluperfect

Like the **passé composé**, the pluperfect (**plus-que-parfait**) is a compound tense, formed with the **imparfait** of the auxiliary + past participle. The agreement of the past participle follows the same rules as for the **passé composé** (example 2).

Mme Dupont est restée au bureau tard parce qu'elle n'**avait** pas **fini** son travail.	*Mrs. Dupont stayed late at the office because she had not finished her project.*
Agnès avait sommeil hier matin parce qu'elle **s'était couchée** tard.	*Agnes was sleepy yesterday morning because she had gone to bed late.*

The pluperfect is a relative past tense that describes an action that took place prior to another past action. As a result, it can only be used in a sentence that has another past tense, or when another past action is clearly implied by the context. We did not include the pluperfect in the unit on relative tenses (Unit 5), because it is not introduced by a specific word, such as **que** or **si**. However, a number of expressions such as **comme** (*as, since*), **parce que** (*because*), and **déjà** (*already*) are often associated with the pluperfect.

Nous avons choisi la table où nous **avions dîné** le soir de notre premier rendez-vous.	*We chose the table where we had had dinner on our first date.*
Comme tu **avais fait** la vaisselle je n'ai pas eu besoin de la faire.	*Since you had done the dishes, I did not have to do them.*
Nous sommes arrivés à la gare en retard, et le train **était déjà parti**!	*We arrived late at the station and the train had already left!*

English usage is not as strict as French; the English pluperfect can be replaced by a preterit. For the use of the pluperfect in an *if*-clause sentence, please see the relevant section in the unit on relative tenses (Unit 5).

Mes amis ne sont pas venus **parce qu'**ils **avaient oublié** l'heure du rendez-vous!	*My friends did not come because they had forgotten the time of our get-together!*
	or: *My friends did not come because they forgot the time of our get-together!*

EXERCICE

3·1

*Complete the sentences with the correct form. Choose the **imparfait**, the **passé composé**, or the pluperfect.*

Dimanche dernier, Paul et Virginie _____ (partir) à la fête de la bière. Tous

leurs amis y _____ (aller) l'année précédente et ils _____

(vouloir) absolument voir ça à leur tour. Ils _____ (penser) qu'ils

s'amuseraient bien. Mais quand ils _____ (arriver), ils _____ (être) déçus. D'abord, il _____ (faire) froid. Ensuite, pour acheter de la

bière ou des saucisses, il fallait attendre vingt ou trente minutes chaque fois. Puis, ils

_____ (vouloir) danser, mais il _____ (y avoir) trop de gens

sur la piste et pendant qu'ils _____ (danser) quelqu'un _____

(renverser) sa bière sur Virginie qui _____ (se mettre) en colère! Alors,

Pierre _____ (décider) qu'il _____ (être) l'heure de rentrer

à la maison. Dans la voiture, il a demandé à Virginie si elle _____

(s'amuser)... Virginie _____ (ne pas répondre) mais dans sa tête elle pensait:

« Si je _____ (savoir), je ne serais pas venue! »

*The following sentences in English are in the past tense. For each underlined verb, say if the French verb should be in the **passé composé**, in the **imparfait**, or if it's not possible to tell.*

1. I (a) came to your house but you (b) were not there.

   _____

2. Last year, I read the paper every morning.

   _____

3. When I was little, I visited my grandmother on Thursdays.

   _____

4. The day they (a) got married (b) was a Thursday.

   _____

5. Yesterday, I (a) went out. I (b) was tired when I (c) got home.

   _____

6. When I (a) was ten, I (b) broke my bike.

_____

7. Last time you (a) traveled, where (b) did you go?

_____

8. What did you wear to travel?

_____

9. It (a) was hot yesterday, so he (b) went swimming!

_____

10. Julie (a) wanted to dance, but her partner (b) did not want to.

_____

11. He (a) used to like cherries, but he (b) ate too many and he (c) was so sick that he won't eat them anymore.

_____

12. I (a) have always liked opera. But my wife does not like it, so (b) I have not been in ages.

_____

_____

EXERCICE

3·3

*Conjugate the verbs in the **passé composé**, the pluperfect, or the **imparfait**. Look for clues!*

1. Quand je _____ (arriver) à la maison, les enfants _____ (ne pas être) là, parce qu'ils _____ (aller) chez les voisins pendant mon absence.

2. Aux dernières élections, ce candidat _____ (perdre) parce qu'il _____ (ne pas dire) la vérité pendant sa campagne.

3. Quand elle _____ (être) jeune, elle _____ (aller) toujours chez sa grand-mère pour les vacances, mais une année, elle _____ (partir) faire du ski dans les Alpes parce qu'elle _____ (ne jamais voir) les Alpes avant.

4. Julie et Paul _____ (ne pas se parler) ce matin parce qu'ils _____ (se disputer) la veille.

5. Ce matin il _____ (se réveiller) malade parce qu'il _____ (trop manger) la veille.

6. Elle _____ (se lever) à 6 heures hier matin parce qu'elle _____ (vouloir) partir au travail tôt.

7. Je _____ (déjà arriver) au restau quand tu me _____ (téléphoner) pour annuler notre diner.

8. Quand nous _____ (se réveiller), il _____ (être) déjà 8h 30!

9. Il _____ (faire) froid ce matin parce qu'il _____ (neiger) toute la nuit.

10. Nous _____ (ne pas encore finir) l'examen quand le prof _____ (dire): « C'est fini ».

11. Quand tu _____ (aller) au lycée, est-ce que tu _____ (se lever) tôt?

12. Hier soir je _____ (ne pas vouloir) regarder le film avec mon mari parce que je le _____ (déjà voir) l'été dernier.

13. Ils _____ (marcher) tranquillement quand soudain, la pluie _____ (commencer) à tomber!

14. Au restaurant ils _____ (s'asseoir) à la table où ils _____ (s'asseoir) pour leur premier rendez-vous.

15. Ce matin, nous _____ (s'habiller) vite et nous _____ (partir) sans petit-déjeuner parce que nous _____ (être) en retard.

16. Pour les élections, mon fils qui _____ (ne jamais voter) _____ (voter) pour la première fois.

17. Pendant que nous _____ (installer) la tente, le vent _____ (commencer) à souffler et la tente _____ (s'envoler)!

18. Est-ce que vous _____ (étudier) le français avant de suivre ce cours de « Français 1 »?

19. La plupart des enfants _____ (déjà ouvrir) leurs cadeaux quand le Père Noël _____ (enfin arriver). Il était en retard parce qu'il _____ (avoir) un accident de traineau!

20. Quand la pluie _____ (s'arrêter), le soleil _____ (commencer) à briller.

21. Samedi soir nous _____ (faire) une chose que nous _____ (ne jamais faire) avant.

22. Maman _____ (demander) aux enfants de faire la vaisselle, mais ils la _____ (déjà faire).

23. Il _____ (déjà se coucher) quand il _____ (se souvenir) qu'il _____ (ne pas encore sortir) la poubelle.

Translating the -ing form into French

The French counterpart of the English gerund, the -ing form (*smiling, running*), is a verb form in **-ant** (**souriant, courant**)—the present participle. The same form is called a **gérondif** when it is preceded by the preposition **en**. Both names will be used in this unit. To simplify things, we'll call the English form a *gerund*. Remember that, when used alone, the French present participle is a literary usage, but the French **gérondif** (**en** + present participle) is commonly used. With the **gérondif** all the verbs of the sentence need to have the same subject. The equivalence of the English gerund to the French present participle is not at all systematic. Several different French verb forms are used to translate the English -ing. In fact, the present participle is little used in French compared to its widespread use in English, and so this unit is divided into sections based on English uses.

Formation of the present participle

The present participle is not conjugated. It is formed by taking the **nous** form of the present tense of a given verb (dropping the subject pronoun **nous**), and replacing the **-ons** ending by **-ant**. Verbs that have a spelling change before **-o** (**c** changes to **ç** + **o/a**, and **g** changes to **g** + **e** + **o/a**) retain that change preceding the **-ant** of the present participle (examples 5 and 6).

nous parlons	parlant	*we speak*	*speaking*
nous finissons	finissant	*we finish*	*finishing*
nous voyons	voyant	*we see*	*seeing*
nous prenons	prenant	*we take*	*taking*
nous commençons	commançant	*we begin*	*beginning*
nous mangeons	mangeant	*we eat*	*eating*

Three verbs have an irregular form: **être: étant, avoir: ayant, savoir: sachant**.

The present participle is not a conjugated form and therefore cannot be used directly after a subject pronoun. As a result, impersonal verbs used only with **il**, like **falloir: il faut** (*it is necessary*), **pleuvoir: il pleut** (*it's raining*), **suffire: il suffit** (*it is enough*), **paraître: il paraît** (*it is said that*), don't have a present participle.

In the negative, the present participle is treated like a conjugated verb: the two negative particles surround it.

Il a arrêté de fumer **en n'achetant plus de** cigarettes.	*He quit smoking by not buying any more cigarettes.*
N'étant pas fatigué, il a continué sa promenade.	*Not being tired (Since he wasn't tired) he continued his walk.*

When a pronominal verb is in the present participle, its reflexive pronoun must match the subject of the conjugated verb, as it would before an infinitive.

J'ai trouvé un chat perdu en **me promenant**.	*I found a lost cat while taking a walk.*
Nous réussirons en **nous appliquant**.	*We will succeed by applying ourselves.*

Differences between the present participle and the past participle

An important difference between the present and the past participle is that the present participle is never used with an auxiliary. Also, unlike the past participle, the present participle never agrees with the subject or the object. Remember that the subject of the present participle is also the subject of the other verb in a given sentence.

Étant malades, **ils** sont restés chez eux.	*Being ill, they stayed home.*
Julie leur a téléphoné **en arrivant**.	*Julie called them upon arriving/when she arrived.*

To be + -ing

In French, there is no progressive verbal form similar to *to be* + *-ing*. Instead, you need to use the verb tense equivalent to the form of *to be*.

Je **parle**.	*I **am** talking.* or *I **talk**.*
Tu **partais**.	*You **were** leaving.*
Je **lisais**.	*I **was** reading.*
Je **pleurerai**.	*I **will be** crying.* or *I **will cry**.*
Nous **ririons**.	*We **would be** laughing.* or *We **would** laugh.*

The French verb can however be "expanded" to match the meaning of the *to be* + *-ing* form more closely, when the context requires it. Use **être en train de** + infinitive (*to be in the process of doing something*) to mark an ongoing action if a simple verb does not seem to suffice.

—Qu'est-ce que tu fais?	*"What are you doing?"*
—Je suis **en train de travailler**, ne me dérange pas.	*"I am working, don't disturb me."*
N'entre pas: je **suis en train de développer** des photos.	*Don't come in: I am developing photos.*

In the past tense, the French equivalent of *was/were* + *-ing* is always in the **imparfait**, never in the **passé composé**.

Qu'est-ce que tu **faisais** quand je t'ai appelé?	*What were you doing when I called you?*
Nous **nous promenions** quand la pluie a commencé.	*We were taking a walk when the rain started.*

In a future context, the French equivalent of *will be* + *-ing* is always the simple future tense, never the **futur immédiat** (**aller** + infintive).

Je **travaillerai** au bureau toute la journée.	*I **will be** working in the office all day.*
Tu **devras** réessayer.	*You **will have to** try again.*

-ing in a sequence of verbs

The English *-ing* structure is translated differently in French depending on whether there is one or more than one subject in a sentence.

Sequence of verbs with the same subject

French uses an infinitive as the equivalent of the English gerund in a sequence of verbs when all the verbs have the same subject. Don't forget that some French verbs require an "empty" preposition before an infinitive (following third and fourth examples).

Tu aimes **danser**?	*Do you like **dancing**?*
Il adore **jouer** du piano.	*He loves **playing** the piano.*
Nous avons passé la soirée **à étudier**.	*We spent the evening **studying**.*
Il s'est arrêté **de pleuvoir**.	*It stopped **raining**.*

Sequence of verbs with multiple subjects

In French, when each verb has its own subject, several things can happen depending on the main verb. What is certain is that each subject in a sentence has a corresponding conjugated verb, with only few exceptions (see Unit 1 for this discussion).

Following certain trigger verbs + **que** (**je veux que**, **il faut que**, etc.), the second subject (highlighted in the following examples) introduces the subjunctive.

J'aime que **mes amis** viennent sans prévenir.	*I like **my friends** coming over unexpectedly.*
Je ne veux pas que **le chien** dorme sur le lit.	*I don't want **the dog** sleeping on the bed.*

In this scenario, in English, the second subject often has the form of a possessive adjective (*my, your,* in the following first two examples), or an object pronoun (*them, her* in examples 3 and 4). In French, the subject of a conjugated verb must be a noun or a subject pronoun: **je** in example 1, **vous** in example 2, **ils** in example 3, and **elle** in example 4.

Ça ne vous dérange pas **que je** vous **appelle** demain?	*Do you mind **my** calling you tomorrow?*
Nous apprécions **que vous soyez** toujours à l'heure.	*We appreciate **your** being always on time.*
Nous ne voulons pas **qu'ils regardent** la télé.	*We don't want **them** watching TV.*
Je préfère **qu'elle** ne **vienne** pas.	*I prefer **her** not coming.*

In French, after a verb of perception, the second subject introduces an infinitive, or a relative clause introduced by **qui.**

Il **a vu** le bateau **partir.** *or:* Il **a vu** le bateau **qui partait.**	*He saw the boat leaving.*
Ils **regardent** leurs enfants **jouer.** *or:* Ils **regardent** leurs enfants **qui jouent.**	*They watch their kids playing.*

English preposition + -*ing*

English prepositions are often followed by a gerund when the same subject rules all the verbs. In French, only a few prepositions, either compound (multi-word) or simple, can be followed by a verb, and when they do, the verb is in the infinitive. They include the "empty" prepositions **à** and **de** as well as the following:

à moins de	*unless*
après (+ past infinitive)*	*after*
au lieu de	*instead of*

au moment de	*at the time of*
avant de	*before*
de façon à	*in order to*
de peur de	*for fear that*
par	*by, through*
pour	*for*
sans	*without*
sauf	*except*

Nous commencerons **par** déguster des hors d'œuvres exotiques.	*We will begin **by** enjoying exotic appetizers.*
Téléphone **avant de** venir, **pour** voir si nous sommes là.	*Call **before** coming **to** see if we are there.*
Il pleut, alors nous regarderons un film **au lieu d**'aller à la plage.	*It is raining, so we will watch a movie **instead of** going to the beach.*

*The preposition **après** is never followed by a simple infinitive in French. A past infinitive is required (auxiliary verb in infinitive + past participle of the main verb) where English uses the gerund. The tense of the main verb has no effect on the **après** clause (the **passé composé** in examples 1 and 2 and the future in example 3).

Après avoir pris une douche, elle **s'est sentie** mieux.	*After showering, she felt better.*
Après avoir lu une heure, elle **s'est endormie**.	*After reading for one hour she fell asleep.*
Nous **regarderons** la télé **après avoir dîné**.	*We will watch TV after eating dinner.*

Preposition or conjunction

The infinitive can only be used after a preposition if one subject rules all the verbs. If the subjects are different, an equivalent conjunction (when there is one) + the subjunctive must be used instead of a preposition (see Unit 6 for the table of equivalence between prepositions and conjunctions). The following examples contrast the two constructions; where subjects are different, both have been highlighted:

Je suis parti **avant de prendre** mon petit déjeuner.	*I left before having breakfast.*
Il est parti **avant que je** lui **dise** au revoir.	*He left before I could tell him good-bye.*
Elle est arrivée **sans nous prévenir**.	*She arrived without warning us.*
Elle est arrivée **sans que personne** ne le **sache**.	*She arrived without anyone knowing.*

Il a écrit son code dans un cahier **de peur de l'oublier**.	*He wrote his code in a notebook for fear of forgetting it.*
Il n'écrit jamais son code dans un cahier **de peur que quelqu'un** ne le **voie**.	*He never writes his code in a notebook for fear someone might see it.*

Note the optional use of the "phony" **ne** in several earlier examples (4 and 6). This use of **ne** is explained later, in Unit 18, "Negative sentences."

Miscellaneous uses of the English gerund

Looking at several other uses of the English *-ing* form will help clarify certain French equivalent constructions.

The gerund as subject

The English gerund is commonly used as subject of a verb. In French, an infinitive can be the subject, but the French present participle can never be the subject of a verb.

Manger est un plaisir.	*Eating is a pleasure.*
Avoir des enfants crée des obligations.	*Having children creates obligations.*

If the French verb has an associated noun, that noun can be used instead of the infinitive as the subject.

Apprendre une nouvelle langue est utile. (*infinitive*)	*Learning a new language is useful.*
or: **L'apprentissage** d'une nouvelle langue est utile. (*noun*)	
En avion, **lire** fait passer le temps.	*On the plane, reading makes time go by.*
or: En avion, **la lecture** fait passer le temps.	

The English gerund expressing simultaneity

After *while* or *upon*, the English gerund expresses simultaneity and must be translated by the French **gérondif**: (tout) **en** + present participle. **En** is the only French preposition which, when followed by a verb, takes the **gérondif** instead of the infinitive.

Elle a perdu une boucle d'oreille **en dansant**.	*She lost an earring **while dancing**.*
Elle regardait la télé (**tout**) **en faisant** la vaisselle.	*She was watching TV **while washing** the dishes.*

If the sentence has multiple subjects, you need to conjugate the second verb rather than using the **gérondif**. English also uses a conjugated verb instead of the gerund in this case.

Elle regardait la télé pendant que **Paul faisait** la vaisselle.	*She was watching TV while **Paul was washing** the dishes.*
Cendrillon travaille pendant que **ses sœurs s'amusent**.	*Cinderella works while **her sisters enjoy themselves**.*

The English gerund expressing a prolonged action

The gerund is often used to describe how someone spends his or her time *doing something*. To render the same idea in French use **à** + infinitive, especially after the expression **passer** (**du temps**). Such a sentence describes how a certain amount of time is entirely occupied by the action presented in the infinitive.

Tu ne travailles pas mais tu passes ton temps **à t'amuser**!	*You don't work but you spend your time **having fun**!*
Il a passé l'été **à faire** des recherches.	*He spent his summer **doing research**.*
Ne perds pas ton temps **à regarder la télé**.	*Don't waste your time **watching TV**.*
On ne gagne rien **à tricher**.	*One does not gain anything (by) **cheating**.*

The following example illustrates a major difference between **en** + **gérondif** and **à** + infinitive:

En observant les animaux nous nous amusons **à les faire parler**.	*While **studying** animals, we have fun **making them speak**.*

With **à** + infinitive, both actions (**s'amuser** and **faire parler**) are assimilated into one.

However, with the **gérondif** (**en** + present participle), the two actions (**observer** and **s'amuser**) are clearly separate.

-ing form as an adjective or noun

Both in French and in English some adjectives and nouns are derived from the present participle. Unlike the verbal form of the present participle which is invariable, such adjectives vary in number and gender, depending on what they describe.

C'est une fille **souriante**.	*She's a smiling girl.*
Ces histoires sont **fascinantes**.	*These stories are fascinating.*
Ce sont des gens **charmants**.	*They are charming people.*

Not all words formed this way have matching forms in both languages. In the following examples, the French adjectives correspond to the present participle form, but the English adjectives do not:

un chien **obéissant**	*an obedient dog*
une tenue **provocante**	*a provocative outfit*
le numéro **précédent**	*the previous issue*

A few of these present participles undergo a spelling change when they are used as adjectives or nouns. These include: **-ant** to **-ent**; **-quant** to **-cant**; and from **-guant** to **-gant**. The following examples reflect some common occurrences of these changes:

Il a fait fortune **en fabriquant** des chaussures.	*He made his fortune making shoes.*
C'est un **fabricant** de chaussures. (*noun*)	*He is a shoemaker.*
Les résultats des experts **différant** beaucoup, l'analyse est nulle.	*The experts' results differing greatly, the analysis is void.*
J'ai obtenu des résultats **différents**. (*adjective*)	*I got different results.*
Il a eu une crise d'asthme **en se fatiguant**.	*He had an attack of asthma by tiring himself.*
Faire la vaisselle n'est pas **fatigant**.	*Washing dishes is not tiring.*
Présidant le conseil, il a une grande responsabilité.	*Presiding over the council, he has great responsibility.*
Son père est le **président** du conseil.	*His father is the president of the council.*
En **provoquant** le directeur, tu auras des ennuis.	*By provoking the director you will get into trouble.*
Elle porte une tenue **provocante**.	*She's wearing a provocative outfit.*
Précédant les autres coureurs depuis le début, il a gagné la course haut la main.	*Leading the other cyclists from the start, he won the race with flying colors.*
J'ai reçu le numéro de septembre, mais je n'ai pas reçu le numéro **précédent**.	*I received the September issue, but I did not get the previous one.*

-ing form to describe a position

When English uses a gerund to describe a position in space, French uses a past participle, a prepositional phrase, or sometimes an adverb (in an adjectival sense) along with its noun or pronoun. If it is a past participle, it must agree with the subject (sentence examples 3 and 4).

accroché	*hanging*
accroupi	*crouching*

à genoux	*kneeling*
allongé/couché	*lying (down)*
appuyé	*leaning*
assis	*sitting*
debout	*standing*
penché	*leaning*
suspendu	*hanging (from)*

Couché dans mon lit, j'entendais la pluie sur le toit.	***Lying** in bed, I could hear the rain on the roof.*
On m'a appris a faire ma prière **à genoux**.	*I was taught to pray **kneeling**.*
De beaux jambons étaient **accrochés** au plafond.	*Nice-looking hams were **hanging** from the ceiling.*
Penchée au-dessus du berceau elle regardait le bébé.	***Leaning** over the crib she was watching the baby.*

Negative commands

In English, generic negative commands, found on signs, for example, are expressed with a gerund instead of a regular imperative form (*No smoking*). French uses the infinitive or a noun such as **defense de** or **interdiction de** + infinitive, or sometimes an impersonal phrase such as **il est interdit/défendu de** + infinitive. Don't forget that the two negative particles are grouped together preceding an infinitive.

Ne pas fumer.	*No smoking.*
Ne pas marcher sur la pelouse.	*No walking on the grass.*
Défense d'entrer.	*No trespassing.*
Interdiction de nager.	*No swimming.*

In French, the infinitive is used for affirmative generic commands found on signs, and also in recipes. As public instructions, they are often preceded by expressions such as **prière de** (*please*).

Ajouter le sucre et **mélanger**.	*Add the sugar and stir.*
Ôter ses chaussures avant d'entrer.	*Remove your shoes before entering.*
Prière d'éteindre son portable.	*Please turn off your cell phone.*

The gerund as a complement of the main verb

The English gerund and the French **gérondif** can complete the action expressed by the main verb by explaining it, or by describing how it is done.

Describing the main action

A sentence with the **gérondif** describes the manner in which the main action is done, almost like an adverb, when the adverb is absent.

Il est parti **en courant**.	*He left **running**.*
Elle m'a regardé **en riant**.	*She looked at me **laughing**.*

For this use of the **gérondif**, it is common to see a "reversed" construction in the English equivalent where the **gérondif** is replaced by a conjugated verb (highlighted in the following examples). This is often the case with verbs of motion (**monter**, **aller** in the examples).

Il travaille **en sifflant**.	*He works whistling. = He **whistles** while he works.*
Je suis monté **en courant**.	*I went upstairs running. = I **ran** upstairs.*
Nous y sommes allés **en nous promenant**.	*We went there walking. = We **walked** there.*

Explaining the main action

The **gérondif** gives the reason why the main action happened (examples 1, 2, and 3) or states how you do something (example 4). Thus, a sentence with the **gérondif** is "lighter" than an explanation with **parce que**: for example, **elle a maigri parce qu'elle a arrêté de grignoter**, or one with **pour** + infinitive (**pour appeler l'ascenseur on appuie ici**).

Il s'est blessé **en coupant** du bois.	*He got hurt cutting wood.*
Elle a maigri **en ne grignotant plus**.	*She lost weight by not snacking anymore.*
J'ai payé mes études **en travaillant** comme assistante.	*I paid for my tuition working as a teaching assistant.*
On appelle l'ascenseur **en appuyant** ici.	*You call the elevator by pushing here.*

The French present participle

Like the **gérondif**, the present participle can be used to explain the main action, but note that use of the present participle allows each verb to have its own subject; in the following first example: both **professeur** and **étudiants**; in example 2: both **lunettes** and **il**. Because this construction with the **gérondif** is rather formal, French alternatives for each example are provided.

Gérondif

Le professeur **étant** fatigué, les étudiants peuvent sortir tôt aujourd'hui.	*The professor being tired, the students can leave early today.*

Alternatives

Comme le professeur est fatigué, les étudiants peuvent sortir tôt aujourd'hui.	*Since the professor is tired, the students can leave early today.*
Les étudiants peuvent sortir tôt aujourd'hui parce que le professeur est fatigué.	*The students can leave early today because the professor is tired.*

Gérondif

Ses lunettes **étant** cassées, il n'y voyait plus.	*His glasses being broken, he could not see anymore.*

Alternatives

Comme ses lunettes étaient cassées, il n'y voyait plus.	*Since his glasses were broken, he could not see anymore.*
Il n'y voyait plus parce que ses lunettes étaient cassées.	*He could not see anymore because his glasses were broken.*

But if you can find only one subject in the sentence, you must assume that it rules all the verbs.

Gérondif

Étant française, **Julie** fête le 14 juillet.	*Being French, Julie celebrates Bastille Day.*

Alternatives

Comme **elle** est française, **Julie** fête le 14 juillet.	*Since she's French, Julie celebrates Bastille Day.*
Julie fête le 14 juillet parce qu'**elle** est française.	*Julie celebrates Bastille Day because she is French.*

Gérondif

Vivant à l'étranger, **elle** ne voit pas souvent ses enfants.	*Living abroad, she does not see her children often.*

Alternatives

Comme **elle** vit à l'étranger, **elle** ne voit pas souvent ses enfants.	*Since she lives abroad, she does not see her children often.*
Elle ne voit pas souvent ses enfants parce qu'**elle** vit à l'étranger.	*She does not see her children often because she lives abroad.*

Compound present participle

This form is made up of the present participle of the auxiliary + past participle of the verb. It is the "past" of the present participle and, like it, it is a literary form. It describes an action that corresponds to the pluperfect tense, as the following alternatives show. The simple **gérondif** cannot be used with an auxiliary.

Gérondif

Ayant fini ses devoirs, il est allé jouer.	*Having finished his homework, he went to play.*

Alternative

Comme il **avait fini** ses devoirs il est allé jouer.	*Since he had finished his homework, he went to play.*

Gérondif

Son fils **ayant quitté** la maison, Mme Martin s'est retrouvée seule.	*Her son having left home, Mrs. Martin was now alone.*

Alternative

Comme son fils **avait quitté** la maison, Mme Martin s'est retrouvée seule.	*Since her son had left home, Mrs. Martin was alone.*

After the auxiliary **étant** the past participle follows the regular rules of agreement, agreeing with the subject. The present participle never agrees.

Gérondif

La pluie **s'étant arrêtée**, nous sommes sortis.	*The rain having stopped, we went out.*

Alternative

Comme la pluie **s'était arrêtée**, nous sommes sortis.	*Since the rain had stopped, we went out.*

Recap: French to English

The following summary will help you determine equivalent French and English structures, especially useful for written translations.

The French present participle

Unlike the **gérondif**, the French present participle and its compound past form (**ayant/étant** + past participle) can be used when each verb has its own subject (both highlighted in the following example).

Ses enfants vivant à l'étranger, **elle** ne les **voit** pas souvent.	*Her children living abroad, she does not see them often.*

However, both forms of the present participle (simple and compound) are rather literary. Note that if all the verbs in the sentence have the same subject, you should use the **gérondif** instead (example 1).

Present participle (formal)

Partant tôt, **tu** évites toujours les embouteillages.

Leaving the house early, you always avoid the traffic jams.

Replace with gérondif

En partant tôt, **tu** évites toujours les embouteillages.

By leaving the house early, you always avoid the traffic jams.

The French gérondif

The **gérondif** is not literary. It can be used only when all the verbs of the sentence have the same subject. Its two main uses in French are (1) to denote simultaneity with the main action (following first two examples), and (2) to complement the main verb by explaining it (example 3). In these uses the **gérondif** is common in French (even though in general it has fewer uses than the English gerund, as the following table demonstrates).

Il chante toujours **en prenant** sa douche. *He always sings while taking his shower.*
Nous passerons à la boulangerie **en rentrant** de l'école. *We'll stop at the bakery on the way home from school.*
Je me suis piqué le doigt **en cousant**. *I pricked my finger while sewing.*

French usage

The following French equivalents correspond to the use of the English present participle or gerund form, shown in the English translations:

Present tense, imparfait, future, conditional

il dort, il dormait, il dormira, il dormirait *He is/was/will/would be sleeping.*

Infinitive or corresponding noun

Aimes-tu danser? *Do you like dancing?*
Aimes-tu la danse?
La natation est agréable. *Swimming is nice.*
Nager est agréable.

Gérondif

Il s'est blessé en courant. *He hurt himself (while) running.*
En partant, il a remarqué quelque chose. *Upon leaving, he noticed something.*

"Trigger verb" + subjunctive

J'aime qu'elle chante pour moi.   *I like her singing for me.*

Verb of perception + infinitive or + relative clause

Je l'entends chanter.   *I can hear her singing.*
Je l'entends qui chante.

Infinitive

Ne pas fumer.   *No smoking.*

EXERCICE
4·1

Put the following sentences into French.

1. We don't want the children eating on the couch.

   _____

2. The girl was wearing a red dress.

   _____

3. The clients left the office laughing.

   _____

4. He watched her leaving.

   _____

5. I don't like singing in public.

   _____

6. Writing in French is hard.

   _____

7. I will get used to sleeping in this new bed.

   _____

8. Stop bugging me!

   _____

9. I'll be thinking of you!

_____

10. She felt her legs weakening.

_____

11. He quit smoking at Christmas.

_____

12. Having paid, he left the store.

_____

13. She took his keys without his noticing.

_____

14. Upon receiving her literary prize, the author cried.

_____

15. Walking into the kitchen, he found the cat drinking his milk.

_____

16. After watching the stars all night, they fell asleep at dawn.

_____

17. "Can I come in?"

"No! I'm getting dressed."

_____

18. She wasted her youth waiting for him.

_____

Using a gerund, explain the cause of the various events. Make all the necessary changes.

1. Elle a eu un accident de voiture parce qu'elle parlait sur son portable.

   _____

2. Je rencontre ma voisine chaque fois que je sors la poubelle.

   _____

3. J'ai attrapé un rhume parce que j'ai embrassé ma fille qui était déjà enrhumée.

   _____

4. Pendant que je mangeais du poulet je me suis cassé une dent.

   _____

5. Elle a perdu dix kilos parce qu'elle n'a mangé que des légumes pendant un mois.

   _____

6. Tu as perdu ton portable pendant une promenade au parc.

   _____

7. Il s'est fait mal parce qu'il a été imprudent en roller.

   _____

8. Julia s'est beaucoup entraînée et elle a fait beaucoup de progrès.

   _____

9. C'est quand j'ai téléphoné à mes amis que j'ai appris la vérité.

   _____

10. Il a appris l'espagnol parce qu'il est allé en Espagne.

    _____

11. Elle a pu payer ses études parce qu'elle a travaillé en même temps.

    _____

12. Nous sommes restés éveillés parce que nous avons bu beaucoup de café.

_____

13. Elle a glissé pendant qu'elle prenait une douche.

_____

14. Avez-vous fermé la porte quand vous êtes partis?

_____

15. Tu t'es perfectionné parce que tu as beaucoup écrit.

_____

_____

Explain how the following people earn a living. You may have to come up with a verb of your own.

1. Charles est chanteur.

_____

2. Virginie est prof.

_____

3. Bernard est docteur.

_____

4. Conrad est écrivain.

_____

5. Wolfgang est pianiste.

_____

6. Josie est vendeuse.

_____

7. Gérard est acteur.

_____

8. Maxime est chauffeur de taxi.

_____

9. Martine est championne de tennis.

_____

10. Sylvie est pharmacienne.

_____

11. Paul est cuisinier.

_____

12. Alain est pilote de course.

_____

13. Pierre est plongeur.

_____

14. Guy est libraire.

_____

15. Francis est fermier.

_____

Relative tenses introduced by **que**

In Unit 1 we talked about sequences of verbs where the second verb is in the infinitive and there are no visible links between the verbs. In the following units we will look at sequences of conjugated verbs related to one another by a linking word, such as **que** (*that*), **quand** (*when*), and **si** (*if*), to only name the major ones. It is the first verb + linking word that determines the form of subsequent verbs. The form of subsequent verbs is therefore said to be "relative" (to what precedes).

Que (*that*) is the most versatile and the most common of those linking words; it can mark different types of relationships between the main verb and the dependent verb, as illustrated in the following examples:

Je pense **que** nous nous amuserons bien cet été.	*I think that we will have fun this summer.*
Elle sait **qu'**ils ont été sages.	*She knows that they were well-behaved.*
Il faut **que** tu fasses tes devoirs.	*You must do your homework.*

In French, there is never an infinitive after **que**, and the dependent verb can be in any tense of the indicative, based on the context, or in a tense of the subjunctive. The English equivalent of this type of construction does not necessarily include *that*, the literal counterpart of **que**. **Que** is never omitted in French.

No subjunctive after **que**

Verbs introducing the subjunctive are verbs that express wish and preference, emotion and feeling, doubt or possibility, necessity, and so on, as long as the main verb expresses subjectivity and a lack of certainty and that its subject and the subject of the dependent verb are different. (See Unit 6.)

Verbs that don't introduce the subjunctive simply establish facts or opinions. Like verbs that do trigger the subjunctive, they are followed by

que (*that*), but unlike in subjunctive sentences, the subject of the dependent verb can be the same as the subject of the main verb. These verbs include verbs of opinion and certainty that are *not* in a negative form or in an inversion, as well as many other transitive verbs. The form of the dependent verb is not obviously determined by the presence of **que**, but by the context. There are many combinations, as the following examples illustrate. The following list provides common examples of verbs + **que** + indicative:

apprendre que	*to learn that*
assurer (quelqu'un) que	*to assure (someone) that*
avertir que	*to warn that*
compter que	*to count/reckon that*
décider que	*to decide that*
découvrir que	*to discover that*
espérer que	*to hope that*
lire que	*to read that*
montrer (à quelqu'un) que	*to show (someone) that*
oublier que	*to forget that*
prévenir que	*to warn that*
promettre que	*to promise to*
réaliser que	*to realize that*
remarquer que	*to notice that*
révéler que	*to reveal that*
se rendre compte que	*to realize that*
se souvenir que	*to remember that*
vérifier que	*to verify that*

Verbs of opinion

considérer	*to consider that*
croire	*to believe that*
estimer	*to deem that*
imaginer	*to imagine that*
penser	*to think that*
prétendre	*to claim that*
supposer	*to assume that*
trouver	*to find that*

Verbs expressing certainty

il est certain/sûr que	*it is certain/sure that*
il est clair que	*it is clear that*
il est évident que	*it is obvious that*
il est vrai que	*it is true that*
je suis certain /sûr que	*I am certain/sure that*
je sais que	*I know that*

Je **trouve que** c'est une bonne idée.	*I think (that) it's a good idea.*
Je vous **assure que** nous **réussirons**.	*I assure you that we will succeed.*
J'**espère que** tu nous **écriras**.	*I hope that you will write us.*
Je **suis sûre que** tu **as compris**.	*I am certain (that) you understood.*
Admets que tu **as** tort!	*Admit (that) you are wrong!*
Il **oubliera** vite **qu**'on l'**a aidé**.	*He will be quick to forget that we helped him.*
Il **a vu que** le café **était** bondé et il n'est pas entré.	*He saw (that) the café was crowded and he did not go in.*
J'**ai lu que** le chômage **avait baissé**.	*I read (that) unemployment had gone down.*
Il **a décidé que** nous **prendrions** nos vacances en mai.	*He has decided that we would go on vacation in May.*

Reported speech after **que**

When you report someone's words without quotation marks (*he said [that] he would . . .*) you are in the indirect mode of reported speech. The introductory verbs must be followed by **que** and a tense of the indicative that has to "match" the main verb (see the following table). Here, the possibilities for tense combination are limited and they must follow rules that are stricter in French than in English. The following verbs associated with **dire** also introduce reported speech:

admettre que	to admit that
affirmer que	to assert that
ajouter que	to add that
annoncer que	to announce that
assurer que	to swear that
chuchoter que	to whisper that
crier que	to shout that
déclarer que	to declare
dire que	to tell that
écrire que	to write that
expliquer que	to explain that
garantir que	to guarantee that
indiquer que	to indicate that
jurer que	to swear that
promettre que	to promise that
raconter que	to tell that
remarquer que	to note that
répondre que	to answer that
riposter que	to reply that
se plaindre que	to complain that
souligner que	to point out that

A number of changes must occur in a sentence when it goes from direct to indirect speech:

- Quotation marks or French **guillemets**, direct punctuation (exclamation points, question marks), and colloquial expressions that can only belong to spoken language disappear (example 1).
- The object and subject pronouns must be changed to follow the logic of the sentence (examples 2 and 3).
- The verb tenses must be changed to match the introductory verb (see the following table).
- Some adverbs, such as **maintenant** (*now*), **ici** (*here*), **demain** (*tomorrow*), **hier** (*yesterday*), **la semaine prochaine** (*next week*), and **la semaine dernière** (*last week*) must change to **à ce moment-là** (*at that moment*), **là** (*there*), **le lendemain** (*the next day*), **la veille** (*the day before*), **la semaine suivante** (*the following week*), and **la semaine précedente** (*the previous week*).

« J'irai à la plage cet été. C'est décidé! »	*"I will go to the beach this summer. That's settled!"*
Elle **a décidé qu'**elle **irait** à la plage cet été-**là**.	*She decided that she would go to the beach that summer.*
« Ma maison est la plus jolie du quartier! »	*"My house is the prettiest in the area!"*
Elle **trouve que** sa maison **est** la plus jolie du quartier.	*She thinks that her house is the prettiest in the area.*
« Tu n'as pas beaucoup changé depuis qu'on se connaît. »	*"You haven't changed much since I've known you."*
Il **trouve qu'elle** n'a pas beaucoup **changé** depuis qu'**ils** se connaissent.	*He thinks that she has not changed much since they've known each other.*

Introductory verb in the present

Both in French and in English, when the introductory verb is in the present (*he says that . . .*), the verbs in the dependent clause do not change (example 1), except for the imperative that changes to an infinitive.

Direct speech	
Il pense: « Je n'ai pas assez dormi. »	*He thinks: "I have not slept enough."*
Reported speech	
Il **pense qu'il** n'a pas assez **dormi**.	*He thinks he has not slept enough.*
Direct speech	
Elle dit: « Dormez! »	*She says: "Sleep!"*

Reported speech

Elle **dit** aux enfants **de dormir**.	*She tells the kids to sleep.*
Le professeur **dit que** ses étudiants **sont** intéressants.	*The professor says that his students are interesting.*
Les enfants **promettent** toujours **qu'ils écriront**...	*Children always promise that they will write . . .*
or: Les enfants **promettent** toujours **d'écrire**...	

Introductory verb in the past

If the introductory verb is in the past (*he said that . . .*) then the verbs in the dependent clause change according to the following patterns (except for the imperative that changes to the infinitive):

TENSE IN THE DIRECT QUOTE	TENSE IN THE REPORTED SPEECH
present	**imparfait**
imparfait	**imparfait**
passé composé	pluperfect
pluperfect	pluperfect
future	conditional
conditional	conditional
imperative	infinitive or subjunctive
subjunctive	subjunctive
near future (**aller** + infinitive)	near future with **aller** in **imparfait**
recent past (**venir de** + infinitive)	recent past with **venir** in **imparfait**

Direct speech

Il a ajouté: « Et je ne **suis** même pas sûr de revenir. »	*He added: "I'm not even sure I'll come back."*

Reported speech

Il a ajouté qu'il n'**était** même pas sûr de revenir.	*He added (that) he was not even sure he would come back.*

Direct speech

Elle a annoncé: « Je **vais** faire des crêpes! »	*She announced: "I am going to make crêpes!"*

Reported speech

Elle a annoncé qu'elle **allait** faire des crêpes.	*She announced (that) she was going to make crêpes.*

Direct speech

Il pensait: « Je **dormirai** mieux **demain**. »

He was thinking: "I will sleep better tomorrow."

Reported speech

Il pensait qu'il **dormirait** mieux **le lendemain**.

He was thinking (that) he would sleep better the next day.

Il a expliqué qu'il **s'était trompé**.

He explained that he had made a mistake.

Le candidat a promis qu'il **donnerait** du travail à tout le monde.

The candidate promised that he would give work to everyone.

Elle a déclaré qu'elle **allait** changer de voiture.

She declared that she was going to get a new car.

After declarative verbs such as **dire que**, and any verb that could introduce a reported command as well as a reported statement, you may find yourself wondering: "Is this a command or a statement?" The answer lies in the dependent verb: if it is in the subjunctive, the sentence expresses a command. Any other verb form after **dire**, and so on, would indicate a reported statement. You will find reported commands in Unit 1, "Sequence of verbs with and without infinitives."

Commands

Elle a dit **qu'il parte**.

She said for him to leave.

Il les a chassés et a ajouté **qu'ils ne reviennent pas**.

He kicked them out and added that they must not come back.

Elle a répondu **qu'ils s'en aillent**.

She answered that they had to scram.

Paul a dit à son frère **qu'il se marie**.

Paul told his brother to get married.

Reported speech

Elle a dit **qu'il était parti**.

She said that he had left.

Il les a chassés et a ajouté **qu'ils ne reviendraient pas**.

He kicked them out and added that they would not come back.

Elle a répondu **qu'ils s'en iraient** sûrement.

She answered that they would certainly take off/scram.

Paul a dit à son frère **qu'il se mariait**.

Paul told his brother (that) he (Paul) was getting married.

Put the following quotes in indirect speech, including reported questions, and make all the necessary changes. (See Unit 7 for the lesson on reported questions.)

1. « Qu'est-ce qui ne va pas? » a demandé le docteur.

   _____

2. « Tu seras malade si tu manges trop, » a dit la mère à l'enfant.

   _____

3. J'ai annoncé: « Bonsoir. Je vais me coucher. »

   _____

4. « Qu'est-ce que tu ferais si tu voyais un Martien? » m'ont demandé les enfants.

   _____

5. J'ai promis: « Je n'arriverai plus en retard. »

   _____

6. « Qui vas-tu inviter à ton anniversaire? » m'ont demandé mes parents.

   _____

7. Sa mère lui a demandé: « Tu t'es brossé les dents? »

   _____

8. Le prof a conseillé: « Étudiez bien avant l'examen. »

   _____

9. « Est-ce que ta fille t'a souhaité bon anniversaire? » lui a demandé son amie.

   _____

10. Julie demande toujours au facteur: « Quelque chose pour moi? »

    _____

11. « Le jour de mon anniversaire je jure que je prendrai une leçon de tango. »

    _____

12. La serveuse: nous a demandé « Vous avez choisi? »

_____

13. « Je te préviens que je ne vais pas y arriver seul. Il faudra que tu m'aides. »

_____

14. « Fais tes devoirs! » a dit sa mère.

_____

15. « Pourquoi faut-il que je fasse mes devoirs maintenant? Je viens d'arriver à la maison! »

_____

16. « Est-ce que tu reviendras nous voir? » ont demandé les amis de Julie.

_____

EXERCICE

5·2

*Complete the sentences with the appropriate verb form. Note that in some cases you may need to add **de**.*

1. La direction a annoncé qu'il y _____ (avoir) des licenciements le mois prochain.

2. Je t'affirme que ce _____ (ne pas être) moi qui t'ai téléphoné à une heure du matin!

3. Tu te rends compte que nous _____ (se rencontrer) il y a exactement vingt ans?

4. Ce prisonnier n'a jamais admis qu'il _____ (commettre) ce crime.

5. Nous sommes certains que tu _____ (réussir). Continue!

6. Je ne t'ai jamais dit _____ (partir)! Tu as rêvé.

7. Je vous avertis que ce _____ (être) dur... mais on y arrivera.

8. Tu as remarqué que les voisins _____ (changer) de voiture?

9. Le comité sportif a déclaré que Paul _____ (gagner) la course.

10. Le prof m'a dit _____ (refaire) ma composition.

11. Je pense que tu _____ (mal fermer) la porte. Vérifie.

12. J'espère que vous _____ (venir) me voir bientôt.

13. Il se plaint toujours que ses étudiants _____ (ne jamais faire) leurs devoirs.

14. Le prof m'a dit que mon devoir _____ (être) excellent.

15. Le conférencier nous a expliqué que ce phénomène _____ (se passer) souvent.

16. Le docteur trouve que je _____ (ne pas dormir) assez.

The subjunctive

You presumably already know quite a bit about the subjunctive, so let's start with a brief review before going on to its more challenging aspects. The subjunctive can be triggered by numerous verbs that we'll call "trigger expressions." These triggers can be impersonal, such as **il faut que** (*it is necessary that*), or they can be a verb conjugated with any subject. They can also be conjunctions. In any case, to a certain degree they all express the subjectivity of their subject. Expressions such as **il faut que**, **vouloir que** (*to want that*), **avoir peur que** (*to fear that*), **il est triste que** (*it is sad that*), **il est impossible que** (*it is impossible that*), **à condition que** (*provided that*) denote the subject's emotions, thoughts, desires, and so on, about what someone else does, did, or will do. In other words, for the subjunctive to occur, the sentence needs two distinct subjects.

Rule of the two subjects

The dependent verb is in the subjunctive because it has its own subject, different from the subject of the main verb (the trigger verb). If both verbs have the same subject, you must, in most cases, use the infinitive instead of the subjunctive. The following examples illustrate this difference:

Il **veut qu'ils** réussissent.	*He wants them to succeed.*
Il veut réussir.	*He wants to succeed.*
Je **voudrais que tu** viennes ici.	*I'd like you to come here.*
Je voudrais venir avec toi.	*I'd like to come with you.*
Il **faut que vous** soyez à l'heure.	*You must be on time.*
Il faut être à l'heure.	*It is necessary to be on time.*
Il est parti **sans qu'on** le sache.	*He left without us knowing it.*
Il est parti sans dire au revoir.	*He left without saying good-bye.*

After the trigger expressions **être** + adjective, **avoir** + noun (**avoir envie/besoin/peur**, etc.), or after the verb **regretter**, when there is a single subject, you must add **de** before the infinitive.

Le prof **a peur que** les étudiants **aient** une mauvaise note.	*The teacher fears that the students will have a bad grade.*
Les étudiants **ont peur d'avoir** une mauvaise note.	*The students are afraid they might have a bad grade.*
Je **regrette que** vous **soyez** si pressés.	*I regret that you (all) are in such a hurry.*
Nous **regrettons d'être** pressés.	*We regret to be in such a hurry.*
Nous **sommes contents que** tu **puisses** nous accompagner.	*We are glad that you can come with us.*
Nous **sommes contents d'avoir** de la compagnie.	*We are glad to have company.*

After some conjunctions, the rule of two subjects/subjunctive, single subject/infinitive does not apply. In those cases, you must maintain the subjunctive, even though both verbs have the same subject. (Refer to the later discussion of conjunctions in this chapter.)

Elle fera un gâteau **pourvu qu'elle ait** assez de temps.	*She will bake a cake provided that she has enough time.*
Je continuerai **jusqu'à ce que je finisse**.	*I will continue until I finish.*
Je t'attendrai **bien que je sois** pressée.	*I will wait for you, even though I am in a hurry.*

Triggers for the subjunctive

You are familiar with verbs expressing desire and want (**je veux**), necessity (**il faut**), possibility (**il est possible**), doubt (**je doute**), emotions (**j'ai peur**, **je suis surpris**). We will focus here on less common, and sometimes confusing, trigger expressions.

Uncommon trigger expressions

Here are several expressions that may not always come to mind as triggers:

avoir de la chance que	*to be lucky that*
ce n'est pas la peine que	*it is not worth the trouble that*
comment se fait-il que... ?	*how come . . . ?*
comprendre que	*to understand that*
être d'accord pour que	*to agree to*
il arrive que	*it may happen/it happens that*
il est temps que	*it is time to/that*
il ne sert à rien que	*it is useless to/that*

il n'est pas question que	there is no way that
il n'y a aucune chance que	there's not a chance of
l'idée que	the thought of/that
on ne pouvait pas croire que	no one could believe that
personne n'aurait pensé que	no one would have imagined
que... !	that . . . !

L'idée que sa fille puisse quitter la maison la rendait triste.	*The thought that her daughter could leave home made her sad.*
Que je lui fasse des excuses? Jamais!	*That I apologize to him? Never!*
Il n'est pas question que tu sortes ce soir.	*It is out of question that you go out tonight.*
Il arrive que les caissiers fassent des erreurs.	*It happens that cashiers make mistakes.*
Comment se fait-il que tu ne m'en **aies** jamais **parlé?**	*How come you never talked to me about it?*
Nous avons eu de la chance qu'il y ait encore des places.	*We were lucky that there were still some seats left.*
Ce n'est pas la peine que nous nous fatiguions à lui expliquer. Il refuse d'écouter...	*It's not worth our getting tired over it. He refuses to listen . . .*

Il faut and il ne faut pas

You have learned that **il faut** means *it is necessary*, but did you know that **il ne faut pas** is *not* the equivalent of *it is not necessary*? In fact, **il ne faut pas** is an extremely strong prohibition. In English, it is translated by *one must not*. To translate *it is not necessary* into French, you may use one of the following personal or impersonal expressions:

ce n'est pas la peine que/de	it is not worth the trouble to
il n'est pas nécessaire que/de	it is not necessary to
il n'est pas obligatoire que	it is not mandatory to
tu n'as pas besoin de	you don't need to
tu n'es pas obligé(e) de	you don't have to

Tu n'as pas besoin de faire la vaisselle ce soir.	*You don't need to do the dishes tonight.*
or: **Il n'est pas nécessaire que tu fasses** la vaisselle ce soir.	*It is not necessary for you to do the dishes tonight.*
or: **Ce n'est pas la peine que tu fasses** la vaisselle ce soir.	*It is not necessary for you to do the dishes tonight.*

But:

| **Il ne faut pas que tu fasses** la vaisselle ce soir! | *You must not do the dishes tonight!* |

Confusing trigger expressions

Some common trigger expressions look very much like expressions that do not introduce the subjunctive. Pay special attention to the following:

INTRODUCES SUBJUNCTIVE		DOES NOT INTRODUCE SUBJUNCTIVE	
douter que	*to doubt that*	se douter que	*to suspect that*
il est heureux que	*it's a good thing that*	heureusement que	*fortunately*
il semble que	*it seems that*	il me semble que	*it seems to me that*
souhaiter que	*to wish that*	espérer que	*to hope that*

Le juge **doute que** l'affaire **soit** sérieuse.	*The judge does not think the case is serious.*
Poirot **se doute que** cet homme **est** le coupable.	*Poirot suspects that that man is the culprit.*
Je **souhaite que** vous **retrouviez** vite vos clés.	*I hope that you'll find your keys quickly.*
J'**espère que** vous **retrouverez** vite vos clés.	*I hope that you'll find your keys quickly.*

When **que** changes to **à ce que**

Some verbs require a little more than **que** to introduce the subjunctive clause. With the following verbs, **que** is expanded into **à ce que**:

contribuer à ce que	*to contribute to*
être attentif (-ive) à ce que	*to be attentive to*
(il) y a intérêt à ce que	*he'd/she'd/it'd/you'd better*
s'attendre à ce que	*to expect to*
se décider à ce que	*to make up one's mind to*
s'employer à ce que	*to work toward*
se refuser à ce que	*to refuse to*
s'habituer à ce que	*to get used to*
s'intéresser à ce que	*to be interested in*
s'opposer à ce que	*to be opposed to*
tenir à ce que	*to insist on*
travailler à ce que	*to work toward*
trouver quelque chose/ne... rien d'étonnant à ce que	*to find it/not find it surprising that*
veiller à ce que	*to ensure that*

Je **tiens à ce que** vous **rentriez** à l'heure.	*I insist that you come home on time.*
Son père **s'est refusé à ce qu'**elle **épouse** ce garçon.	*Her father refused that she marry that boy.*

Tu **ne trouves rien d'étonnant à ce qu'**ils ne **répondent** pas?	*Aren't you surprised that they are not answering?*
Il y a interêt à ce que ça **marche**, après tous nos efforts!	*It'd better work, after all our efforts!*

Il y a interêt à ce que is reserved for spoken, colloquial French and pronounced **y'a interêt à s'que**.

Subjunctive after a conjunction

Verbs are not the only possible triggers for the subjunctive. Conjunctions can also serve that function. Like any trigger expression, a conjunction can introduce a second subject (+ subjunctive) or not (+ infinitive). The following examples have two subjects:

Ils iront à la piscine **pourvu qu'il fasse** beau.	*They will go to the pool, provided that the weather is nice.*
Je préparerai le dîner **en attendant que vous rentriez.**	*I will cook dinner while waiting for you to come home.*
Il est trop tôt **pour que nous puissions** l'appeler.	*It is too early for us to call him.*

In the absence of a second subject, the conjunction is replaced by the equivalent preposition (see following list) + infinitive (examples 1 and 2). Note the following exceptions: after the conjunctions **bien que**, **à moins que**, **jusqu'à ce que**, and **pourvu que**, you must maintain the subjunctive whether or not the sentence has a second subject (examples 3 and 4).

J'ai acheté ce livre **pour le lire.**	*I bought this book (in order) to read it.*
Je mets la clé en lieu sûr **de peur de** la **perdre.**	*I'm putting the key in a safe place for fear of losing it.*

But:

Il sortira avec nous **à moins qu'il (n')ait** trop de travail.	*He will go out with us unless he has too much work to do.*
Nous serons en retard **à moins que nous (ne) partions** immédiatement.	*We will be late unless we leave at once.*

In the two previous examples, the use of **ne/n'** is optional and does not have a negative meaning. **Ne/n'** can accompany the subjunctive after **à moins que**, **avant que**, and **de peur/de crainte que**.

CONJUNCTION	EQUIVALENT PREPOSITION	
à condition que	à condition de	*provided that*
à moins que	—	*unless*
avant que	avant de + infinitive	*before*
bien que	malgré	*although/in spite of*
de peur/de crainte que	de peur/crainte de + infinitive	*for fear of*
en attendant que	en attendant de + infinitive	*while*
jusqu'à ce que	—	*until*
pour que/afin que	pour/afin de + infinitive	*in order to*
pourvu que	—	*provided that*
sans que	sans + infinitive	*without*
trop/assez/pas assez... pour que	trop... pour	*too much/enough/not enough . . . to*

Phony triggers: verbs that don't always trigger the subjunctive

In the same way that some verbs always trigger the subjunctive, others can *never* introduce it, even when they are followed by **que** + dependent clause with its own subject. Since we covered them in the previous unit (see Unit 5) we won't repeat them here. Still other verbs alternate between subjunctive and indicative. Let's start with those:

Verbs of opinion

Verbs expressing opinion (**penser que, trouver que**) or certainty (**il est certain que, il est évident que...**) introduce a dependent verb that alternates between the indicative and the subjunctive. We use the indicative in affirmative sentences and the subjunctive in negative sentences, as well as in interrogative sentences with inversion. The subjunctive reinforces the idea of uncertainty expressed by the interrogative or negative form.

Mon père **pense que** les Martiens **sont** réels.	*My dad believes (that) Martians are real.*
Mon prof de sciences **ne pense pas que** les Martiens **soient** réels.	*My science teacher does not believe (that) Martians are real.*
Il **estime que** cette décision **est** juste.	*He deems this decision fair.*
Estimez-vous que cette décision **soit** juste?	*Do you deem this decision fair?*
Nous **pensons qu'**il **peut** battre le champion.	*We think (that) he can beat the champion.*
Pensez-vous qu'il **puisse** battre le champion?	*Do you think (that) he can beat the champion?*

Alternatives to the subjunctive

Under certain circumstances you can replace the subjunctive by an infinitive or even simply by a noun. The construction without the subjunctive is "lighter" and often preferred.

Infinitive for reported commands

To report a command or a request, a construction with the *infinitive* is generally used, even though it is also possible to use the subjunctive (given in parentheses in the following third and fourth examples). The verbs expressing indirect commands typically have an indirect object (you tell *someone*—**à quelqu'un**—to do something). The recipient of the order also serves as the subject of the dependent infinitive. (See the section on reported commands in Unit 1.)

Maman a dit **aux enfants de rentrer**.	*Mom told the children to come home.*
Il **m**'a empêché **de finir** mon travail.	*He prevented me from finishing my work.*
Je **lui** ai demandé **de m**'**aider**.	*I asked him to help me.*
(Je **lui** ai demandé **qu**'**il** m'**aide**.)	
Papa **nous** a permis **de faire** du vélo.	*Papa allowed us to ride our bikes.*
(Papa a permis **que nous fassions** du vélo.)	*Papa allowed us to ride our bikes.*

However, it isn't always possible to use the infinitive for reported commands. Some main verbs, such as **exiger** and **avoir envie** (the following examples 1 and 3) do not take an indirect object. Using the infinitive construction with such a verb would lead to a mistranslation. Examples 2 and 5 show the correct translation of the French.

Il a exigé qu'elle s'en aille.	*He demanded that she go away.*
Il a exigé de s'en aller.	*He demanded (the right) to go away.*
Bébé a envie que tu le prennes dans tes bras.	*Baby wants you to pick him up.*
Je souhaite que tu t'excuses.	*I wish that you would apologize.*
Je souhaite t'excuser.	*I wish to excuse you.*

Sometimes the indirect object is not expressed. The next two examples show the verb **demander**, first, without an indirect object and then, with the indirect object (**au pâtissier**).

Elle a demandé **que le gâteau ait** un glaçage blanc.	*She requested that the cake have white icing.*
Elle a demandé *au pâtissier de faire* un glaçage blanc.	*She asked the baker to make a white icing.*

The following verbs cannot take the infinitive construction with a second subject. After these verbs, the conjugated verb is always in the subjunctive.

accepter que	to accept/agree
attendre que	to wait for
avoir envie que	to want
être d'accord pour que	to agree
exiger que	to demand
préférer que	to prefer
souhaiter que	to wish for
tenir à ce que	to insist on
vouloir que	to want

Je vais attendre **que tu finisses**.	I will wait for you to finish.
Je tiens à ce **que tu t'excuses**.	I insist that you apologize.
Il veut **que vous soyez** les premiers à le savoir.	He wants you to be the first ones to know.

Infinitive after il faut

The subjunctive is normally used after **il faut**. But it is also common to use an indirect object pronoun + infinitive instead of a subject + subjunctive, as follows:

Il **faut que je fasse** la vaisselle.	I need to do the dishes.
Il *me* **faut faire** la vaisselle.	I need to do the dishes.
Il **faut qu'il réussisse** son bac.	He must pass his baccalaureate.
Il *lui* **faut réussir** son bac.	He must pass his baccalaureate.

Noun instead of a clause in the subjunctive

With some verbs it is even possible to replace the subjunctive clause by a simple noun, with no verb at all. You may do this when the verb in the subjunctive has an appropriate noun equivalent.

Je refuse **qu'il démissionne**.	I refuse that he resign.
Je refuse **sa démission**.	I refuse his resignation.
La grève a empêché **que nous partions**.	The strike prevented us from leaving.
La grève a empêché **notre départ**.	The strike prevented our departure.
Grand-père apprécie **que nous soyons** à l'heure.	Grandpa appreciates that we are on time.
Grand-père apprécie **notre exactitude**.	Grandpa appreciates our punctuality.
Elle ne supporte pas **que les enfants crient**.	She can't stand that the kids shout.
Elle ne supporte pas **les cris des enfants**.	She can't stand the kids' screams/ shouting.

If the subjunctive is introduced by a conjunction, sometimes the equivalent preposition + noun is possible, as follows:

Ils écouteront **jusqu'à ce que tu finisses** ton discours.	*They will listen until you finish your speech.*
Ils écouteront **jusqu'à la fin** de ton discours.	*They will listen until the end of your speech.*

Other uses of the subjunctive

There are several additional uses of the subjunctive that deserve more detailed discussion.

Subjunctive versus the future

There cannot be a future tense or an "immediate future" after a trigger verb. Thus, when the context of a sentence that begins with a trigger verb is the future, the subjunctive is your only choice.

Il faut **que vous soyez** à l'heure **demain**.	*You will have to be on time tomorrow.*

This may sometimes leave you with an ambiguous sentence in French (example 1). To remedy this, you can use expressions that indicate time (**demain, la prochaine fois**, etc., as in the previous example) or use a more precise verb, one that already expresses an idea of the future, such as **compter** or **avoir l'intention de** (*to intend to do*), seen in example 2.

Ils sont contents **que leur patron** leur **donne** un congé.	*They are glad that their boss is giving them a day off.*
	or: *They are glad that their boss is going to give them a day off.*
Ils sont contents **que leur patron compte** leur **donner** un congé.	*They are glad that their boss is going to give them a day off.*

Subjunctive in a relative clause

Normally the relative pronouns (**qui, que, dont, où**) do not introduce the subjunctive (see Unit 10). There are however two scenarios where they do:

Queries and negative answers

In a sentence beginning with **Je cherche une personne qui...** (*I am looking for someone who . . .*), **Y a-t-il une chose que... ?** (*Is there something that . . . ?*), **Connaissez-vous une chose que... ?** (*Do you know one thing that . . . ?*), and so on, the subjunctive is used in the subordinate clause to reinforce the idea of query.

The subjunctive is also used in the relative clause following the *negative* of such sentences (**Il n'y a rien qui...**, **Je ne connais personne qui...**), where its use reinforces the idea of non-fact. When the same verbs do not express a query or a negative, *do not* use the subjunctive. The following examples highlight the verbs in the relative (subordinate) clause:

—Connaissez-vous quelqu'un **qui puisse** m'aider?	*"Do you know someone who might be able to help me?"*
—Je connais quelqu'un **qui peut** vous aider.	*"Yes, I know someone who will be able to help you."*
—Je ne connais personne **qui puisse** vous aider.	*"I know no one who might be able to help you."*
Il n'y a pas de mots **qui puissent** décrire ma joie.	*There are no words that can describe my joy.*
Il y a une quantité de mots **qui peuvent** décrire ma joie.	*There are lots of words that can describe my joy.*

Superlatives

After a superlative, the verb in the relative clause must be in the subjunctive.

C'est le plus beau bébé **qui soit**.	*He/She is the most beautiful baby ever.*
Fred et Ginger sont les plus gracieux danseurs **que j'aie jamais vus**.	*Fred and Ginger are the most graceful dancers I've ever seen.*

Subjunctive as a third-person imperative

You have learned that the imperative has only three forms: **tu**, **nous**, and **vous**: **Parle! Parlons! Parlez!** (*Speak! Let's speak! Speak!*) However, you may sometimes need to express a command in the third person, singular or plural, for example, an order addressed to an absent person, or a wish made out loud. To do so you can use the expression **pourvu que** (*may he/she . . .*) + subjunctive, or a sentence that begins directly with **Que** + subjunctive, without even an introductory verb.

Pourvu que le docteur **arrive** à temps!	*May the doctor arrive in time!*
Qu'il fasse ce dont il parle au lieu de continuer à en parler!	*May he do what he's talking about instead of continuing to talk about it!*

Total subjectivity

In addition to being triggered by the expressions we have just reviewed, the subjunctive can also be triggered by the underlying tone one wants to impart to the sentence—without the use of a trigger verb. It can express someone's intellectual or emotional input or his or her subjectivity (highlighted in the following examples).

Mon avis est que ce travail est mauvais.	*My opinion is that this work is bad.*
Mon espoir est que ce travail **soit** meilleur.	*My hope is that this work can be better.*
L'idéal n'existe pas.	*The ideal does not exist.*
L'idéal serait que nous **vivions** sur une île tropicale.	*The ideal (life) would be if we could live on a tropical island.*

The past subjunctive

The past can be expressed in a subjunctive sentence, but only in one case: when the subordinate action (the action of the verb you're about to conjugate in the subjunctive) is prior to that of the trigger verb. In other words, when it comes to the *past subjunctive*, not all pasts are equal, and you should not automatically use the past subjunctive in the subjunctive clause, even if the trigger verb is in the past. For example, the present subjunctive would be used in the following example :

Il **était** content que ses amis **soient** là.	*He was happy that his friends were there.*

The rules and examples below will help you sort it out.

♦ When the action of the verb in the subjunctive is simultaneous (first example) or after (second example) the action of the trigger verb, use the *present subjunctive*.

Papa veut que nous **réussissions**.	*Dad wants us to succeed.*
J'ai peur qu'il **pleuve** demain.	*I'm afraid it may rain tomorrow.*

♦ When the action of the verb in the subjunctive is before that of the trigger verb, use the *past subjunctive* (second example).

Les enfants avaient peur que le Père Noël les **oublie**.	*The kids were afraid that Santa would forget them.*
Les enfants ont été gatés. Ils sont heureux que le Père Noël ne les **ait** pas **oubliés**.	*The kids were spoiled. They are glad that Santa did not forget them.*

Formation of the past subjunctive

The past subjunctive is formed just like the *passé composé*: by using the auxiliary verb *avoir* or *être* in the present subjunctive + a past participle, and applying all the rules of agreement of the past participle.

Passé composé	**Past subjunctive**
J'ai (*présent*) dormi	que j'aie (*subjonctif*) dormi
J'ai parlé	que j'aie parlé
Je suis venu(e)	que je sois venu(e)

Alternatives to the past subjunctive

Just as the infinitive can be used instead of the present subjunctive (see previous discussion, page 81), so can the past infinitive (second example).

Les profs n'aiment pas **annuler** les cours.	*Professors don't like to cancel classes.*
Le prof regrette d'**avoir annulé** le cours mardi dernier.	*The professor regrets having (to have) canceled class last Tuesday.*

The past infinitive is formed by using the the auxiliary verb *avoir* or *être* in the infinitive + a past participle.

infinitive	**past infinitive**
dormir	avoir dormi
parler	avoir parlé
venir	être venu

EXERCICE

6·1

Replace the following subjunctive constructions by an infinitive construction when possible (some will use the noun replacement construction). Be sure to make all necessary changes.

1. Les parents ont permis que les enfants regardent la télé jusqu'à minuit.

   _____

2. La police ordonne que les citoyens restent chez eux.

   _____

3. La petite fille demande que les autres ne prennent pas ses jouets.

   _____

4. Le club interdit que les enfants jouent sur le terrain de golf.

   _____

5. Il faut que je finisse ce travail aujourd'hui.

   _____

6. Les grévistes ont empêché que le train parte.

   _____

7. Il faut qu'elle choisisse le bon numéro.

   _____

8. Il n'est pas nécessaire que vous veniez.

   _____

9. Je souhaite que vous vous rétablissiez vite.

   _____

10. Elle a dit aux enfants qu'ils dorment.

    _____

11. Je sortirai sans que mes parents le sachent.

    _____

12. Il t'aidera bien qu'il soit fatigué.

    _____

13. Je préfère que vous rentriez tôt.

    _____

EXERCICE
6·2

Complete the following sentences with the correct form of the verb. Choose between the present subjunctive or any tense of the indicative (present, past, or future).

1. As-tu vraiment besoin que je _____ (faire) ça pour toi?

2. J'espère que tu _____ (venir) à notre soirée samedi prochain.

3. Je sais que tu _____ (rentrer) tard hier soir.

4. Ma mère me dit toujours que je _____ (être) trop gentille avec les inconnus.

5. Croyez-vous que les politiciens _____ (être) toujours honnêtes?

6. C'est dommage que tu _____ (ne pas pouvoir) rester plus longtemps.

7. Ça m'étonnerait que tu _____ (se souvenir) de cette histoire.

8. Thomas est puni parce que son père sait qu'il _____ (ne pas dire) la vérité quand on lui a posé des questions.

9. Mes parents croient que je _____ (être) très sérieux, mais en fait je m'amuse beaucoup!

10. Est-ce que ça vous dérange que je _____ (prendre) une photo de votre bébé?

11. Est-ce que tu trouves que ce chapeau me _____ (aller) bien?

12. Il est clair qu'elle _____ (ne pas avoir) assez d'argent pour payer.

13. Je ne pense pas qu'elle _____ (avoir) assez d'argent pour payer.

14. Je suppose que vous _____ (trouver) ça drôle?

15. Nous sommes choqués que vous _____ (trouver) ça drôle!

16. Nous espérons qu'il y _____ (avoir) du soleil dimanche prochain.

17. Je trouve que cette affaire _____ (être) assez sérieuse pour que nous lui _____ (donner) la priorité sur toutes les autres.

18. Je sais que vous _____ (faire) des efforts constamment, mais ce n'est pas suffisant.

19. Il est terrible que nous _____ (avoir) cours à 8 heures du matin!

20. Vos amis sont contents que vous _____ (se marier) en été parce qu'ils sont sûrs qu'il _____ (faire) beau pour la cérémonie.

21. Est-ce que tu te souviens que tu _____ (devoir) aller chercher les enfants ce soir?

22. As-tu remarqué que Julie _____ (avoir) une nouvelle voiture?

23. Ça me surprend que Pierre ne _____ (vouloir) pas te raconter cette histoire.

24. Continuez jusqu'à ce que vous _____ (finir) le travail.

25. Il aime que ses enfants lui _____ (servir) le café au lit le dimanche.

26. J'aimerais mieux que tu _____ (ne pas prendre) ma voiture aujourd'hui.

27. Les enfants n'aiment pas aller chez le dentiste parce qu'ils ont peur qu'il leur _____ (faire) mal.

28. Si vous avez souvent mal à la tête, je recommande que vous _____ (prendre) une aspirine par jour.

29. Nous espérons qu'il _____ (comprendre) notre décision.

30. Les enfants seront contents que tu _____ (sortir) au parc avec eux samedi après-midi.

Put the following into French. All the yous *are* **tu** *unless otherwise noted.*

1. I will wait until you finish your work.

   _____

2. It is time for you to leave.

   _____

3. He will stay here until you tell him the truth.

   _____

4. I asked Julie to hurry.

   _____

5. What do you want me to do? (**vous**)

   _____

6. I will do it even though I don't feel like it.

   _____

7. Do you think that it will rain tomorrow? (**vous**)

   _____

8. I would be afraid of someone who could read people's thoughts.

   _____

9. This is the most surprising story I have ever heard!

   _____

10. I am sorry that you could not come. (**vous**)

_____

11. It is too bad that you don't want to meet them.

_____

12. We are glad you're here.

_____

13. We want you to come with us.

_____

14. I would like to give you this book before you leave.

_____

_____

EXERCICE
6·4

Read the first two contextual sentences in each example, and then choose between the present subjunctive or the past subjunctive to complete the third sentence.

1. Si tu es en retard, il faut que tu préviennes tes parents.

   Tu les as prévenus.

   Ils sont contents que tu les _____ (prévenir).

2. Vos parents avaient peur que vous buviez de l'alcool avant de prendre le volant, samedi dernier.

   Mais vous n'avez pas bu.

   Ils sont fiers que vous _____ (être) raisonnables, et que vous _____ (ne pas boire).

3. Le prof a demandé que vous écriviez une bonne composition.

   Vous l'avez fait.

   Le prof est content que vous _____ (écrire) une bonne composition!

4. Julie voulait sortir avec cet horrible garçon.

   Finalement elle n'est pas sortie avec lui et sa mère est soulagée!

   Sa mère est soulagée qu'elle _____ (ne pas sortir) avec lui.

5. Un sportif a triché pour gagner.

   On lui a repris son titre de champion.

   Était-il juste qu'on lui _____ (reprendre) son titre?

6. Je voulais que mes amies viennent à mon anniversaire.

   Elles n'ont pas pu venir.

   Je suis triste qu'elles _____ (ne pas venir).

7. Je voudrais que mes amies viennent à mon anniversaire.

   Elles ne pourront pas y être parce qu'elles seront en vacances.

   Je suis triste qu'elles _____ (ne pas venir).

8. Tu es parti du restaurant trop tôt.

   Nous sommes arrivés 10 minutes après ton départ. Nous nous sommes ratés.

   C'est dommage que tu _____ (ne pas attendre) un peu plus pour nous voir.

9. Cet étudiant ne manque jamais les cours.

   Il est absent depuis une semaine.

   Les autres étudiants sont surpris qu'il _____ (être) absent.

Relative tenses *not* introduced by **que**

In this unit, we'll look at the relationship between the first verb and the subsequent verb(s) in a sentence marked by linking words other than **que**, including **quand** (*when*), **si** (*if*), and the words that introduce reported speech.

When sentences

When expressing the future, constructions with **quand** and similar expressions behave quite differently in French than in English. Other tenses with **quand** are parallel in both languages.

quand in the present and past

In present and past contexts, French and English follow similar rules: when the verb of the **quand** clause is in the present, the verb outside the clause is also in the present, when the verb of the **quand** clause is in the past, the verb outside the clause is also in a past tense. The difference between using the **imparfait** or the **passé composé** is not determined by **quand**, but rather by the normal context (examples 2, 3, and 4).

Quand il **fait** chaud, nous **mettons** la climatisation.	*When it is hot we turn on the A/C.*
Quand j'**avais** quinze ans, je n'**aimais** pas l'école.	*When I was fifteen, I did not like school.*
Quand j'**avais** quinze ans, je **me suis cassé** la jambe.	*When I was fifteen, I broke my leg.*
Quand j'**ai eu** mon bac, mes parents m'**ont acheté** un scooter.	*When I passed the baccalaureate, my parents bought me a moped.*

quand in the future

When the context is in the future, French and English show an important difference. In French, the verbs that follow **quand**, and similar expressions such as **dès que**, **aussitôt que** (*as soon as*), **au moment où** (*at the time when*), and so on, must be in the future or **futur antérieur**:

Cet été, **dès qu'il fera** chaud, **nous mettrons** la climatisation.	*This summer as soon as it is hot we will turn on the A/C.*
Quand elle sera grande **elle sera** docteur.	*When she grows up she will be a doctor.*
Dès que tu arriveras en France **tu devras** trouver un hôtel.	*As soon as you arrive in France you will have to find a hotel.*

The futur antérieur

The rationale for using the **futur antérieur** (**aura fait** in example 1) is that in French, you cannot introduce a "pure" past tense in a future context as you do in English (*have finished* in example 1).

Tu iras jouer quand tu **auras fait** ton travail.	*You will go play when you have finished your homework.*
Que fera-t-il quand il **aura terminé** ses études?	*What will he do when he is done with school?*

In this type of sentence, English often uses *after* and a present tense. French rarely uses **après** to introduce a conjugated verb. It uses **quand** + **futur antérieur**, or **après** + noun.

Lave-toi les mains **quand** tu **auras fini**.	*Wash your hands after you're done.*
Tu pourras sortir **quand** tu **auras mangé** tes légumes.	*You can go out after you have eaten your vegetables.*
Que fera-t-il **après ses études**?	*What will he do when he is done with school?*
Tu pourras sortir **après le dîner**.	*You will be able to go out after dinner.*

If sentences

In this type of sentence, English and French follow similar rules: **si**/*if* + present tense is used in the dependent clause (i.e., after **si**), with a future or imperative in the main clause. (Note that the "main" clause is often the second clause.)

Si je **suis** chez moi ce soir, je **regarderai** la télé.	*If I'm home this evening, I'll watch TV.*

Si/*if* + past tense (often, the **imparfait**) is used in the dependent clause, with the conditional in the main clause.

> S'ils **avaient** l'argent, ils **iraient** en voyage.   *If they had the money, they'd take a trip.*

Note that the forms of the verbs are different in English and French: the present conditional is a simple tense in French (**nous irions**), whereas it is a compound tense in English (*we would go*). Similarly, the French past conditional is a two-word compound tense (**nous serions allés**), whereas it is a three-word compound tense in English (*we would have gone*).

Remember that **si** (*if*) can only be elided to **s'** before the subject pronoun **il**, *not* before **elle** or **on**.

S'il est seul ce soir, invite-le.	*If he's alone tonight, invite him.*
Si elle veut venir, elle est la bienvenue.	*If she wants to come, she's welcome.*
Si on est en retard, on ratera le train.	*If we are late, we will miss the train.*

Expressing a possibility

In a present context, something will happen if something else requires it, or causes it to happen. The verb in the **si** clause is usually in the present, but the main verb can be in the future (examples 1 and 2), the immediate future (**aller** + infinitive, as in example 3) or the imperative (examples 4 and 5).

Nous **mettrons** la climatisation **s'il fait** chaud.	*We will turn on the A/C if it is hot.*
Le prof **sera** content **si** nous **avons** de bonnes notes.	*The prof will be pleased if we make good grades.*
Si tu **montes** sur cette chaise, tu **vas** la casser!	*If you climb on that chair, you are going to break it!*
Étudie, si tu **veux** réussir tes examens.	*Study if you want to pass your exams.*
Mets la climatisation **s'il fait** chaud.	*Turn on the A/C if it is hot.*

The verb in the **si** clause (the dependent verb) can also be in the **passé composé** or **imparfait** when it expresses that something will happen if something else *has caused* it. The main verb remains in the future or imperative. None of these uses express a hypothesis.

S'il n'**a** pas **fini** à temps, nous **devrons** partir sans lui.	*If he is not done on time, we'll have to leave without him.*
Si vous n'**avez** pas encore **lu** le livre, vous ne **comprendrez** pas la discussion.	*If you have not read the book yet, you will not understand the discussion.*

Si c'est toi qui **as fait** ça, **dis**-le moi!	*If you did that, tell me!*
Si elle **parlait** espagnol dans sa jeunesse, elle **se débrouillera** très bien au Mexique.	*If she used to speak Spanish in her youth, she'll manage very well in Mexico.*

Making a hypothesis in a present context

The speaker imagines (now) what could happen (now or in the future) if something were different (now). The verb of the **si** clause is in the **imparfait** or pluperfect, the main verb is in the conditional (or in the past conditional when the pluperfect is in the dependent clause).

Context or fact

Aujourd'hui il **pleut**, et nous ne **sortons** pas.	*It is raining today and we aren't going out.*

Hypothesis contrary to fact

Nous **irions** au parc **s'il faisait** beau.	*We would go to the park if the weather were good.*

Context or fact

Elle **a** peur en avion et elle ne **voyage** jamais.	*She is scared in a plane and never travels.*

Hypothesis contrary to fact

Si elle n'**avait** pas peur en avion, elle **voyagerait**.	*If she were not scared on a plane she would travel.*

Context or fact

Julie n'**aime** pas Paul, et elle ne **se mariera** pas avec lui.	*Julie does not love Paul and will not marry him.*

Hypothesis contrary to fact

Si Julie **aimait** Paul, elle **se marierait** avec lui.	*If Julie loved Paul she would marry him.*

Making a hypothesis in a past context

In a past context, a hypothesis with **si** + pluperfect can have consequences that are either present or past. If the consequences are in the present, use the conditional to express them. If they are in the past, use the past conditional.

With consequences in the present

The speaker imagines (now) what things would be like (the consequences now) if something had been different (then). The verb of the *if*-clause is always in the pluperfect, the main verb is in the conditional.

Context or fact

Tu **as raté** ton bac et maintenant tu **dois** redoubler.

You failed your baccalaureate and now you have to redo your senior year.

Hypothesis

Si tu **avais réussi** ton bac, tu ne **redoublerais** pas ta terminale.

If you had passed your baccalaureate you would not be redoing your senior year.

Context or fact

Tu **as mangé** du poisson et maintenant tu **es** malade.

You ate some fish and now you are sick.

Hypothesis

Tu ne **serais** pas malade **si** tu n'**avais** pas **mangé** ce poisson.

You would not be sick if you had not eaten that fish.

Context or fact

Il n'**a** pas **rangé** ses clés, et maintenant ils les **cherche** à la dernière minute.

He did not put his keys away, and now he has to look for them at the last minute.

Hypothesis

Il ne **chercherait** pas ses clés à la dernière minute **s'**il les **avait rangées** hier soir.

He would not be looking for his keys at the last minute if he had put them away last night.

With consequences in the past

The speaker imagines (now) what things would have been like (the consequence then) if something had been different (then also). In this scenario the main verb is in the past conditional. This sentence construction expresses regret over something that did or did not happen, particularly with the past conditional of verbs like **devoir** (**j'aurais dû**), **aimer** (**j'aurais aimé**), **vouloir** (**j'aurais voulu**), and **falloir** (**il aurait fallu**), as in the parenthetical examples following examples 2 and 3).

Context or fact

Dimanche il **a plu**.

It rained on Sunday.

Hypothesis and regret

Nous **serions allés** au parc s'il **avait fait** beau dimanche.

We would have gone to the park if the weather had not been bad on Sunday.

Context or fact

Marie n'a pas **fait** ses devoirs parce qu'elle **avait oublié** son livre à l'école.

Marie could not do her homework because she had forgotten her book at school.

Hypothesis and regret

Marie **aurait fait** ses devoirs **si** elle n'**avait** pas **oublié** son livre à l'école.

Marie would have done her homework if she had not forgotten her book at school.

(Il **aurait fallu** qu'elle pense à son livre!)

(She should have thought about her book!)

Context or fact

Le Petit Chaperon Rouge **est allé** dans la forêt et le loup l'**a mangé**!

Little Red Riding Hood went into the woods and the wolf ate her!

Hypothesis and regret

Si elle n'**était** pas **allée** dans la forêt, le loup ne l'**aurait** pas **mangée**.
(Elle n'**aurait** pas **dû aller** dans la forêt!)

If she had not gone into the woods, the wolf would not have eaten her.
(She should not have gone into the woods!)

Context or fact

Ses parents n'**habitaient** pas en France au moment de sa naissance.

Her parents did not live in France when she was born.

Hypothesis and regret

Si ses parents **avaient habité** en France, elle **aurait appris** le français très jeune.

If her parents had lived in France, she would have learned to speak French very young.

(Elle **aurait voulu apprendre** le français très jeune.)

(She would have liked to learn French at a young age.)

More expressions with si

A number of linking words include **si**. The most common ones include **comme si** and **même si**.

comme si (*as if*)

The verb that follows **comme si** must be in the pluperfect or the **imparfait** and it denotes something *contrary to fact*.

Ne me parle pas **comme si** j'**avais** quatre ans!	*Don't talk to me as if I were four years old!*
Ils nous ont traités **comme si** nous **étions** des pachas.	*They treated us as if we had been/were royalty.*
Le chat fait toujours **comme s'**il ne nous **entendait** pas.	*The cat always acts as if he did not hear us.*

même si (*even if, even though*)

After **même si**, the verb can be in any tense except the tenses in **-r-** (namely, futures and conditionals) and the subjunctive. **Même si** + indicative is a good alternative to the conjunction **bien que** (*even though*) + subjunctive (last example).

Dis merci, **même si** tu **n'as** pas **aimé** son gâteau.	*Say thanks, even if you did not like her cake.*
Julie est toujours en short, **même s'**il **fait** froid.	*Julie always wears shorts, even if it is cold out.*
Il fallait t'arrêter au carrefour **même si** tu n'**avais** pas **vu** de stop.	*You needed to stop at the intersection, even if you had not seen a stop sign.*
Tu iras à ta retenue, **même si** tu **dis** ne pas la mériter.	*You will go to detention even if you say you don't deserve to.*
Tu iras à ta retenue, **bien que** tu **dises** ne pas la mériter.	*You will go to detention even though you say that you don't deserve to.*

Reporting questions

When you are reporting a question someone asked, you need an introductory verb such as **demander, se demander, vouloir savoir** and a dependent clause introduced by **si** for *yes/ no* questions, and the corresponding question words—some may require changes when reporting—for all other questions. Reported questions do not allow for the use of inversion or **est-ce que**. To determine the tense of the dependent verb, follow the same rules as for reported speech (see Unit 5).

Reported yes/no questions

The *yes/no* question is introduced by **si** in reported speech.

Pierre **voulait savoir si** j'**irais** au match vendredi soir.
Pierre wanted to know if I would go to the game Friday night.

Grand-mère **demande** toujours **si** on **a** assez **mangé**.
Grandma always asks if we have eaten enough.

Je **me demande si** j'**ai** déjà **pris** mes vitamines ou non.
I'm wondering if I have already taken my vitamins or not.

Reported information questions

Most question words don't change in indirect questions, but a few change as follows:

DIRECT QUESTION	REPORTED QUESTION	
Qu'est-ce qui... ?	ce qui	*what*
Je veux savoir **ce qui** se passe ici!	*I want to know what is going on here!*	
Qu'est-ce que... ?	ce que	*what*
Que... ? (object)	ce que	*what*
Elle m'a demandé **ce que** je voulais.	*She asked what I wanted.*	
Je ne comprends pas **ce que** vous dites.	*I don't understand what you're saying.*	
Qui est-ce que... ?	qui	*who*
Qui est-ce qui... ?	qui	*who*
Il veut que je lui dise **qui** a pris son livre.	*He wants me to tell him who took his book.*	
Dis-moi **qui** tu voudrais inviter pour ton anniversaire.	*Tell me who(m) you would like to invite to your birthday.*	

The words **ce qui**, **ce que** that replace the direct question words listed previously are neutral relative pronouns. (See Unit 10 for details.)

In reported speech the questions **Quelle heure est-il?** (*What time is it?*) and **Quel temps fait-il?** (*What is the weather like?*) change to **l'heure qu'il est** and **le temps qu'il fait** with the appropriate verb tenses.

Pourriez-vous me dire **l'heure qu'il est**, s'il vous plaît?
Could you tell me what time it is, please?

Il voulait savoir **le temps qu'il faisait** ici.
He wanted to know what the weather was like here.

Be sure to make a distinction between **demander que** (*to ask that*) and **demander si/comment/pourquoi...** (*to ask if/how/why . . .*). **Demander que** is a command and is followed by the subjunctive, whereas **demander si...** is a true reported question and requires the indicative.

Elle **a demandé qu'**on nous **serve** rapidement. (*command*)	*She asked that we be served quickly.*
Elle **a demandé si** nous **pouvions être servis** rapidement. (reported question)	*She asked if we could be served quickly.*
Il **demande** toujours **qu'**on ne lui **fasse** pas de cadeaux. (*command*)	*He always asks that people don't bring him any gifts.*
Il **a demandé si** on lui **avait apporté** des cadeaux. (reported question)	*He asked if anyone had brought him any gifts.*

In doing the following exercises, you may also review the section on relative tenses in reported questions presented in Unit 1.

EXERCICE
7·1

Complete the following sentences with the correct form of the verb. There is no subjunctive in this exercise.

1. Est-ce que tu savais qu'ils _____ (avoir) un accident le mois dernier?

2. La radio a annoncé qu'il _____ (faire) beau demain.

3. Si j'avais de mauvaises notes, mes parents _____ (être) en colère.

4. Qu'est-ce que tu feras quand tu _____ (ne plus avoir) de devoirs?

5. Si nous nous étions dépêchés, nous _____ (ne pas rater) le train.

6. Le candidat a promis qu'il _____ (boire) du champagne avec son opposant.

7. Si elle avait su, elle _____ (ne pas sortir) avec ce garçon.

8. Il ne serait pas arrivé en retard s'il _____ (prendre) un taxi au lieu du métro.

9. Tu m'avais dit que tu me _____ (aider).

10. Sherlock Holmes pensait qu'il _____ (pouvoir) arrêter l'assassin.

11. Elle n'a pas voulu admettre qu'elle _____ (se tromper).

12. Tu as remarqué que Paul _____ (ne plus porter) son alliance?

13. Je te promets que je _____ (ne pas oublier) l'heure de notre prochain rendez-vous.

14. Je t'aiderai, même si ce _____ (être) fatiguant.

15. Si j'avais su que tout le monde serait là, je _____ (apporté) mon appareil photo. Quel dommage!

*Translate the following sentences into French. The sentences include all the relative tenses, including the subjunctive. All the yous are **tu**.*

1. If they had known, they would never have done that.

_____

2. I will take my glasses next time I go to the movies.

_____

3. As soon as you open the door, you will see your surprise.

_____

4. I told the salesman I wanted to return that item.

_____

5. I told the salesman to help me.

_____

6. They hoped that the movie would be interesting.

_____

7. She wanted you to come see her.

_____

8. That morning he told us he was leaving.

   _____

9. My grandparents will go to Florida after they sell their house here.

   _____

10. My friend told me she ran after a thief.

    _____

11. My friend told me to run after the thief.

    _____

12. Sometimes my cat looks at me as if he did not know me!

    _____

Articles

You know that in French, a noun must almost always be accompanied by a *determiner*. A determiner can be a *demonstrative adjective*, such as **ce** (*this*) or **ces** (*these*); a *possessive adjective*, like **mon** (*my*) or **ton** (*your*); an *article*, such as **des** (*some*) or **le** (*the*); or an *expression of quantity*, such as **beaucoup de** (*a lot of*). In this unit we will study the articles as determiners. Other determiners are studied in Unit 9.

Indefinite articles

Indefinite articles refer to an object or objects that are not otherwise specific: **un**, **une**, **des**, and **de** in a negative sentence (*a, one, some* in the sense of "several," and *not any*).

Elle porte **une** jolie robe.	*She wears a pretty dress.*
Je n'ai pas acheté **de** pommes.	*I did not buy any apples.*
Je t'ai apporté **des** bonbons.	*I brought you some sweets.*
Avez-vous **une** moto ou **un** vélo?	*Do you have a motorcycle or a bicycle?*

After a negative verb

In the negative, **un**, **une**, and **des** become **de** or **d'** (examples 1 and 2), *unless* the verb in the negative is **être** and the negative implies a contrast (examples 3, 4, and 5), or the speaker insists on the fact that there is "only one" or "not even one" (examples 6 and 7).

Il **n'**a plus **d'**argent.	*He does not have any more money.*
Je **n'**ai **jamais** vu **d'**éléphants roses.	*I have never seen pink elephants.*
Ce garçon **n'**est **pas un** étudiant de notre cours.	*This boy is not a student from our class.*
Regarde! Ce **n'**est **pas un** oiseau! C'est un avion.	*Look! It's not a bird! It's a plane.*
Paul **n'**est **pas un** prof sérieux.	*Paul is not a serious professor.*

Il **n'a pas un** centime en poche.	*He does not have one cent in his pocket.*
Je **n'ai qu'une** minute à te consacrer!	*I only have one minute to give you!*

des: indefinite article (**des**) or contraction of preposition (**de**) + definite article (**les**)

Some verbs require the preposition **de** before a noun (see following list). When the noun that follows such verbs has the definite article **les**, the preposition **de** and **les** are contracted into **des** (*of the*)—which is also the form of the plural indefinite article! The distinction between **des** (the contraction of **de** + **les**) and **des** (the plural indefinite article) is important to understand, since, with the definite article, one denotes a specific thing (as in examples 1, 2, and 3), whereas the plural indefinite article describes unspecified objects. (See also "**des** changing to **de**: After certain verbs.")

de + les = des

Je me sers **des** ciseaux.	*I am using the scissors.*
Elle s'occupe souvent **des** enfants de sa sœur.	*She often looks after her sister's kids.*
Je me souviens **des** histoires que j'ai lues.	*I remember the stories I read.*

des as an indefinite article

Il y a **des** ciseaux sur la table.	*There are some scissors on the table.*
Elle a vu **des** événements dramatiques.	*She saw some dramatic events.*
Il raconte toujours **des** histoires drôles.	*He always tells funny stories.*

A few common verbs are followed by the preposition **de**:

avoir besoin de	*to need*
avoir envie de	*to want*
avoir l'habitude de	*to be used to*
avoir peur de	*to fear*
entendre parler de	*to hear about*
être + adjectif (content/déçu) de	*to be + adjective (happy/sad) with/about*
faire la connaissance de	*to meet*
jouer de	*to play an instrument*
manquer de	*to lack/not have enough of*
parler de	*to talk about*
profiter de	*to take advantage of*
rêver de	*to dream of*
s'apercevoir de	*to realize*
se moquer de	*to make fun of*

s'occuper de	to take care of
se servir de	to use
se souvenir de	to remember

The partitive article

The partitive article refers to a partial quantity or a partial category, and usually translates to English *some* (but *not* in the sense of "several"). The partitive articles are **du**, **de la**, **de l'**, **des**, and **de** in a negative sentence.

Partial quantities

The partitive article refers to a partial quantity, a portion taken from a larger whole. Let's consider coffee, and the ways it can be served. In the morning, someone in the household makes a pot of coffee, and everyone will have *some* of that coffee (example 1). But when you order coffee in a restaurant, the waiter usually brings you a *cup of* coffee, not a pot, and you drink **un café** (example 2). Similarly, you could perhaps eat *an entire* pumpkin pie (**une tarte**), but typically, one eats only *some* of it (**de la** tarte, as in example 3).

Le matin il boit **du café**.	*In the morning he drinks (some) coffee.*
« Je voudrais commander **un café**, s'il vous plaît. »	*"I'd like to order a coffee, please."*
Maman a fait **une tarte**. Nous allons manger **de la tarte** ce soir!	*Mom made a pie. We are going to have (some) pie tonight!*
Prenez-vous **du sucre** dans votre thé?	*Do you take (any) sugar in your tea?*

Partial categories

General categories require the definite article when they represent that category as a whole, in general: **l'argent** ("money" in general), **le sport** ("sports" in general), **la chance** ("luck" in general), **les enfants** ("children" in general). When you refer to such a category only partially, not in general (not as "luck" in general, but as "some luck"), you must use the partitive article: **de la chance** (not all the luck in the world as a whole, but some of it), **de l'argent** (not all the money in the world as a whole, but some of it), **du sport** (not all the sports in the world as a whole, but some of them). (See also "Naming general categories.")

Quand on travaille, on gagne **de l'argent**.	*When one works, one earns (some) money.*
Il a **de la chance**.	*He has (some) luck.*
Elle est au chômage, mais elle cherche **du travail**.	*She is unemployed, but she is looking for (some) work.*

When a partitive article + noun that refers to a partial category is modified by an adjective, you need to use the *indefinite* article instead of the partitive, as shown in the examples.

Il a **de la** chance.	*He has luck.*
Il a **une grande** chance.	*He has great luck.*
Je vois **de la** lumière.	*I see some light.*
Je vois **une petite** lumière.	*I see a little light.*
Il fait **du** sport.	*He plays sports.*
Il fait **un** sport **dangereux**.	*He practices a dangerous sport.*

faire + sports, musical instruments, and school subjects

To express that one practices a sport, a musical instrument, or studies a particular subject, use **faire** + partitive article + name of that activity.

On doit faire **du sport** pour rester en forme.	*One should practice sports to stay in shape.*
Alice fait **de la natation** mais son frère fait **du judo**.	*Alice practices swimming but her brother does judo.*
Ce semestre elle fait **du français** et **de l'histoire**.	*This semester, she studies French and history.*

However, the *definite* article must be used with those nouns when they occur after the verbs **apprendre** and **étudier**.

Quand il était jeune il **a appris l'allemand**.	*When he was young he learned German.*
Je voudrais **étudier le violon** mais je n'aurai jamais assez de patience.	*I'd like to study the violin, but I will never have enough patience.*

Note that another way to express the practice of a sport or of a musical instrument is to use **jouer du/de la/de l'/des** + instrument and **jouer au/à la /à l'/aux** + sport. The difference is in the preposition: **à** versus **de**. Note that some sports are found in both constructions whereas others are only possible in one. A tip, but not a rule, is that team sports can use either construction, but more individual sports like **la natation** (*swimming*), **l'équitation** (*equestrian*), and **l'athlétisme** (*track and field*) can only take the **faire de** construction.

des changing to de

Whether **des** is the indefinite article plural or the partitive article, it changes to **de** in certain circumstances.

In a negative sentence

After a negative verb, **des** becomes **de**, except when the verb in the negative is **être** (third example). See also the earlier section on "Indefinite articles."

Ils ne veulent **pas d'enfants**.	*They don't want any children.*
Si tu continues, tu n'auras **pas de dessert**.	*If you continue, you will not have any dessert.*

But:

Ne sois **pas un sauvage**! Mange avec ta fourchette.	*Don't be a savage! Eat with your fork.*

This rule also applies to negatives without a verb.

Pas de chaussures, pas de service!	*No shoes, no service!*

After certain verbs

The plural indefinite article **des** can never be used after verb/verbal expression + **de**, such as **avoir envie de** or **se souvenir de** (see the following list). In fact, the preposition **de** that is part of the verb replaces any article beginning with a **d-**. All other articles may follow the preposition **de**. When *de* is followed by the definite articles *le* or *les* they contract to *du* and *des* respectively.

Can't use a d- article after de

Elle **a envie de** fraises.	*She wants (some) strawberries.*
Je **me sers de** ciseaux pour couper.	*I use (some) scissors to cut.*
Il **a besoin de** lunettes pour regarder la télé.	*He needs (some) glasses to watch TV.*
Ce plat **manque d'**épices.	*This dish lacks (some) spices.*
Nous **rêvons de** vacances à la plage.	*We dream of a vacation on the beach.*
En été, je **m'occupe d'**enfants.	*In the summer I take care of children.*
On **se souvient** toujours **d'**événements étranges.	*One always remembers strange events.*

Other articles allowed after de

Ils ont envie **d'une** pizza.	*They want a pizza.*
As-tu besoin **de la** voiture?	*Do you need the car?*
Je me sers **d'un** couteau pour couper.	*I use a knife to cut.*
On se souvient toujours **des** (**de** + **les**) amis qu'on a au lycée.	*We always remember the friends we have in high school.*
Sers-toi **d'un** dictionnaire.	*Use a dictionary.*
En été, profitez **du** (**de** + **le**) soleil.	*In the summer take advantage of the sun.*

Before an adjective

Des becomes **de** when a preceding adjective stands between **des** and most nouns. Adjectives likely to occur in that position are those referring to beauty, age, goodness/kindness, size, and a few more listed here:

Il y a **de beaux livres** sur l'étagère.	*There are some nice books on the shelf.*
J'ai acheté **de bons gâteaux** pour le déssert.	*I bought some good pastries for dessert.*
Nous avons mangé **de très bonnes choses**.	*We ate some very good things.*
Ce sont **de jeunes enfants** polis.	*They are polite young children.*
Ma chatte a eu **de beaux chatons**.	*My cat had beautiful kittens.*

Adjectives that precede the noun

As a general rule, when an adjective has one syllable, such as **tel/telle** (*such*) and **faux/fausse** (*false*), and the noun it describes has two or more syllables, the adjective precedes the noun. Also included in this category are adjectives (of one or more syllable) referring to beauty (**beau/belle**, **joli[e]**), age (**nouveau/nouvelle**, **jeune**, **vieux/vieille**), goodness and kindness (**bon[ne]**, **gentil[le]**, **mauvais[e]**), size (**petit[e]**, **bref/brève**, **grand[e]**, **gros[se]**, **long[ue]**, **vaste**, **haut[e]**, and **large**), to name only the most common that are likely be found before a plural noun.

Il y avait **de tels** embouteillages que je suis arrivé en retard.	*There was so much bad traffic that I arrived late.*
J'ai **de longues** conversations avec ma mère.	*I have long conversations with my mother.*
Cet élève a eu **de mauvaises** notes.	*That student had some bad grades.*
Il voyage avec **de faux** papiers!	*He travels with fake papers!*

With certain fixed compound nouns formed by adjective + noun (there are other types of compound nouns) **des** remains as is.

J'ai acheté **des petits fours** pour le dessert.	*I bought (some) petits fours for dessert.*
Ce sont **des jeunes gens** bien élevés.	*They are well-mannered young people.*
Ces grands-parents ont **des petits-enfants** adorables.	*Those grandparents have lovely grandchildren.*

Before **autres**

Before the word **autres** in the plural, the article **des** always becomes **d'**.

Singular

Elle a besoin **d'un autre** stylo. Celui-là est cassé.	*She needs another pen. This one is broken.*

Donnez-moi **une autre** feuille de papier.	*Give me another sheet of paper.*

Plural

Elle a besoin **d'autres** stylos. Ceux-là sont cassés.	*She needs other pens. These are broken.*
Donnez-moi **d'autres** feuilles de papier.	*Give me other sheets of paper.*

If you do encounter **des** in front of **autres**, it will *not* be the plural indefinite article, but rather the contraction of the preposition **de** + the article **les** (**des**).

Elle a besoin **des** (**de** + **les**) **autres** lunettes, pas de celles-ci.	*She needs the other glasses, not these.*
Nous avons fait la connaissance **des** (**de** + **les**) **autres** cousins de Julie.	*We have met Julie's other cousins.*

Expressions of quantity

An expression of quantity replaces any article. Most expressions of quantity end with **de**, except for **quelques** (*several*), **plusieurs** (*several*), and **aucun(e)** (*no*) (as in examples 7 and 8), and the expression of quantity **la plupart de** (*most/the majority of*), must be followed by a definite article (last two examples). The following examples contrast an article and an expression of quantity:

Mets **du jambon** dans ton sandwich.	*Put some ham in your sandwich.*
Mets **une tranche de jambon** dans ton sandwich.	*Put a slice of ham in your sandwich.*
L'eau est bonne pour la santé.	*Water is good for your health.*
Nous buvons **beaucoup d'eau** quand il fait chaud.	*We drink a lot of water when it is hot.*
Nous adorons **les cacahuètes**.	*We love peanuts.*
Achète **un paquet de cacahuètes**.	*Buy a bag of peanuts.*
A-t-il **de la chance**?	*Is he lucky?*
Ce garçon **n'a aucune chance**.	*That boy has no luck.*
Aimes-tu **les œuvres** de Boris Vian?	*Do you like the works of Boris Vian?*
J'ai **quelques livres** de Vian.	*I have a few books by Vian.*
Aujourd'hui, **la plupart des** (**de** + **les**) **gens** ont une voiture.	*Nowadays, most people have a car.*
La plupart du (**de** + **le**) **temps**, nous dînons chez nous.	*Most of the time we eat dinner at home.*

Definite articles

The *definite articles* are: **le, la, l'**, and **les**. The definite article is not the most common article in French, and you should only use it when you have a good reason to do so. Here is a list of those reasons:

Elision and contraction

The form of the definite article can change: **le** and **la** are elided to **l'** before a vowel or a mute **h**. **Le** and **les** are contracted to **au/aux** after the preposition **à** and to **du/des** after the preposition **de**.

> **Elision**
>
> l'eau (*f.*)   l'oiseau (*m.*)   l'omelette (*f.*)   l'homme (*m.*)
>
> **Contractions**
>
> Allons **au** zoo. (**à** + **le**)   *Let's go to the zoo.*
> Il va **aux** toilettes. (**à** + **les**)   *He goes to the restroom.*
> Je rentre **du** bureau. (**de** + **le**)   *I just arrived from the office.*
> Ils viennent **des** quartiers nord. (**de** + **les**)   *They come from the north side.*

Naming specific things

Use the definite article when talking about something that has been previously mentioned (in context or in the sentence itself) or something qualified by what follows immediately: in the first example, **le livre** is qualified by the relative clause **qu'elle voulait** which follows it.

> Il lui a offert **le livre qu'elle voulait**.   *He gave her the book that she wanted.*
> Nous cherchons **le chemin de la gare**.   *We are looking for the way to the station.*
> On a retrouvé **les bijoux qui avaient**   *They found the jewels that had been*
>   **été volés**.   *stolen.*
> Vive **le premier jour des vacances**!   *Hooray for the first day of vacation!*

Naming general categories

When naming a class of things or a concept in general, you refer to it in its entirety, and the noun must be preceded by the *definite article*. In English, you would not use an article here. (However, that's not the only case where the English article would be omitted, so don't rely on this "rule" too much.) This includes *preferences* in French: when you like or dislike something you like or dislike it "in general" (examples 4 and 5).

> **La vie** est douce.   *Life (in general) is sweet.*
> **Les carottes** sont orange.   *(All the) Carrots are orange.*
> Il est allergique **aux** (**à** + **les**) chats.   *He is allergic to cats (in general).*

| Mes enfants adorent **le chocolat**. | *My kids love chocolate (in general).* |
| Il préfère **la musique classique**. | *He prefers classical music (in general).* |

However, when a noun that describes a class as a whole is not referred to in its entirety but rather in a "partial" way, the partitive article is used. The following examples contrast the two ways a category can be referred to: in its entirety or partially. See also "The partitive article."

Whole category

Tu aimes **le poisson**.	*You like fish (in general).*
Les enfants sont intéressants.	*(All) Children are interesting.*
La chance est un cadeau.	*Luck (in general) is a gift.*
On doit **le respect** à ses parents.	*We owe our parents respect (in general).*
L'eau est bonne pour la santé.	*Water (in general) is good for your health.*

Partial category

Tu as mangé **du poisson** à midi.	*You had (some) fish for lunch.*
Ils ont **des enfants** intéressants.	*They have (some) interesting children.*
Il a **de la chance**.	*He has luck/He is lucky.*
Paul a **du respect** pour ses parents.	*Paul has respect for his parents.*
Pour ma santé, je bois **de l'eau**.	*For my health, I drink water.*

Here is a little trick that will help you when you're not sure whether you are dealing with a whole category or a partial one. If you can add "in general" after the noun, you should use the definite article. However, after some nouns, in particular those referring to food, adding "in general" may not help, and could even prove confusing. So with food items in particular, use the phrase "all the (water/meat/fish) in the world" instead of "in general."

The following examples demonstrate why. In the first one, you drink *water* "in general" for your health, true, but it is not "all the water in the world" that you drink. Same with *ham*: it is some ham "in general" that the French eat, yet it is still not "all the ham in the world."

Pour ma santé, je bois **de l'eau**.	*For my health, I drink water.*
Le soir, beaucoup de Français mangent **du jambon**.	*In the evening, many French people eat ham.*
Le matin nous prenons **du café**.	*In the morning, we drink coffee.*

For dates

When the definite article is used before a date, it expresses either a recurrence or it names a specific date, depending on what follows it.

Recurrences

Before the name of a day, the definite article expresses recurrence, something you do regularly. If you don't intend to express recurrence, do not use the definite article.

Nous avons cours **le lundi** et **le mercredi**.	*We have class on Mondays and Wednesdays.*
Il fait du yoga **le lundi soir**.	*He goes to yoga every Monday night.*
Le samedi nous allons au restaurant.	*On Saturdays we eat out.*

But:

Lundi il a fait beau.	*On Monday the weather was nice.*

Specific dates

Use the definite article before a date that includes a number. In the absence of a number, don't use the definite article (if you do, you'd express recurrence instead of a specific date).

Mon fils est né **le jeudi 2 mars**.	*My son was born Thursday, March 2.*
Noël est toujours **le 25 décembre**.	*Christmas is always on December 25.*
Nous partirons **le 15 juillet** et nous rentrerons **le 21**.	*We will leave on July 15 and return on the 21st.*
Mon anniversaire est **le 26 janvier**.	*My birthday is on January 26.*

Holidays

A definite article usually precedes the name of a holiday. **Pâques** (*Easter*) and **Noël** (*Christmas*) are exceptions, with no article, although you may see (rarely) **la Noël**.

L'Ascension (*f.*)	*Ascension Day*
La Fête nationale	*Bastille Day*
Hanoukka (*f.*)	*Hanukkah*
Le Fête du Travail	*Labor Day (May 1)*
La Pâque (juive)	*Passover*
La Pentecôte	*Pentecost*
Le Ramadan	*Ramadan*
La Saint-Sylvestre	*New Year's Eve*
La Toussaint	*All Saints' Day*

In superlatives

As in English, the definite article is used in a superlative construction.

C'est **le passage le moins intéressant** de ce livre.	*This is the least interesting passage in this book.*
Voilà **la meilleure photo** de nos vacances.	*Here is the best picture of our vacation.*

To express choice

To offer a choice between two things that have already been described, you can use the definite article + adjective (used alone, without a noun). This construction is not typically used to describe people.

Quelle valise veux-tu? **La grande** ou **la petite?**	*Which suitcase do you want? The big one or the little one?*
J'ai loué deux films. Tu veux regarder **le français** ou **l'italien?**	*I rented two movies. Do you want to watch the French one or the Italian one?*

If the two (or more) objects have not already been described, the indefinite article should be used.

Allons louer un film. Tu préférerais un français ou un italien?	*Let's go rent a movie. Would you prefer a French one or an Italian one?*

With geographical names

Before countries, regions, some cities, oceans, and so on, including famous architectural landmarks such as **Le Louvre**, **Le Carlton**, **La tour Eiffel**, **L'Odéon**, and **Le Vatican**, use the definite article. Depending on the style of writing, the definite article will be capitalized or not. For famous landmarks that already include another determiner in their name such as, **Notre-Dame de Paris**, or if their name includes a name (often a saint's name), such as the churches **Saint-Pierre de Rome** and **Saint-Sulpice**, do not use the definite article.

La Méditerranée est dangereuse.	*The Mediterranean (Sea) is dangerous.*
Ils sont en vacances dans **le Périgord**.	*They are vacationing in the region of Périgord.*
As-tu visité **la France?**	*Have you visited France?*
Nous sommes montés au sommet de **la tour Eiffel**.	*We climbed to the top of the Eiffel Tower.*

If a preposition precedes the definite article, they are contracted as follows:

à + le = **au**
à + les = **aux**

de + le = **du**
de + les = **des**

Ils vont **au (à + le) Maroc** en voyage de noces.
They are going to Morocco for their honeymoon.

Mes amis rentrent **du (de + le) Sénégal.**
My friends are back from Senegal.

Remember that names of cities are never preceded by an article, except for a few whose names always include the definite article: **Le Havre, Le Mans, La Ciotat, La Nouvelle-Orléans,** and **Le Caire.**

With people's titles and functions

The definite article must be used before a person's title.

Le premier ministre va prendre sa retraite.
The prime minister is going to retire.

« Je vous présente **le capitaine Boutin.** »
"Allow me to introduce Captain Boutin."

Do not use the article when you are directly addressing the person (example 1), or after **être, paraître, devenir, sembler, être élu(e),** or **nommer** (or **faire** in the same sense).

« Allô, **Professeur** Prévost? »
"Hello, Professor Prévost?"

Pierre **a été nommé délégué** syndical.
Pierre was nominated as union spokesman.

Il **est devenu cardinal** assez jeune.
He became a cardinal fairly young.

With people's names

Proper names should not be preceded by any article, unless the name is qualified by an adjective (see highlighting in the following examples), or when it describes an entire family (last example).

Chopin était un grand pianiste.
Chopin was a great pianist.

Le grand Chopin a écrit des sonates merveilleuses.
The great Chopin composed wonderful sonatas.

« Vous connaissez **Julie?** »
"Do you know Julie?"

« **L'adorable Julie** qui habite à côté? »
"The adorable Julie who lives next door?"

Catherine de Russie fut une grande impératrice.
Catherine of Russia was a great empress.

La grande Catherine de Russie parlait très bien français.	*The great Catherine of Russia spoke French very well.*
Les Paret sont des gens agréables.	*The Parets are pleasant people.*

Use of articles in physical descriptions

The determiners used when referring to parts of the body can vary depending on the verbs used in each sentence. Definite and indefinite articles as well as possessive adjectives are used.

Definite article

When naming parts of the body in a generic description (**avoir** + body part), the definite article is used in French. The sentence simply states what the person or animal looks like in general.

Elle a **les cheveux longs**.	*She has long hair.*
Les loups ont **les dents longues**.	*Wolves have long teeth.*

French also uses the definite article following a pronominal verb (even though English uses the possessive adjective).

Brosse-toi *les* **dents** trois fois par jour.	*Brush your teeth three times a day.*
Elle **s'est cassé** *le* **bras** au ski.	*She broke her arm skiing.*
Qu'est-ce que tu **t'es fait** *au* (à+ **le**) **nez**?	*What happened to your nose?*

The definite article also follows any other verb, as long as the owner (of the body part) is obvious. Note that the owner is represented by the indirect object pronoun **lui** in the last two examples:

Ne hausse pas **les** épaules.	*Don't shrug (your shoulders).*
J'ai mal à **la** tête.	*I have a headache.*
Ouvre **la** bouche et dis « Aah ».	*Open your mouth and say "Ah."*
Il **lui** a coupé **les** cheveux.	*He cut his/her hair.*
Le docteur **lui** a examiné **la** gorge.	*The doctor examined his/her throat.*

The possessive adjective

Use the possessive adjective instead of the definite article whenever it is not obvious whose hair, hand, teeth, and so on, are being mentioned (see following first two examples), and when that noun is the subject of the verb (examples 3 to 5)

Elle a dû vendre **ses** cheveux.	*She had to sell her (own) hair.*
Il a ouvert **sa** grande bouche et le Petit Chaperon Rouge a eu peur.	*He opened his large mouth and Little Red Riding Hood got scared.*

Ses dents sont si blanches!	*His teeth are so white!*
Mon doigt est tout enflé.	*My finger is all swollen.*
Ses cheveux sont devenus blancs en une nuit.	*His hair turned white overnight.*

Assessment versus description

Expressing an opinion or judgment about a description can require constructions different from the possessive adjective.

With avoir

When **avoir** + body part is a personal assessment instead of a simple description, the indefinite article must be used instead of the definite article: **un/une** in the singular, **des** in the plural, and **de** before a preceding plural adjective. The "personal" aspect is likely to be an adjective expressing admiration (**beaux**, **toute petite**, **extraordinaires**) or disgust (**vilaines**).

Elle a **les** cheveux longs. (*fact*)	*She has long hair.*
Elle a **de beaux** cheveux. (*judgment*)	*She has beautiful hair.*
Ce bébé a **une** toute petite bouche.	*This baby has a tiny little mouth.*
Édith Piaf avait **des** mains extraordinaires.	*Edith Piaf had incredible hands.*
Elle se ronge les ongles: elle a **de vilaines** mains.	*She bites her fingernails: she has ugly hands.*

With a verb other than avoir

If the sentence has a subjective adjective, use the possessive with a part of the body. Note that you can't use a reflexive verb in this type of sentence. If there were no adjective in these sentences, the first example would be **elle s'est brûlé le doigt**, and in the second it would be **elle s'est coupé les cheveux**.

Elle a brûlé **son pauvre doigt**.	*She burned her poor finger.*
Elle a coupé **ses beaux cheveux**.	*She cut her beautiful hair.*

Omission of articles

In English, it is very common to omit the article in front of a noun, particularly in the plural. In French, the article is omitted only in certain cases:

After an expression of quantity

An expression of quantity replaces the article. Most expressions of quantity include **de**, but note also **plusieurs** (*several*), **quelques** (*some*), and **aucun(e)** (*no*), as well as all the cardinal numbers (**un, deux, trois...**).

Il a **peu d'**amis.	*He has (very) few friends.*
Elle a **plusieurs** enfants.	*She has several children.*
Achète **un paquet de** bonbons.	*Buy a bag of candies.*
Nous partons dans **deux** jours.	*We leave in two days.*

After verb + de

Remember that after verb/verbal expression + **de**, you cannot use an article that begins with a **d-: du, de la, de l', des**. (See "**des** changing to **de**.")

J'ai envie **de** chocolat.	*I want (some) chocolate.*
(*Instead of:* J'ai envie de + du chocolat.)	
Mes plantes ont besoin **d'**eau.	*My plants need some water.*
(*Instead of:* Mes plantes ont besoin de + de l'eau.)	
La piscine est couverte **de** feuilles.	*The pool is covered with leaves.*
(*Instead of:* La piscine est couverte de + des feuilles.)	

After the preposition sans

The indefinite and partitive articles are not used after **sans**. However, if the noun is qualified, you have to use the definite article (example 3).

Je voudrais du café **sans sucre**.	*I would like some coffee without sugar.*
Il est sorti **sans manteau** et il a pris froid.	*He went out without a coat and caught a cold.*

But:

L'équipe est revenue **sans le trophée qu'elle convoitait**.	*The team came home without the trophy they coveted.*

After the prepositions **par** and **avec**

The prepositions **par** and **avec** occur in many fixed and conventional expressions.

par/avec + abstract noun

When an abstract noun follows **par** or **avec**, no article is used (see later exceptions):

Elle lui a donné de l'argent **par bonté d'âme**.	*She gave him money out of kindness.*
J'ai pu avoir des places **par miracle**.	*Miraculously, I was able to get tickets.*
Ils se sont rencontrés **par accident**.	*They met by accident.*
C'est **avec plaisir** que j'accepte.	*I accept with pleasure.*
Elle répond toujours **avec dédain**.	*She always answers scornfully.*

Some common expressions with **par** + noun (without an article):

par alliance	*by marriage*
par avion	*air mail*
par beau temps	*when the weather is nice*
par centaines	*by the hundreds*
par cœur	*by heart (i.e., memorized)*
par erreur	*by mistake*
par excellence	*par excellence*
par exemple	*for instance*
par hasard	*by chance*
par intérêt	*out of self-interest*
par mois/semaine/an...	*per month/week/year . . .*
par personne	*per person*
par terre	*on the floor*

par/avec + adjective + abstract noun

If an adjective modifies an abstract noun, you have to use an article—definite, indefinite, or partitive, according to the context. Here are some contrasting examples:

Il écrit **avec** application.	*He writes with care.*
Il écrit **avec une grande** application.	*He writes with great care.*
Certains jeunes conduisent **avec** désinvolture.	*Some young people drive with abandon.*
Certains jeunes conduisent **avec une** désinvolture **inquiétante**.	*Some young people drive with worrisome abandon.*

J'ai trouvé ce livre **par** hasard.	*I found this book by accident.*
J'ai trouvé ce livre **par un pur** hasard.	*I found this book by sheer luck.*

You will find some fixed phrases, used as adverbs, that don't follow this rule. A few such phrases are: **avec grand appétit** (*with a healthy appetite*), **avec grand plaisir** (*with great pleasure*), and **avec bonne humeur** (*with a good temper*).

par/avec + concrete noun

An article—definite, indefinite, or partitive, according to the context—is normally used after **par** and **avec** before a concrete (not abstract) noun. Don't forget that **par** is the preposition that introduces the "agent" of a passive form (last example).

Je voudrais un thé **avec du citron**.	*I'd like a tea with lemon.*
C'est une maison **avec un toit rouge**.	*It is a house with a red roof.*
Le voleur est entré **par la fenêtre** du salon.	*The thief came in though the living room window.*
Je suis arrivée **par le train** de neuf heures.	*I arrived by the nine A.M. train.*
Le voleur est emmené **par la police**.	*The thief is taken away by the police.*

After en

The preposition **en** can indicate many different things: location, material, time, manner, and so on, but it is never followed by an article. When **un** or **une** follows **en** (example 4), it is the number *one*, not the indefinite article.

en grande pompe	*with great pomp*
Nous n'aimons pas voyager **en** avion.	*We don't like traveling by plane.*
Il habite **en** France.	*He lives in France.*
Tu as fini ton travail **en une** heure!	*You finished your work in just one hour!*
Elle porte une bague **en** or.	*She wears a gold ring.*
C'est un film **en** français.	*The movie is in French.*
Il se spécialise **en** sciences politiques.	*He majors in political science.*
Elle est sortie **en** chemise de nuit!	*She went out in her nightgown!*

After quel

As both exclamative or interrogative adjectives, **quel** (*which/what*) and its forms are never followed by an article:

Quelle horreur!	*What a horrible thing!*
Quels amours de bébés!	*What adorable babies!*
Quel jour sommes-nous?	*What day is it?*
À **quelle** heure rentres-tu?	*What time do you come home?*

After **comme**

The meaning of **comme** changes with the addition of an article.

comme: no article

If you omit the article after **comme**, it means *as, in the quality of*:

Cette chanteuse est nulle **comme actrice**.	*This singer is awful as an actress.*
J'ai travaillé **comme secrétaire** pendant mes études.	*While I was in school, I worked as a secretary.*

comme + article

Followed by any article, **comme** is the equivalent of the English comparatives *like, as*:

Cet enfant parle **comme** une grande personne.	*This child speaks like an adult.*
Elle rit **comme** une sorcière!	*She laughs like a witch!*
Il est beau **comme** le soleil.	*He is as handsome as the sun.*

In expressions with **à** or **de** and two nouns

In French, a noun can be described by a short prepositional phrase made up of **à** or **de** + another noun. The article is always omitted before the second noun. In English, this description is conveyed by an adjective. (See also Unit 12.)

des lunettes de lecture	*reading glasses*
une station de métro	*a subway station*
la sortie de secours	*the emergency exit*
une assiette à soupe	*a soup bowl*
un panier à pain	*a bread basket*

Recap

Sometimes the French use of articles follows English. For example, when the English sentence has a definite article, chances are the French sentence will, too.

Regarde **la voiture** qu'il vient d'acheter!	*Look at **the car** he just bought!*
Tu te souviens de **l'histoire** que je t'ai racontée?	*Do you remember **the story** I told you?*

Unfortunately, the parallel construction doesn't happen too often. Difficulties start to appear when English does not use an article or simply omits it: then you must choose between the the definite or the partitive article (plural indefinite) in French. One trick will help you with plural nouns: if you can put the word *several* in front of the English noun without changing its meaning, then you need the plural **des** in French.

Nous avons **des** chats.	*We have (several) cats.*
Les chats sont des animaux formidables.	*Cats are great animals.*
Il y a **des** pommes sur l'arbre.	*There are (several) apples on the tree.*
Voudrais-tu **des** pommes?	*Would you like (several) apples?*
Aimes-tu **les** pommes?	*Do you like apples (in general)?*

The following sets of examples will help you review all the uses of the articles:

Nous avons **un** chat.	*We have a cat.*
Nous avons **des** chats.	*We have (several) cats.*
Nous avons **de gentils** chats.	*We have (several) nice cats.*
(*indefinite plural before an adjective:* **de**)	
Nous aimons **les** chats.	*We like cats.*
(*a class of animals taken in its entirety*)	
Voici **le** chat que nous venons d'adopter.	*Here is the cat we have just adopted.*
(**chat** *is determined by the relative clause that follows, as in English*)	
Il y a **du** pain sur la table.	*There is (some) bread on the table.*
Il y a **une** baguette sur la table.	*There is a (one) baguette on the table.*
(**baguette** *is countable*)	
Il n'y a **pas de** pain sur la table.	*There is no bread on the table.*
(*negative verb*)	
J'ai envie **de** pain.	*I want (some) bread.*
(*no d- article after* **avoir envie de**, *a verb/verbal expression followed by the preposition* **de**)	
J'ai envie **du** pain qui est sur la table.	*I want the bread that is on the table.*
(*preposition* **de** + **le** *contract to* **du**)	
J'aime **le** pain.	*I like bread (in general).*
(*a class of food taken in its entirety*)	

Complete the following sentences with the correct article or an X to signify no article. You may need to contract or elide some forms.

1. Maman s'occupe _____ enfants de ma meilleure amie un jour par _____ semaine.

2. Elle ne prend jamais _____ dessert! Quel _____ dommage!

3. Si tu travailles bien, tu auras _____ succès dans ta carrière.

4. As-tu envie de _____ fruits ou _____ glace comme dessert?

5. Ce chat manque de _____ affection.

6. Le loup a _____ longues dents.

7. Ce semestre, nous faisons _____ italien à l'école.

8. _____ chien des voisins fait beaucoup _____ bruit.

9. Elle est enceinte et elle a constamment envie de _____ chocolat.

10. Julie n'aime pas _____ sport, mais elle sait que _____ sport est bon pour la santé et elle en fait.

11. Il ne va jamais au bureau sans _____ cravate.

12. La voisine porte toujours _____ jolis petits chapeaux.

13. Tu te souviens de _____ jour où nous nous sommes rencontrés?

14. Si tu achètes _____ vélo, tu auras aussi besoin de _____ casque.

15. Cet enfant a _____ cheveux bouclés comme un ange.

16. J'ai _____ amis qui parlent portugais.

17. Grand-mère me brossait toujours _____ cheveux le soir.

18. Ces soldats ont _____ courage.

19. Ils ont _____ appareil photo numérique.

20. Ils vont garder _____ chat de leurs voisins qui sont en vacances.

21. Le coiffeur a abîmé _____ beaux cheveux! Je suis furieuse.

22. Ta chambre est en _____ désordre. Range-la!

23. Cette femme est devenue _____ ministre par _____ accident.

24. Elle n'a jamais besoin de _____ barrettes: elle a _____ cheveux courts!

25. Dans _____ maison avec un bébé, y a-t-il _____ instruments dangereux?

EXERCICE
8·2

As with the previous exercise, complete the following sentences with the correct article or an X to signify no article. You may need to contract or elide some forms.

1. Ne m'apporte pas ces vieux ciseaux. J'ai besoin _____ autres, ceux qui sont neufs.

2. Qu'est-ce que tu proposes comme _____ activités de plein air?

3. Maman pense que _____ bonnes manières sont _____ qualités essentielles dans _____ vie.

4. Pierre aime beaucoup _____ boissons sucrées.

5. Tu as fait tout ça sans _____ aide de personne?!

6. Une blonde a évidemment _____ cheveux blonds.

7. Il prend toujours son café sans _____ sucre ni _____ lait.

8. Il y a souvent _____ vent au printemps.

9. Connaissez-vous _____ docteur Picaud? Il est _____ dentiste.

10. Cet arbre produit toujours _____ très belles pommes.

11. Je me croise _____ doigts: jusqu'ici je ne me suis jamais cassé _____ jambe en skiant.

12. On ne met pas _____ chocolat dans une salade de fruits parce que _____ chocolat n'est pas _____ fruit!

13. Aux derniers Jeux olympiques, plusieurs _____ athlètes ont battu leur propre record.

14. Quand l'été arrive, les moustiques arrivent aussi par _____ centaines.

15. As-tu envie _____ pâtes ou _____ riz pour le dîner?

16. Ma nièce est restée chez nous plusieurs _____ jours.

17. Nous avons revu ce vieux classique avec _____ grand plaisir.

18. Louis XVI avait _____ nez de tous les Bourbons, c'est à dire qu'il avait _____ gros nez.

19. J'ai ouvert cette lettre par _____ erreur.

20. À midi, il a mangé _____ petite salade et _____ fruits de mer.

21. Connaissez-vous _____ cuisine mexicaine?

22. Après un long sommeil, la princesse a enfin ouvert _____ yeux.

23. En _____ France, _____ fromage est toujours servi après _____ salade.

24. Il faut que je m'achète _____ autre paire de lunettes.

25. Il faut toujours avoir _____ eau dans sa voiture.

26. Les étudiants n'ont pas _____ droit de se servir _____ dictionnaire pendant un examen.

27. Nos voisins ont _____ jeunes enfants.

28. La plupart _____ temps, c'est moi qui fait la vaisselle.

29. Les pommes sont à 8 euros _____ kilo! Ce sont _____ pommes _____ plus chères que j'aie jamais vues.

30. Quelle _____ horreur! Mon portefeuille est tombé par _____ fenêtre.

Complete the following negative sentences with the correct article.

1. Je n'ai plus _____ lait pour le chat.

2. Ne te sers pas de _____ affaires de ton frère quand il est absent.

3. N'achète pas _____ poisson parce que personne n'aime _____ poisson à la maison.

4. Ce n'est pas _____ oiseau! C'est une branche.

5. Elle n'aime pas beaucoup _____ avion parce qu'elle a peur.

6. Je ne prends jamais _____ sucre dans mon café.

7. Ces gens n'ont pas _____ sou mais ils sont toujours contents.

8. Nous n'avons pas _____ cours aujourd'hui. Allons au ciné.

9. Je ne comprends pas pourquoi tu n'aimes pas _____ épinards!

10. Ce bébé n'a pas _____ cheveu sur la tête, il est drole!

11. Il ne se souvient jamais de _____ dates importantes.

12. On ne met pas _____ viande dans la soupe de légumes parce que la viande

    n'est pas _____ légume.

13. Il ne s'est pas brossé _____ dents ce matin!

14. Il n'y a pas _____ autre solution.

15. Grand-mère n'a pas besoin de _____ lunettes pour lire.

16. Cette année, le citronnier n'a donné aucun _____ citron.

17. Ce n'est pas _____ problème.

EXERCICE
8·4

Translate the following sentences into French.

1. He turned his back to me.

   _____

2. Most students had a good grade.

   _____

3. I don't need the pens that are on the table.

   _____

4. I like neither snails nor shrimp.

   _____

5. They have young children.

_____

6. I need eggs and flour.

_____

7. Mr. Esslin is a famous doctor. His father was a doctor, too.

_____

8. Do you take your coffee with sugar or without sugar?

_____

9. I want some chocolate. (use **avoir envie de**)

_____

10. He eats neither meat nor fish.

_____

11. There is water on the road. Be careful.

_____

12. The children got beautiful presents.

_____

13. This is not a happy story.

_____

14. For All Saints day, we will go to the old cemetery.

_____

15. Cardinal Wolsey had a terrible death.

_____

16. Who will be elected president?

_____

17. They live in Michigan.

_____

18. On Sundays, they like to rest.

_____

19. You need other socks!

_____

20. I dreamed of the day of our wedding.

_____

Other determiners

In this unit, we explore the use of demonstrative adjectives (**ce/cet/cette/ces**) and possessive adjectives (**mon/ma/mes**, etc.).

Demonstrative adjectives

There are two main things to remember about the French demonstrative adjective **ce** (*this* or *that* in English): (1) the distinction between *this* and *that* does not exist in French (but there's a way to mimic the English meaning), and (2) it is an adjective, and as such it has a variable form.

Simple demonstrative adjectives

They are:

ce + masculine noun

cet + vowel sound, singular masculine noun

cette + feminine noun
ces + plural feminine or masculine noun

Tu as vu **cette** fille?	*Did you see that girl?*
Qui sont **ces** gens?	*Who are these/those people?*
Ce petit bistro est formidable.	*This/That little bistro is great.*
Cet homme va tomber...	*That man is going to fall . . .*
Je n'aime pas **ces** fleurs rouges.	*I don't like these/those red flowers.*
Cette histoire est incroyable!	*That/This story is incredible!*

Compound demonstrative adjectives

They are:

ce + masculine noun-**ci** or -**là**
cet + vowel sound, singular masculine noun-**ci** or -**là**
cette + feminine noun-**ci** or -**là**
ces + plural feminine or masculine noun-**ci** or –**là**

ce chien-**ci**	*this or that dog*
cet homme-**ci**	*this or that man*
Cette fille-**ci** ou **cette** fille-**là**?	*This girl or that girl?*
Ces filles-**ci** ou **ces** filles-**là**?	*These girls or those girls?*

-ci versus -là

When **-ci** or **-là** is added to the demonstrative adjective + noun, it does not truly indicate *this* versus *that* with the idea of something close as opposed to something at a distance, as it does in English. In fact, **-ci** or **-là** are almost never used in that sense! French uses **-ci** versus **-là** when one needs to make a choice between two things of the same type.

Tu veux voir **ce** film-**ci** ou **ce** film-**là**?	*Do you want to see this movie or that (other) movie?*
Je mets **ces** chaussures-**ci** ou **ces** chaussures-**là**?	*Should I wear these shoes or these other shoes?*

-là

The demonstrative adjective + noun-**là** is also frequently used alone in French as a simple demonstrative, not in contrast with noun + **-ci**, even when there is no choice. This use belongs to spoken, colloquial language.

Donnez-moi **ce** gâteau-**là**, s'il vous plaît.	*Give me this/that cake, please.*
Nous avons besoin de **ce** livre-**là**.	*We need this/that book.*
Dans **ce** cas-**là**...	*In this/that case . . .*
Passe-moi **ce** truc-**là**!	*Hand me that thing there!*

The only instance in French where noun + **-là** truly denotes distance is in expressions of time. Using noun + **-là** indicates absolute remoteness in time, as found in stories. In this case it is not in contrast to noun + **-ci**.

en ce temps-là	*in those days*
cet hiver-là	*that winter*
ce jour-là	*that day*
à cette époque-là	*at that time*

Possessive adjectives

French and English look differently at the expression of ownership. As the rightmost column of the following table shows, English makes no distinction between a plural object and a singular object when French does (fourth column: **mes** versus **mon**). On the other hand, English marks the gender of a singular owner (**his** versus **her**) when French does not. See the following table and examples:

OBJECT IS:

OWNER	MASCULINE	FEMININE	PLURAL	ENGLISH
je	mon	ma	mes	*my*
tu	ton	ta	tes	*your*
il	son	sa	ses	*his*
elle	son	sa	ses	*her*
nous	notre	notre	nos	*our*
vous	votre	votre	vos	*your*
ils	leur	leur	leurs	*their*
elles	leur	leur	leurs	*their*

Ils ont acheté **leur** maison il y a dix ans.	*They bought their house ten years ago.*
Leurs enfants sont toujours bien habillés.	*Their children are always well dressed.*
Vos amis parlent-ils aussi français?	*Do your friends speak French as well?*
Comment s'écrit **votre** nom?	*How is your name spelled?*
Mon oncle habite en Amérique.	*My uncle lives in America.*
Paul était content de **sa** note.	*Paul was happy with his grade.*
Julie n'aime pas **sa** nouvelle coupe.	*Julie does not like her new haircut.*

Remember that any singular noun (masculine or feminine) beginning with a vowel or a mute **h** must be preceded by the masculine form *mon, ton,* or *son.*

Jeanne d'Arc est **mon** héroïne.	*Joan of Arc is my heroine.*
Son histoire est incroyable.	*His/her story is incredible.*
Est-ce que **son** amie viendra avec lui?	*Will his girlfriend come with him?*
Aimes-tu **ton** école?	*Do you like your school?*

Before an abstract noun and any noun that a person can only have one of, the French possessive is very often singular. For example, in the first example, each of the multiple owners only has one life, in the second, only one hat, and so on. Note that English tends to use the plural. Modern French informal language also frequently uses the plural.

Laisse-les faire **leur vie**.	*Let them live their lives.*
En entrant dans l'église ils ont enlevé **leur chapeau**.	*Upon entering the church they took off their hats.*
Les enfants, il fait froid: mettez **un bonnet** sur votre tête.	*Children, it's cold outside: put a cap on your head.*

Complete the sentences with the possessive adjective as indicated.

1. _____ oncle est gentil. (*her*)

2. Je vais inviter _____ amies. (*my*)

3. _____ professeurs sont tous intéressants. (*our*)

4. _____ parents sont riches: _____ père est directeur d'une banque. (*his*)

5. _____ amie Colette est malade. (*my*)

6. _____ parents sont en Amérique. (*their*)

7. Poupou est _____ chien. (*our*)

8. _____ maison est très agréable. Tu l'entretiens bien. (*your*)

9. _____ fils est avocat. (*their*)

10. Ce sont _____ filles. (*his*)

11. _____ amies sont en France. (*their*)

12. C'est _____ voiture. (*his*)

13. Les jeunes passent _____ temps à la mer. (*their*)

14. Il va prendre _____ vacances en juin. (*his*)

15. Vous devez montrer _____ passeport et _____ bagages à la police. (*your*)

Complete the sentences with the correct demonstrative adjective.

1. _____ hotel est confortable.

2. Tu connais _____ fille?

3. N'écoute pas _____ homme!

4. Je préfère _____ gâteau-_____.

5. _____ fruits ne sont pas mûrs.

6. _____ idée est absurde.

7. _____ article est intéressant.

8. On a tourné _____ film en Russie.

9. _____ voitures sont en panne.

10. _____ acteur est célèbre dans le monde entier.

11. Elle va arriver _____ après-midi ou _____ soir.

12. _____ amie n'est pas fidèle.

13. _____ étudiants sont sérieux.

14. Je viens d'acheter _____ lunettes. Tu les aimes?

15. _____ hôpital a un hélipad sur le toit.

16. Je trouve _____ femmes totalement extravagantes.

17. C'est _____ héros américain que mon fils veut rencontrer.

18. _____ été- _____, ils ne sont pas partis en vacances.

19. _____ avocats viennent de gagner leur procès.

20. _____ étendue d'eau est un très grand lac.

21. Regardez _____ enfants! Ils sont amusants.

22. En _____ temps-_____ vivait un magicien.

23. Nous avons trouvé _____ portefeuille dans la rue.

24. _____ hasard est extraordinaire.

25. Nous savons que _____ armes sont dangereuses.

Relative pronouns

·10·

A relative pronoun introduces a relative clause that determines a noun in the same way an adjective does. Like an adjective, the relative clause follows the noun. So rather than thinking of relative pronouns as pronouns that replace a noun, view them as a link between a noun and the clause that describes it.

The relative pronouns are **qui**, **que**, **dont**, **où**, and **lequel**. The choice is determined by the verb of the dependent (or subordinate) clause: the relative pronoun can be the subject or the object of that verb, the object of a preposition tied to that verb, or the object of noun + **de** to express possession. In any case, look for the logical link between the two clauses (exercise 1 at the end of the unit shows you how). Note that in English, relative pronouns are often omitted, but in French, you can never omit the relative pronoun.

Relative pronoun subject

The relative pronoun subject of the dependent verb is **qui**. The verb of the relative clause must be singular if **qui**'s antecedent is singular, plural if **qui**'s antecedent is plural (example 1). The antecedent of a relative pronoun (highlighted in the following examples, along with the pronoun) is the noun that pronoun describes: **des gens** in example 1, **moi** in 2, and **le témoin** in 3.

Ce sont **des gens qui** n'aiment rien!	*These are people who don't like anything!*
C'est toujours **moi qui** fais la vaisselle!	*I am always the one washing dishes!*
Voici **le témoin qui** a tout entendu.	*This is the witness who heard it all.*

Qui is never elided before a vowel (see the third example). If it were, one would not be able to distinguish it from **que** which is elided (**qu'**).

133

Relative pronoun object

The relative pronoun object of the dependent verb is **que** (**qu'** before a vowel sound). In the following examples, the antecedent of **que** is highlighted, along with the pronoun:

C'est **une amie que** j'ai depuis l'école primaire.	*She's a friend (that) I have had since high school.*
Il a **un travail qu'**il aime beaucoup.	*He has a job (that) he likes a lot.*

When the verb of the relative clause is in the **passé composé** (or any compound tense) with **avoir**, the past participle must agree with **que**'s antecedent. For details, see Unit 2 on the agreement of the past participle.

Il adore **les jouets qu'**il a reçus à Noël.	*He loves the toys (that) he got for Christmas.*
Les chaussures que tu lui as donn**ées** étaient trop petites.	*The shoes (that) you gave him/her were too small.*

Relative pronoun object of the preposition de

The very useful relative pronoun **dont**, used as the object of the preposition **de**, does not have a simple English equivalent. It is helpful to study the construction of the example sentences with **dont** by "dismantling" them.

Verbs and adjectives + de

When the preposition **de** is tied to the verb (examples 1, 2, and 3) or to **être** + adjective (examples 4 to 5) in the dependent clause, the relative pronoun **dont** is used. If the verb is in a compound tense, the past participle always remains invariable.

L'erreur **dont il s'est rendu compte** était grave.	*The error he discovered was serious.*
La fille **dont je te parle** est blonde.	*The girl I am telling you about is blonde.*
L'enfant **dont je m'occupe** est adorable.	*The child I am taking care of is adorable.*
L'homme **dont elle est amoureuse** est un acteur.	*The man she is in love with is an actor.*
Voici un travail **dont je suis** assez **fier**.	*This is a work that I am quite proud of.*

Compound prepositions with **de** are treated like prepositions other than **de**.

de expressing possession

In French, possession can be expressed using a possessive adjective (**mon, ton, leur...**) + noun, or using noun + **de** + noun. To express possession with a relative clause, use **dont** *after* the noun referring to the owner (person or thing), similar to *whose* in English.

Ce sont les enfants de mes amis.	*They are my friends' kids.*
Mes amis **dont les enfants sont si mignons** viennent en vacances avec nous.	*My friends whose kids are so cute are coming with us on vacation.*
Regardez les chapeaux de la reine.	*Look at the queen's hats.*
La reine **dont les chapeaux sont célèbres** a assisté au Derby.	*The queen whose hats are famous attended the Derby.*
Cette dame n'a pas vu que son sac était ouvert.	*This lady did not notice that her purse was open.*
La dame **dont le sac est ouvert** va perdre quelque chose.	*The lady whose purse is open is going to lose something.*
L'auteur de ce roman est une très jeune femme.	*The author of this novel is a very young woman.*
C'est un roman **dont l'auteur est une très jeune femme**.	*This is a novel whose author is a very young woman.*

Relative pronoun object of other prepositions

After prepositions such as **à**, **en**, **sur**, **pour**, **avec**, and compound prepositions with **de** (see following list), the rules are different. There you need look only at the gender of the antecedent rather than its function. When the antecedent is a thing, use preposition + **lequel**; when the antecedent is a person, use preposition + **qui**, or preposition + **lequel**.

Here are some common compound prepositions with **de**:

à cause de	*because of*
à côté de	*next to*
auprès de	*with/at the side of*
au sujet de	*about*
le long de	*along*
loin de	*far from*
près de	*near*

Preposition + things

The relative pronoun **lequel** varies in gender and number and must match its antecedent.

The forms of **lequel** are **lesquels** (masculine plural), **laquelle** (feminine singular), and **lesquelles** (feminine plural).

Les sports **pour lesquels** il se passionne n'intéressent pas sa femme.	*The sports for which he has a passion don't interest his wife.*

Tu as des idées **avec lesquelles** je ne suis pas d'accord.	*You have ideas with which I disagree.*
La rivière **le long de laquelle** je me promène est presque à sec.	*The river along which I am walking is almost dry.*
C'est une chose **à laquelle** je n'avais pas pensé.	*This is something I had not thought about.*

When combined with the **de** of a compound preposition, **lequel** changes to **duquel**, and **lesquels/lesquelles** to **desquels/desquelles**. The same type of contraction occurs with the preposition **à**: **lequel** changes to **auquel**, and **lesquels/lesquelles** to **auxquels/auxquelles**.

Le problème **au sujet duquel** ils se sont disputés était grave.	*The issue they argued about was serious.*
Je veux connaître toutes les choses **auxquelles** tu penses.	*I want to know all the things you're thinking about.*

The antecedent of **lequel** must be the noun it sits closest to, even if it may not seem logical because of its gender (*le yoga* and *une* **chose** in example 1).

Le yoga est **une chose pour laquelle** il n'a aucune patience.	*Yoga is a thing he has no patience for.*
Une table est **un objet sur lequel** on écrit.	*A table is an object people write on.*

Preposition + people

When the relative pronoun describes a person, use preposition + **qui** or preposition + **lequel**. Usage prefers preposition + **qui**, except with **parmi** and **entre**, with which you can only use a form of **lequel** (last example).

Ma sœur est une personne **avec qui** je m'entends bien.	*My sister is a person I get along well with/with whom I get along well.*
or: Ma sœur est une personne **avec laquelle** je m'entends bien.	
Mon docteur est une personne **en qui** j'ai confiance.	*My doctor is a person (whom) I trust.*
or: Mon docteur est une personne **en laquelle** j'ai confiance.	
C'est la femme **auprès de qui** je veux finir mes jours.	*She is the woman with whom I want to spend the rest of my life.*
or: C'est la femme **auprès de laquelle** je veux finir mes jours.	

Sa mère et sa grand-mère sont les deux femmes **entre lesquelles** il a grandi.	*His mother and grandmother are the two women between whom he grew up.*

When the antecedent is the indefinite **personne** or **quelqu'un**, always use **qui** after the preposition. Do not confuse **personne** (*no one*) and **une personne** (*a person*).

Il n'y a personne **avec qui** parler ici.	*There's no one to talk to here.*
Ce prof est quelqu'un **avec qui** on a envie de discuter.	*This prof is someone you want to chat with/with whom you want to chat.*
Julie est quelqu'un **sur qui** on peut compter.	*Julie is someone whom you can count on.*

Relative clauses of place and time

A dependent (subordinate) clause can refer to place and time, as well as persons and objects (discussed earlier).

Place

The relative pronoun used to indicate place can be **où**, or a more specific preposition + **lequel**, as illustrated in the following examples. The difference between **où** and **dans laquelle**, for instance, is insignificant in examples 1 and 2. You can use either one. But do not use **où** if the sentence has a specific preposition, just as you could not use *where* instead of *in the middle of which* (example 4) in English.

Voila la maison **où** je suis né.	*This is the house where I was born.*
Voilà la maison **dans laquelle** je suis né.	*This is the house in which I was born.*
C'est un endroit **d'où** on peut voir le coucher de soleil.	*It is a place from where you can see the sunset.*
C'est un lac **au milieu duquel** il y a une île.	*It's a lake in the middle of which sits an island.*

Time

A relative clause that indicates time uses **où**, or a preposition + **lequel** if the sentence has a specific preposition (last two examples).

Au moment où j'ai ouvert la porte, le chat a filé.	*The minute I opened the door, the cat ran out.*
Le jour où il est arrivé, il pleuvait à verse.	*The day (when) he arrived, it was pouring.*
C'est la minute d'inattention **pendant laquelle** il a volé la clé.	*That's the minute of inattentiveness during which he stole the key.*
Je ne me souviens pas du dîner **au cours duquel** je t'ai rencontré.	*I don't remember the dinner party during which I met you.*

Building a sentence with a relative pronoun: recap

A relative clause acts almost as an adjective and describes a noun (except for the relative clause that expresses possession). The first step is to decide or find the noun to which it refers.

Let's say "you have a friend named Paul" and "he is someone you can really count on." At this point, we can safely say that "your friend" or even "your friend Paul" is the noun to describe, and we could start our sentence with: **J'ai un ami...** Now let's describe that friend: **Il s'appelle Paul** (*His name is Paul*). **Je peux compter sur lui** (*I can count on him*). Now, let's combine this into one complex sentence: **J'ai un ami** *qui* **s'appelle Paul et** *sur qui* **je peux compter.**

How did we get there? By understanding how the verbs relate to Paul: Paul is the subject of **s'appelle**, so we used the relative subject pronoun **qui**. Paul is also the object of **compter sur**, and the relative pronoun object of a preposition is **(sur) qui/lequel**. Easy, no?

The one/those who . . .

A demonstrative pronoun (**celui, celle, ceux, celles**) can be the antecedent of the relative pronoun. Everything works the same as with a noun antecedent. **Celui, celle, ceux,** and **celles** can refer to people and things alike.

Regarde mes beaux iris, **ceux qui** sont sortis les premiers sont les jaunes.	*Look at my pretty irises, those that bloomed first are the yellow ones.*
J'ai lu tous ces romans. **Celui que** j'ai préféré est le plus long.	*I have read all these books. The one that I preferred is the longest.*
Toutes mes amies sont mariées, mais **celles qui** ont des enfants sont toujours prises.	*All my friends are married, but those who have kids are always busy.*
J'ai invité tous mes amis, sauf **ceux qui** ne m'avaient pas donné leur adresse!	*I invited all my friends, except those who had not given me their addresses!*

To those/with those . . .

When a demonstrative pronoun is combined with a preposition (*à, avec, pour,* etc.) build the sentence that includes the relative pronoun just like you would for a noun combined with a preposition:

demonstrative pronoun (or noun) + preposition + relative pronoun...

Tu as écris à tes amies? Je veux dire **celles à qui** tu écris toujours à Noël.	*Did you write to your friends? I mean the ones you always write to at Christmas.*
Il y avait trois fourchettes propres sur la table mais **celle dont** tu t'es servi était sale.	*There were three clean forks on the table, but the one you used was dirty.*

A few notes:

- ◆ *Traiter quelqu'un d'un emanière* and *se comporter d'une manière* + feminine adjective is always replaced with the relative pronoun **dont**.
  La manière dont il s'est comporté...   *The way in which he behaved...*

- ◆ *Fois* (expression of time) combined with a number is used with the relative pronoun *que*, not *où*.
  C'est la première fois que tu fais ça?   *Is it the first time you do that?*
  Used without a number, *fois* is used with *où*.
  La fois où je me suis trompé.   *The time I made a mistake.*

- ◆ In front of a vowel, the relative pronoun *que* will be elided into *qu'* (first example), whereas *qui* will never be elided. (second example)
  Le chat qu'il regarde.   *The cat that he is watching.*
  C'est un chien qui aime le fromage.   *It's a dog that likes cheese.*

EXERCICE
10·1

Using a compound relative pronoun (prepositions + relative pronoun), compose one single sentence instead of two. If there is more than one way of rewriting the sentence, give both (even if the second way is not with a compound relative).

1. Le journal parle d'un accident. Nous avons été en retard au cours à cause de cet accident.

   _____

2. Je t'ai vu dire bonjour à un homme, mais je ne connaissais pas cet homme.

   _____

3. Regarde ce vieux bureau. Balzac a écrit Eugénie Grandet sur ce bureau.

   _____

4. Sur mon balcon il y a une plante. Un oiseau y a fait son nid.

   _____

5. Il y a un problème, et je pense souvent à ce problème.

   _____

6. Depuis qu'elle est au chômage elle a droit à des allocations. Ça l'aide beaucoup financièrement.

   _____

7. La ville de la Ciotat est un endroit merveilleux. Elle y a passé les vacances.

   _____

8. Tu te souviens de ce match de foot? A la fin, il y a eu une grosse bagarre!

   _____

9. Dans l'avion Julie se trouvait assise entre deux passagers. Ils étaient très bavards.

   _____

10. J'aimerais bien poser la question, mais il n'y a personne.

   _____

11. Les Martin sont des gens très gentils. Nous avons diné avec eux récemment.

   _____

12. Ces animaux vivaient dans des conditions épouvantables. La SPA (Société
    Protectrice des Animaux) a été choquée.

   _____

   _____

EXERCICE
10·2

*Fill in the blanks with the correct simple relative pronoun. Choose either **qui,
que, dont**, or **où**.*

1. Paul est une personne _____ nous connaissons bien.

2. C'est un petit bistro _____ on mange bien.

3. Quel est l'auteur du roman _____ vous m'avez parlé?

4. Au moment _____ il s'est aperçu de son erreur, il a rougi.

5. Recyclez les journaux _____ vous avez lus.

6. Mes amis sont des gens _____ je vois souvent.

7. Je suis ravie des soldes _____ j'ai pu profiter.

8. Je vous présente l'ami _____ je vous avais parlé.

9. Tu te souviens de la fois _____ le chat est tombé dans ton bain?

10. C'est une fille _____ s'ennuie partout.

11. Il n'y a personne_____ puisse te remplacer.

12. As-tu vu le film _____ je t'avais recommandé?

13. L'instrument _____ il joue est une harpe.

14. L'enfant _____ tu t'es moqué à la récréation veut se venger.

15. Le jour _____ j'arriverai à résoudre ce problème, nous boirons du champagne.

16. Lire le journal est une chose _____ je n'ai pas le temps de faire.

17. Un bikini n'est pas une chose _____ tu auras besoin en Alaska.

18. C'est un sujet _____ intéresse tout le monde.

19. C'est la deuxième fois _____ il reçoit une lettre d'elle.

20. Mon meilleur ami est une personne _____ ne me critique jamais.

21. La manière _____ il parle à ses parents est choquante.

22. Connais-tu l'endroit _____ il garde son trésor?

23. Grand-père nous a parlé des choses _____ il a souffert pendant la guerre.

24. Elle a reçu des nouvelles d'une étudiante _____ était dans sa classe il y a un an.

25. Il a un chien adorable _____ il est fou.

26. Je viens de finir un livre _____ j'ai oublié le titre!

27. Pour Noël, bébé a eu beaucoup de cadeaux _____ il ne méritait pas vraiment!

28. Nous avons fait connaissance d'une femme intéressante _____ la fille est dans le même cours de danse que notre fille.

EXERCICE

10·3

Put the following sentences into French. Remember that English often omits the relative pronouns, but French never does. Also pay attention to the prepositions!

1. The stories he told me are funny.

   _____

2. In the career he is thinking about, he will make lots of money.

   _____

3. Name the person you have the most admiration for.

   _____

4. The kids she takes care of are very rambunctious.

   _____

5. The trophy he is so proud of is on his nightstand.

   _____

6. What is the name of the people we met last night?

   _____

7. He has a friend (f) he does not get along with any more.

   _____

8. There is no one I trust more.

   _____

9. The lake next to which we camped last summer is dry this year.

   _____

10. His wife is someone he shares everything with.

    _____

11. It is they (them) who did it!

    _____

12. The sports my brother is interested in are of no interest to me!

    _____

13. Painting is something he has no talent for.

    _____

14. The cases this lawyer deals with are interesting.

    _____

15. Those who want to stay home should tell me so.

    _____

16. I am the one who told you that.

    _____

17. Once you are finished, turn in your exams.

    _____

18. There is someone here to whom they will give an award.

    _____

19. I like the paper with which you wrapped my gift.

    _____

20. The woman whose husband got fired had to go back to work.

    _____

Neutral relative pronouns: translating a different kind of *what*

We established that a relative clause describes a noun. However some sentences include a relative pronoun that does not describe a noun, and therefore does not have an antecedent either! What could that be? It is a sentence such as *Finish **what** you started*, where *what* is not a question word and should not be translated as a question (that is, no **quoi** or **que**!).

The same type of *what* is found in indirect questions in English, such as *I don't know **what** they want*, where *what* is an indirect question word. What you need for this type of indirect question is the neutral relative pronoun: in French, **ce qui** (*what* as subject), **ce que** (*what* as object), **ce dont** (*what* as object of **de**), or **ce** + preposition + **quoi** (*what* as object of that preposition), with **ce** acting as a "dummy" antecedent. There is no "who" neutral relative pronoun.

Finis **ce que** tu as commencé.	*Finish what you started.*
Il parle de **ce qu'**il ne connaît pas.	*He's talking about what he doesn't know.*
Je ne sais pas **ce qui** s'est passé.	*I don't know what happened.*
Ce qu'il me faut c'est du repos.	*What I need is rest.*

tout ce qui, tout ce que, and tout ce dont

It is common to see **tout** (*all*) immediately before the neutral relative pronoun.

Demande-lui **tout ce que** tu veux savoir.	*Ask him all you want to know.*
Tout ce qui brille n'est pas d'or.	*All that glitters is not gold.*
Raconte-moi **tout ce que** tu sais.	*Tell me all you know.*

143

With a preposition

The relative pronoun **que** changes to **quoi** after all prepositions, including compound prepositions with **de**. Pay attention to the word order in the following examples: **ce** precedes preposition + **quoi**.

La comptabilité n'est pas **ce pour quoi** il est fait!	*Accounting is not what he is made for!*
Ce avec quoi je ne suis pas d'accord c'est le mode de paiement.	*What I disagree with is the payment method.*
C'est exactement **ce à quoi** je pensais.	*That is exactly what I had in mind.*

Use the neutral relative pronoun **ce dont** when the preposition is **de** alone.

Tu ne connais pas **ce dont** je parle. (parler de)	*You are not familiar with what I am talking about.*
Ce dont j'ai besoin c'est de calme! (avoir besoin de)	*What I need is some peace and quiet!*

ce for the previous sentence

Ce can refer back to the thought of a previous phrase, as *which* does in English. In that scenario, it must be preceded by a comma.

Julie veut travailler pour Médecins sans frontières, **ce à quoi** ses parents s'opposent.	*Julie wants to work for Doctors Without Borders, which her parents oppose.*
Rachel va travailler cet été, **ce qui** lui permettra d'acheter une voiture à la rentrée.	*Rachel will work this summer, which will allow her to buy a car when she starts school.*

Reported questions

The neutral relative pronouns are used to ask *what* in indirect questions. They replace the direct question words **qu'est-ce qui...** , **qu'est-ce que...** , and **que** (object), all of which ask *what*. See Unit 7 on reporting questions for details.

Je voudrais savoir **ce qui** te rend triste.	*I'd like to know what makes you sad.*
Dis-moi **ce que** tu veux pour ton anniversaire.	*Tell me what you want for your birthday.*

Stylistic note

You may find a neutral relative pronoun other than **ce qui** and **ce que** in an indirect question. In that case, and because they have no antecedent, they emphasize the verb of the question, as illustrated in the English translation of the following examples:

Je te demande **ce à quoi** tu fais allusion.	*I am asking you what (on earth) you are alluding to.*
Je voudrais savoir **ce à quoi** sert cette machine!	*I would like to know what (on earth) that machine is for!*

Also, the sentences that use the neutral relative pronoun can resemble indirect questions. Sometimes only a fine line separates them! In such cases usage is somewhat flexible. In example 1, **ne pas comprendre** can be considered an introductory verb for reported questions . . . or not! Both versions of the sentence are acceptable, although the version with the neutral pronoun is more formal.

Personne ne comprend **ce à quoi** sert cette machine.	*Nobody understands what that machine is for.*
or: Personne ne comprend **à quoi** sert cette machine.	
Je ne veux pas savoir **ce à quoi** vous pensez.	*I don't want to know what you're thinking about.*
or: Je ne veux pas savoir **à quoi** vous pensez.	

Recap

The neutral relative pronouns **ce que**, **ce qui**, **ce dont**, and **ce** + preposition + **quoi** (all meaning *what*) are used:

◆ As the subject

Ce n'est pas **ce à quoi** tu penses.	*It's not what you are thinking about.*

◆ After **être**

C'est **ce que** je viens de te dire!	*That's what I just told you.*

◆ As the direct object

Prends **ce qui** te plaît.	*Take what you like.*

◆ As the object of a preposition

Souviens-toi **de ce que** je te dis.	*Remember what I am telling you.*

The neutral relative pronouns **ce que** and **ce qui** (meaning *what*) replace the question words **qu'est-ce qui...** , **qu'est-ce que...** , and **que** (object) in indirect questions.

Qu'est-ce qui se passe?	*What is happening?*
Dis-moi **ce qui** se passe.	*Tell me what is happening.*
Qu'est-ce que tu veux?	*What do you want?*
or: **Que** veux-tu?	
Dis-moi **ce que** tu veux.	*Tell me what you want.*

EXERCICE

11·1

Fill in the blanks with the correct neutral relative pronoun.

1. Nous voudrions savoir _____ va arriver à Harry Potter.

2. « Garçon, ce n'est pas _____ j'ai commandé. »

3. As-tu oublié _____ je t'ai dit hier?

4. Avez-vous vu _____ s'est passé?

5. Cette dame ne sait pas _____ elle veut.

6. Ils ont pensé à tout, ou presque. C'est _____ ils n'ont pas pensé qui m'inquiète!

7. Dites-moi _____ vous pensez de ce film.

8. Le prof explique aux étudiants _____ ils doivent faire.

9. Expliquez-moi _____ vous fait mal.

10. Je ne comprends pas _____ tu veux dire.

11. Je vais jeter tout _____ je n'ai pas besoin.

12. La pollution est _____ les écologistes parlent le plus.

13. Regarde par la fenêtre et dis-moi _____ tu vois.

14. Tout _____ j'ai besoin c'est de tranquillité.

15. Explique-moi _____ les enfants ont eu peur.

16. J'ai de l'aversion pour _____ est malhonnête.

17. Julie raconte à son ami _____ elle a rêvé.

18. Si tu savais _____ je pense...

19. Quand il dit ça, il fait de la peine à son père. _____ il ne se rend pas compte c'est qu'il fait de la peine à sa mère aussi.

20. Dis-moi _____ tu vas faire demain.

21. Est-ce que le Père Noël t'a apporté _____ tu voulais?

22. Je ne sais pas _____ se passera si j'appuie ici.

23. Vous devez m'expliquer _____ les étudiants sont mécontents.

Determining a noun with prepositions

French prepositions can be a real challenge because their usage is very different from English. This is particularly true when French prepositions determine a noun; English rarely uses a preposition for this purpose. This unit identifies several broad categories of expressions to help you understand the main prepositions used with nouns (**à**, **de**, and **en**), and how to use them. Note that these categories are not fixed; there are exceptions. The following examples illustrate how French never has two nouns side by side, as English does:

des souvenirs **d'**enfance	*childhood memories*
des affaires **de** famille	*family business*
un bateau **à** voile	*a sailboat*

When to use à

À frequently links two nouns or a noun and an infinitive.

à introducing a characteristic

The noun or verb infinitive that follows the preposition describes a fundamental quality. **À** is usually not followed by an article in this construction. You may think of **à** as a synonym of **avec**:

un drapeau **à** damiers	*a checkered flag*
un pull **à** col roulé	*a (sweater with a) turtleneck*
un four **à** gaz	*a gas oven*
un train **à** grande vitesse	*a high-speed train*

Important exceptions, in which the definite article is combined with the preposition **à**, include expressions that describe people (physical traits and clothing), and the composition of things, such as prepared foods (last two examples).

un enfant **aux** cheveux blonds	*a child with blond hair*
l'homme **au** chapeau noir	*the man in the black hat*
un gâteau **au** chocolat	*a chocolate cake*
une tarte **aux** fraises	*a strawberry pie/tart*

à introducing a function

The expression that follows the preposition describes the function of the noun, that is, what it is for. It could answer the question: **À quoi ça sert?** (*What is it for?*). You may think of **à** here as a synonym of **pour**:

un panier **à** provisions	*a grocery basket*
un rouge **à** lèvres	*lipstick*
une cuillère **à** café	*a coffee spoon*
un étui **à** lunettes	*a glasses case*
la salle **à** manger	*the dining room*
une machine **à** laver	*a washing machine*
un sac **à** dos	*a backpack*

Note that **de** can also express function, although it is less common. There is no way to tell when it should be used rather than **à**. One general use with **de** describes the function of articles of clothing (see later discussion). Here is a list of some common expressions with **de** used to describe the function of a noun:

une bague **de** fiançailles	*an engagement ring*
une salle **de** bains	*a bathroom*
une salle **de** séjour	*a living room*
la salle **d'**attente	*the waiting room*
une table **de** nuit	*a nightstand*
des lunettes **de** lecture	*reading glasses*
des lunettes **de** soleil	*sunglasses*
une robe **de** plage	*a beach robe*
des chaussures **de** ski	*ski boots*
un maillot **de** bain	*a bathing suit*
une chemise **de** nuit	*a nightgown*

When to use de

Many nouns are described by a prepositional phrase introduced by **de**. Such phrases can express origin, ownership, or contents, much like *of* and *from* in English.

Origin and ownership

An expression introduced by **de** indicates the origin of the noun being described, or it introduces the owner of the preceding noun (last 2 examples).

des nouvelles **de** France	*news from France*
un poulet **de** ferme	*a farm-raised chicken*
du sel **de** mer	*sea salt*
du poivre **de** Cayenne	*Cayenne pepper*
un balai **de** sorcière	*a witch's broom*
une robe **de** mariée	*a wedding (bridal) gown*

Sometimes, **de** needs to be expanded in order to avoid confusion between ownership and origin.

Ambiguous

le train **de** Nice
*the train **to** Nice* or: *the train **from** Nice*

Clear

le train **en provenance de** Nice
*the train (**coming**) **from** Nice*

Ambiguous

un cadeau de Paul
a gift from Paul or: *one of Paul's gifts*

Clear

un cadeau **de la part de** Paul
*a gift **from** Paul*

Contents

When it expresses the contents of an object, **de** is the literal equivalent of *of*.

une boîte **de** petits pois	*a can of peas*
une bouteille **d'**eau	*a bottle of water*
une douzaine **d'**œufs	*a dozen eggs*

(See also "When to use **en**: Shape and material," later.)

To introduce a number

When the expression that describes the noun includes a number (for example, for age and size), **de** is often used.

une fille **de** quinze ans	*a fifteen-year-old girl*
une piscine **de** cinquante mètres	*a fifty-meter pool*
un billet **de** 100 euros	*a 100 euro bill*
un diamant **d'**un carat	*a one-carat diamond*

Cause

De + noun or infinitive can express that something is *caused by* or is done *out of*.

un cri **de** désespoir	*a cry of despair*
une larme **de** joie	*a tear of joy*
un geste **de** colère	*an angry gesture*

When to use en

Deciding whether to use **en** or **de** in a descriptive noun phrase can be tricky. Your skill in this will grow with experience.

Shape and material

A noun introduced by **en** describes the shape or make of an object when no adjective exists. It is a synonym of **en forme de** (*in the shape of*) or **fait en** (*made in/of*).

des yeux **en** amandes	*almond-shaped eyes*
une serviette **en** papier	*a paper napkin*
un bracelet **en** argent	*a silver bracelet*
un plat **en** céramique	*a ceramic dish*

Note that the preposition **de** can also be found in this usage. The difference between **en** and **de** is often parallel to the difference between *in* and *of* in English. In the following examples, we don't use **en** in French, just as we would not use *in* in the equivalent English expressions:

un chapeau **de** paille	*a straw hat*
une toque **de** fourrure	*a fur hat*
une boule **de** neige	*snowball*
une boulette **de** viande	*meatball*
une feuille **de** papier	*a sheet of paper*

Some common expressions with **de** describing material often have an abstract meaning.

un cœur **d'**or	*a heart of gold*
une santé **de** fer	*excellent (strong as iron) health*

To describe what something is made of, if the preposition + noun or infinitive follows the verb **être** instead of following the noun it describes, **en** must be used, never **de**.

une feuille **de** papier	*a sheet of paper*
Cette feuille est **en** papier.	*This sheet is made of paper.*
un chapeau **de** paille	*a straw hat*
Ce chapeau est **en** paille.	*This hat is made of straw.*
une assiette **en** céramique	*a ceramic plate*
cette assiette est **en** céramique	*This plate is ceramic.*

Recap

Here are some helpful tips you should keep in mind when using a noun or an infinitive to describe another noun:

- A prepositional link is necessary between two nouns or a noun and an infinitive in French.

des souvenirs **d'**enfance	*childhood memories*

- **De** is never followed by an infinitive. However, an infinitive may follow **à**.

une salle **à** manger	*dining room*
des tâches **à** accomplir	*tasks to accomplish*

- Like *of* in English, **de** conveys an idea of *contents* that **à** does not.

une tasse **de** thé	*a cup of (filled with) tea*
une tasse **à** thé	*a teacup (for tea)*
une assiette **de** soupe	*a bowl of (filled with) soup*
une assiette **à** soupe	*a soup bowl (for soup)*
un verre **d'**eau	*a glass of (filled with) water*
un verre **à** eau	*a water glass (for water)*

*Fill in the blanks with the correct preposition. Choose among **à** (**au** and **aux**), **de**, and **en**.*

1. C'est une bague _____ or. C'était la bague _____ ma grand-mère.

2. Le blessé pousse des cris _____ douleur.

3. Pour le pique-nique, prenez des fourchettes _____ plastique et des serviettes _____ papier. J'apporterai des verres et des bouteilles _____ eau.

4. Il porte une chemise _____ manches longues et un chapeau _____ paille.

5. Un couteau _____ pain peut être dangereux.

6. « Je prendrai une tasse _____ thé, s'il vous plaît. »

7. La cathédrale mesure cinquante-cinq mètres _____ haut.

8. Le thon est un poisson _____ mer.

9. Pour son baptême, il a reçu une gourmette _____ argent.

10. À midi j'ai pris une assiette _____ crudités.

11. Nous sommes restés quarante-cinq minutes dans la salle _____ attente!

12. Ils viennent d'acheter une jolie table _____ salon.

13. C'est un virage _____ épingle àcheveux.

14. Elle veut des tasses _____ thé _____ porcelaine _____ Chine.

15. Les statues de Rodin sont _____ bronze.

16. Cette petite tasse est ravissante, mais elle sert _____ quoi? C'est une tasse _____ thé, ou _____ café?

17. Un mur médiéval fait souvent un mètre _____ épaisseur.

18. Les enfants mangent des œufs _____ chocolat à Pâques.

19. C'est une femme _____ cheveux blonds et _____ yeux bleus.

20. Ce vase est _____ terre cuite.

21. Préférez-vous les statues _____ marbre ou _____ bronze?

22. Elle est devenue toute rose _____ plaisir.

23. Quand tu auras trouvé le couteau _____ fromage, nous pourrons manger ce gouda.

24. La chambre _____ coucher et la salle _____ bains sont au premier étage.

25. Elle rêve d'un manteau _____ fourrure.

26. Quoi? Tu n'aimes pas le gâteau _____ chocolat?

27. Ma sœur est une blonde _____ yeux bleus.

28. Je n'ai pas bu ma tasse _____ café ce matin: je suis encore endormi.

29. J'ai pris ma serviette _____ plage et mon maillot _____ bain.

30. Comme dessert, il y a une tarte _____ abricots.

Object pronouns

A pronoun can be the direct object of a verb, or the object of a preposition attached to a verb. It is this preposition or its absence that determines which object pronoun is used: either a direct or indirect object pronoun. The antecedent of the pronoun is also important: does the object being replaced by the pronoun represent a thing or a person?

The direct object

The direct object answers the question *what* or *whom* after the verb, and is not introduced by a preposition. The direct object pronoun replaces nouns referring to things or people.

> Remember that there is never a contraction between the prepositions **de** or **à** and the object pronouns **le** or **les** that may follow.
>
> | | |
> |---|---|
> | Il s'amuse **à les** regarder nager. | *He has fun watching them swim.* |
> | Nous avons besoin **de le** voir. | *We need to see him.* |

Direct object describing a thing

If the object's antecedent is a noun that refers to a thing or an animal, use **le**, **la**, **l'**, or **les** before the verb:

Il regarde **la télé**.	*He watches TV.*
Il **la** regarde.	*He watches it.*
Ils ont oublié **leurs livres**.	*They forgot their books.*
Ils **les** ont oubliés.	*They forgot them.*

If the object's antecedent is an entire clause, use **le** (**l'**) as the object pronoun. When a clause is the direct object of the main verb, its verb can be either conjugated (examples 1 and 2) or in the infinitive (example 3).

In both cases it is replaced by the object pronoun **le (l')**, and it is either translated by *it* in English or simply omitted (last example).

Je ne t'ai pas dit **que j'allais quitter mon poste?**	*I did not tell you that I was quitting my job?*
Je ne te **l'**ai pas dit?	*I did not tell it to you/you that?*
Je ne comprends pas **qu'ils soient fâchés.**	*I don't understand that they are cross.*
Je ne **le** comprends pas.	*I don't understand it.*
Voulez-vous **les aider?**	*Do you want to help them?*
Oui je **le** veux.	*Yes, I want to./Yes, I do.*

To avoid ambiguity, use **ça**. When the main verb expresses preference (**aimer, détester, préférer**), French prefers **ça** (*it, that*) instead of **le, la, l'**, or **les** to make a clear distinction between human and non-human objects.

Tu aimes **le chocolat?**	*Do you like chocolate?*
J'adore **ça!**	*I love it!*
Il déteste **manger seul.**	*He hates to eat alone.*
Il déteste **ça.**	*He hates it.*

Also, after a verb where the direct object is human, **ça** is used instead of the regular pronoun to avoid ambiguity when referring to a whole clause or a situation. Note the contrast in the following two examples:

Il s'occupe d'enfants handicapés. Je **le** trouve formidable.	*He takes care of handicapped children. I find **him** great.*
Il s'occupe d'enfants handicapés. Je trouve **ça** formidable.	*He takes care of handicapped children. I find **that** great.*

Direct object describing a person

If the direct object describes a person, use **me (m')**, **te (t')**, **le (l')**, **la (l')**, **les**, **nous**, or **vous**.

Ils aiment **leurs parents**. Ils **les** aiment.	*They love their parents. They love them.*
Nous **t'**aimons.	*We love you.*
Ils vont **nous** écouter.	*They are going to listen to us.*
Elle **m'**a regardé.	*She looked at me.*

Object of the preposition à

The object introduced by the preposition **à** is an indirect object and should be replaced by the indirect object pronoun if it describes a person (or in some cases a stressed pronoun—see later "exceptions"), or by the pronoun **y** if it describes a thing.

à + human object

Verbs that call for a human indirect object include: **répondre à, ressembler à, téléphoner à, parler à**, and so on.

Il ressemble **à son père**.	*He looks like his dad.*
Il **lui** ressemble.	*He looks like him.*
Nous n'avons pas téléphoné **à nos parents**.	*We did not call our parents.*
Nous ne **leur** avons pas téléphoné.	*We did not call them.*

Many of these verbs also have a direct object that is non-human. (See the following list of verbs with a double object construction.) With a double object, the direct object immediately follows the verb, and the indirect object comes second. The order may vary when object pronouns are used, as the following examples demonstrate:

Il va donner des roses à sa femme.	*He is going to give his wife some roses.*
Il va **lui** donner des roses.	*He is going to give her some roses.*
Il va **lui en** donner.	*He is going to give her some.*
Les jeunes demandent des conseils aux adultes.	*Young people ask adults for advice.*
Les jeunes **leur** demandent des conseils.	*Young people ask them for advice.*
Les jeunes **leur en** demandent.	*Young people ask them for some.*

Verbs with a double object construction

apprendre quelque chose à quelqu'un	*to teach someone something*
conseiller quelque chose à quelqu'un	*to advise someone about something*
défendre/interdire quelque chose à quelqu'un	*to forbid something to someone*
demander quelque chose à quelqu'un	*to ask someone something*
dire quelque chose à quelqu'un	*to tell someone something*
donner quelque chose à quelqu'un	*to give someone something*
offrir quelque chose à quelqu'un	*to offer someone something*
passer quelque chose à quelqu'un	*to hand something to someone*
prendre quelque chose à quelqu'un	*to take something from someone*
promettre quelque chose à quelqu'un	*to promise someone something*
proposer quelque chose à quelqu'un	*to propose something to someone*
rappeler quelque chose à quelqu'un	*to remind someone of something*
refuser quelque chose à quelqu'un	*to refuse something to someone*
rendre quelque chose à quelqu'un	*to return something to someone*
reprocher quelque chose à quelqu'un	*to blame something on someone*
servir quelque chose à quelqu'un	*to serve something to someone*
suggérer quelque chose à quelqu'un	*to suggest something to someone*
vendre quelque chose à quelqu'un	*to sell something to someone*

Object of the verb falloir

To avoid a subjunctive construction after **falloir**, replace the subjunctive by an infinitive, and change the former subject into the corresponding indirect object pronoun. The pronoun must precede **falloir**, instead of the infinitive.

With subjunctive

Il faut **que je finisse** ce travail. *It is necessary for me to finish this work.*

Alternative construction

Il **me** faut **finir** ce travail. *It is necessary for me to finish this work.*

With subjunctive

Il faut **qu'ils arrivent** à l'heure. *It is necessary for them to be on time.*

Alternative construction

Il **leur** faut **arriver** à l'heure. *It is necessary for them to be on time.*

à + human object: exceptions

A few verbs that require the preposition **à** before a human object cannot, however, take the indirect object pronoun. The stressed pronoun is used instead, as listed below.

When using the stressed pronoun, you must retain the preposition in the sentence. The following examples illustrate the contrast between the use of the indirect object pronoun and the stressed pronoun. If you look up such a verb in the dictionary, you will find the preposition that accompanies that verb. But only the dictionary examples will show if the verb uses a regular indirect object pronoun or the stressed pronoun. You will learn these verbs with time and experience.

Janine **parle à** ses parents. *Janine talks to her parents.*
Elle **leur** parle. *She talks to them.*

Janine **pense à** ses parents. *Janine thinks about her parents.*
Elle pense **à eux**. *She thinks about them.*

Il **fait confiance à** ses employés. *He trusts his employees.*
Il **leur** fait confiance. *He trusts them.*

Il **se fie à** ses employés. *He trusts his employees.*
Il se fie **à eux**. *He trusts them.*

Some common examples of verbs that require a stressed pronoun include:

être à (*possession*) *to belong to*
faire attention à quelqu'un *to pay attention to someone*
penser à quelqu'un *to think about someone*
renoncer à quelqu'un *to give up someone*

s'attacher à quelqu'un	*to become attached to someone*
s'attaquer à quelqu'un	*to attack someone*
se consacrer à quelqu'un	*to devote oneself to someone*
se fier à quelqu'un	*to trust someone*
s'habituer à quelqu'un	*to get used to someone*
s'intéresser à quelqu'un	*to be interested in someone*
tenir à quelqu'un	*to hold someone dear*

We established that the indirect object pronouns **lui/leur** could only replace human objects. However, some of those verbs + **à** + human object (verbs of communication) can have a non-human object. Can you still use the indirect object pronouns? Yes, because you don't have an alternative. Note that **ça**, which can be an alternative in some cases, cannot be used after a verb of communication.

L'économie est stagnante, il faut **lui** donner un coup de fouet.	*The economy is stagnant, it needs a big push.*
C'est le comité qui décidera. Nous devons **lui** parler.	*The committee decides. We need to talk to them/him/it.*
—À quelle heure ferme l'épicerie?	*"At what time does the grocery store close?"*
—Je ne sais pas. Téléphone-**lui** vite.	*"I don't know. Call it/them quickly."*

à + thing object: y

If the object of **à** is a noun that refers to a thing, use the pronoun **y**.

Je pense **à nos dernières vacances**.	*I think about our last vacation.*
J'**y** pense.	*I think about it/them.*
Il s'intéresse **à la politique**.	*He is interested in politics.*
Il s'**y** intéresse.	*He is interested in it.*
Tu t'habitues **à tes nouvelles lunettes**?	*Are you getting used to your new glasses?*
Tu t'**y** habitues?	*Are you getting used to them?*

If the object of **à** is a clause, use the pronoun **y**. **Y** can replace **à** + dependent clause with conjugated verb, or **à** + dependent clause with verb in the infinitive. Note that if the dependent verb is conjugated, **à** changes to **à ce que** + verb in the subjunctive (example 2).

Il pense **à créer son entreprise**.	*He's thinking about creating his company.*
Il **y** pense.	*He's thinking about it.*
Je tiens **à ce que tu finisses ce travail**.	*I insist that you finish this work.*
J'**y** tiens.	*I insist on it.*

Y is also used to replace most prepositional phrases that indicate a *place*, except those introduced by **de** and by certain very specific prepositions for which **y** would be too vague. (See "Objects of other prepositions.")

Je n'ai pas vu le chat **dans ta chambre**.	*I did not see the cat in your room.*
Je n'**y** ai pas vu le chat.	*I did not see the cat there.*
Tu es déjà **au lit**!	*You are already in bed!*
Tu **y** es déjà.	*You are already there.*
Ils n'aiment pas aller **chez le dentiste**.	*They don't like to go to the dentist's.*
Ils n'aiment pas **y** aller.	*They don't like to go there.*

When **y** occurs before the verb **aller** in a conjugated form that begins with **i** (that is, the future and the conditional), it not used. (This is because the two sounds are identical.)

Vous **iriez à Rome** si vous parliez italien?	*Would you go to Rome if you spoke Italian?*
Oui, nous **irions**.	*Yes we would go (there).*
Tu **iras chez eux** samedi?	*Will you go to their house on Saturday?*
Oui, **j'irai**.	*Yes, I will go (there).*

In the following idiomatic expressions, do not try to find an English equivalent for **y**:

Ça **y** est!	*That's done!/Finished!*
On **y** va?	*Shall we?*
Il s'**y** prend bien/mal.	*He is going about it wrong/well.*
Tu t'**y** connais en (tortues)?	*Do you know much about (turtles)?*
Il **y** va de (sa réputation).	*(His reputation) is on the line/at stake.*
Y compris...	*. . . included*
Tu n'**y** connais rien.	*You don't know what you're talking about.*
Je n'**y** suis pour rien.	*I have nothing to do with it.*

Object of the preposition **de**

You have already studied many of the verbal constructions with **de** in other contexts, but it is also important to understand how they function when the noun must be replaced by a pronoun.

de + human object

When the object of a verb that takes the preposition **de** is a person or a group of persons, use the stressed pronoun to replace the noun, unless you're dealing with a *quantity* of people (last example), in which case you use **en**.

Il parle **de Julie**.	*He talks about Julie.*
Il parle **d'elle**.	*He talks about her.*
Je me souviens **de mon premier prof**.	*I remember my first teacher.*
Je me souviens **de lui**.	*I remember him.*
Elle est fière **de ses enfants**.	*She is proud of her kids.*
Elle est fière **d'eux**.	*She is proud of them.*

But:

—Combien **de frères** as-tu?	*"How many brothers do you have?"*
—J'**en** ai deux.	*"I have two."*

Verbs that require the preposition **de** include:

avoir besoin de quelqu'un	*to need someone*
avoir peur de quelqu'un	*to be afraid of someone*
avoir pitié de quelqu'un	*to have pity for/on someone*
dépendre de quelqu'un	*to depend on someone*
entendre parler de quelqu'un	*to hear about someone*
être + *adjective* + de quelqu'un	*to be + adjective + about someone*
parler de quelqu'un	*to talk about someone*
répondre de quelqu'un	*to vouch for someone*
se débarrasser de quelqu'un	*to get rid of someone*
s'éloigner de quelqu'un	*to get away from someone*
s'occuper de quelqu'un	*to take care of someone*
se passer de quelqu'un	*to do without someone*
se souvenir de quelqu'un	*to remember someone*

And also, with two objects, the direct object is non-human:

obtenir (quelque chose) de quelqu'un	*to get something from someone*
recevoir (quelque chose) de quelqu'un	*to receive something from someone*

de + inanimate object

When the object of a verb that takes the preposition **de** is a thing, the pronoun **en** must be used. Such verbs include the same ones discussed earlier and some additional verbs that can only have a non-human object such as:

accuser de	*to accuse of something*
avoir envie de	*to want something*
bénéficier de	*to benefit from something*
jouer de	*to play an instrument*
manquer de	*to lack something*
profiter de	*to take advantage of*
raffoler de	*to be crazy for/about something*
s'apercevoir de	*to realize something*
s'excuser de	*to apologize for something*
tenir compte de	*to take something into account*

Il parle **de ses vacances**.	*He talks about his vacation.*
Il **en** parle.	*He talks about it.*
Êtes-vous content **de votre victoire**?	*Are you happy with your victory?*
En êtes-vous content?	*Are you happy with it?*
Occupe-toi **de tes affaires**!	*Mind your own business!*
Occupe-t'**en**!	*Mind it!*
—Répondez-vous **de sa conduite**?	*"Do you vouch for his behavior?"*
—J'**en** réponds.	*"I do."*
Il raffole du **golf**. Il **en** est fou.	*He loves golf. He is crazy about it.*
Son mari bénéficiera **de son assurance maladie**.	*Her husband will benefit from her medical coverage.*
Son mari **en** bénéficiera.	*Her husband will benefit from it.*

De can also express *from*. Even though this type of prepositional phrase represents a location, the pronoun **en** must be used instead of **y**.

Tu viens **de la maison**?	*Are you coming from the house?*
J'**en** viens.	*I'm coming from there.*
Sortez **de la piscine**.	*Get out of the pool.*
Sortez-**en**.	*Get out of it.*

de + clause object

When the object of the preposition **de** is a clause, a distinction must be made between the types of clauses: does the clause have an infinitive or a conjugated verb? The choice of the pronoun depends on that distinction.

de + clause with an infinitive

De between a verb and an infinitive can have two functions: it is either required by the main verb, as in **avoir peur** *de* (*to be afraid of*) and **se souvenir de** (*to remember*), or it indicates an indirect command (**dire à quelqu'un** *de* **faire quelque chose**).

Verbs that report commands usually have a double object construction, like **demander quelque chose à quelqu'un** (*to ask someone something* or *something of someone*), where the direct object is non-human (*to ask something*). So the pronoun that replaces the dependent clause (*something*) must be the direct object pronoun **le**. The **de** that follows the verb is part of the reported command construction and is irrelevant for the choice of the pronoun. That is, the object of the verb begins with **de**.

Je te demande **de ne pas crier**.	*I am asking you not to shout.*
Je te **le** demande.	*I am asking it of you.*
Elle leur a dit **de partir**.	*She told them to leave.*
Elle **le** leur a dit.	*She told it to them.*

When **de** is part of the verb, however, we have instead an indirect transitive construction: verb + **de** + object, so any non-human object of that verb, including a dependent clause, will be replaced by **en**.

Il **a besoin de** prendre des vacances.	*He needs to take a vacation.*
Il **en a besoin**.	*He needs it.*
Il n'**est** pas **question de** partir!	*Leaving is out of the question!*
Il n'**en est** pas **question**!	*It is out of the question!*

To find out what the true construction of the verb is (with or without **de**), replace the clause by a noun: if **de** must be kept before the noun object, use the pronoun **en** to replace the clause. If it is not kept, use **le**. In the first example, **demander** is transitive direct as shown by the version in parentheses, so you will need to replace the clause with the direct object pronoun **le**. In the second example, on the other hand, *de* is part of the original verb *avoir envie de* so choose the pronoun *en*.

Ils lui ont demandé **de chanter**.	*They asked him to sing.*
Je n'ai pas envie **de** me mouiller les pieds.	*I don't want to get my feet wet.*
Je n'**en** ai pas envie.	*I don't want to (do that).*

de + clause with a conjugated verb

But watch out! The pronoun **en** can replace a clause that is not introduced by **de**, but rather by **que**! When a verb, such as **avoir peur de**, that usually takes **de** + object, introduces a conjugated dependent verb, the preposition **de** (which only introduces an infinitive) will not appear in the sentence. Instead, the conjugated verb is introduced by **que**. Use the pronoun **en** to replace the dependent clause object of the verb.

J'ai peur **que nous soyons en retard**.	*I am afraid (that) we may be late.*
J'**en** ai peur.	*I am afraid of it.*
Elle a besoin **que tu l'aides**.	*She needs you to help her.*
Elle **en** a besoin.	*She needs it.*
—Êtes-vous contents **que vos enfants arrivent demain?**	*"Are you happy that your children are arriving tomorrow?"*
—Nous **en** sommes ravis.	*"We are delighted (about it)."*

Idiomatic expressions with en

Do not try to find English equivalents for **en** in the following expressions:

Vite! Le train s'**en** va. (s'en aller)	*Hurry! The train is leaving.*
Ne t'**en** fais pas. (s'en faire)	*Don't worry.*
Le héros s'**en** sort toujours. (s'en sortir)	*The hero always makes it.*
Je m'**en** tiendrai à l'essentiel. (s'en tenir à)	*I will stick to the essentials.*
Elle **en** veut à ses parents. (en vouloir à)	*She holds a grudge against her parents.*
Ç'**en** est fait de sa réputation.	*That's the end of his reputation.*
J'**en** ai assez!	*I've had enough!*
Je n'**en** peux plus!	*I can't take it anymore!*
Je n'**en** sais rien.	*I have no clue.*
Je n'**en** ai pas la moindre idée.	*I don't have the faintest idea.*

Objects of other prepositions

Prepositions other than **à** and **de** can also have an object. Unlike **à** and **de** they cannot be replaced entirely by a pronoun. Because of their meaning, they must remain in the sentence, and that affects and limits the choice of pronoun. As a general rule remember the following:

- A stressed pronoun can only refer to a person (or a pet).
- When using a stressed pronoun, retain the preposition in the sentence. All other pronouns incorporate the preposition.
- Sometimes you cannot use any pronoun at all (see following list).

Here is a list of common prepositions:

à côté de	*next to*
avec	*with*
chez	*at (someone's house or business)*

contre	*against*
loin de	*far from*
malgré	*in spite of*
parmi	*among*
pour	*for*
sans	*without*
selon	*according to*
sur	*on*
vers	*toward*

Preposition + human object

Always use the stressed pronoun after "meaningful" prepositions such as **pour, avec**, and **chez** (see previous list), and retain the preposition.

J'ai acheté ce livre **pour toi**.	*I bought this book for you.*
Elle est partie **avec eux**.	*She left with them.*
Tu peux compter **sur moi**.	*You can count on me.*
Je suis tombée **sur elle** par hasard.	*I ran into her by chance.*
Je vais m'asseoir **à côté de toi**.	*I will sit next to you.*
Quand il a reconnu son maître, le chien a couru **vers lui**.	*When he recognized his master, the dog ran toward him.*

A number of prepositions that are made of preposition + **de** follow a different route. When **au sujet de** and **à propos de**, (*about/on the subject of* - literally "*at the subject of*") or **au profit de** (*at the benefit of*) are replaced by a pronoun, the whole prepositional phrase is replaced by possessive adjective + noun, as illustrated below.

au sujet de sa fille	*about (on the subject of) her daughter*
à son sujet	*about her (on her subject)*
à propos de ses enfants	*about (on the subject of) her kids*
à propos	*about them (on their subject)*
au sujet de Julie et moi	*about (on the subject of) Julie and me*
à notre sujet	*about us (on our subject)*
au profit de son héritier	*at the benefit of his heir*
à son profit	*at his benefit*
au profit de ses héritiers	*at the benefit of his heirs*
à leur profit	*at their benefit*

Preposition + inanimate object

Usually, those "meaningful" prepositions can't be removed from a sentence, as **à** or **de** can, because without them, the sentence would lose meaning. Stressed pronouns are the only pronouns that would allow you to keep the preposition . . . but they can only be used for people! What to do? If the object of such prepositions is a thing, there are two outcomes: no pronoun is used, and the preposition ends the sentence . . . an unusual construction in French. Or, with some prepositions that can't be left at the end, you may be able to use **cela**, **ceci** or **ça** (*this, that, it*).

No pronoun

When the object of such prepositions is a thing, no pronoun is used and the preposition ends the sentence.

Il a oublié d'enlever ses pantoufles et il est sorti **avec**.	*He forgot to take his slippers off and went out with them on.*
Ma tente s'est envolée. Il faut courir **après**.	*My tent flew away. We must run after it.*

Several prepositions have to undergo a transformation in order to end a sentence on their own. The following table presents the most common ones that will change, with their translations. Note how the English equivalent often includes the object pronoun *it* afterwards. In French, add nothing (other than a period) to the words listed below.

sur (*on*)	dessus (*on it*)
sous (*under*)	dessous (*under it*)
dans (*in*)	dedans (*in it*)

preposition + *de*	**preposition alone**
à côté de (*next to*)	à côté (*next to it*)
à l'arrière de (*in the back of*)	à l'arrière (*in the back of it*)
à l'intérieur de (*inside*)	à l'intérieur (*inside of it*)
au-delà de (*beyond*)	au-delà (*beyond it*)
au-dessus de (*above*)	au-dessus (*above it*)
autour de (*around*)	autour (*around it*)
en-dessous de (*below*)	en-dessous (*below it*)
en échange de (*in exchange for*)	en échange (*in exchange for it*)
en face de (*across from*)	en face (*across from it*)
en plus de (*in addition to*)	en plus (*in addition to it*)
le long de (*along*)	tout le long (*along it*)

In any case where you need to use a compound preposition, one ending with **de** that is not listed here, keep in mind that **de** is only used to introduce a noun. If no noun follows, don't use **de**, especially at the end of a sentence.

Je n'ai pas vu l'arbre et je suis rentré **dedans**.	*I did not see the tree, and I ran **into it**.*
Il y avait un chat sur le banc, et la dame s'est assise **à côté**.	*There was a cat on the bench, and the lady sat down **next to it**.*
Il a perdu ses clés, il ne peut plus mettre la main **dessus**.	*He lost his keys, he can't get his hands **on them** anymore.*

ça, ceci, cela

Prepositions such as **selon, malgré, pour, par, d'après, à propos de, à cause de, à l'exception de, en dépit de**, and **compte tenu de**, just to name the most common ones, can't be left as is at the end of a sentence. However, they must also not be dropped. The only option here is to keep the preposition, followed by the neutral pronouns **ceci/cela** (in a more literary context, example 1) or **ça** (in most other cases). **Ceci/cela** and **ça** are mostly used as demonstrative pronouns, but here they are used as "neutral stress pronouns" of sorts and can replace a noun object or an infinitive clause object (last two examples).

| Il se mit à crier et à courir en rond. Il fit cela dans le but de troubler son adversaire. | *He started to shout and run in circles. He did that in order to confuse his adversary.* |

Note that the above example is in the **passé simple.**

Le budget est important et nous allons commencer **par ça**.	*The budget is important and we will begin with it.*
Ce sondage dit qu'une personne sur deux gagnera le loto. **D'après ça**, nous avons donc des chances!	*That survey says that one person out of two will win the lottery. According to it, we have a chance!*
S'amuser est important et il faut garder du temps **pour ça**.	*It is important to enjoy oneself, and one must save some time for that.*
Il est malade, mais il reste de bonne humeur **malgré ça**.	*He is sick, but he remains in a good mood in spite of it.*

Using a demonstrative to supplement pronoun usage occurs also with compound prepositions such as **au sujet de** (*about*) and **à l'occasion de** (*for*). **À l'exception de** (*except*) belongs here as well with one little twist: add **près** after it.

au sujet de + *noun*	à ce sujet (*about that*)
à l'occasion de + *noun*	à cette occasion (*for this event*)
à l'exception de + *noun*	à cette exception près (*except for that*)
À l'occasion du retour de leurs enfants pour les vacances d'été, ils voulaient faire une grande fête.	*For the return of their kids for the summer break, they wanted to have a big party.*
À cette occasion, ils voulaient faire une grande fête.	*For this event, they wanted to have a big party.*

Expressions of quantity

Expressions of quantity often include **de** (see following list), but some don't. With or without **de**, an expression of **quantity** + noun (referring to things or people) is replaced by the pronoun **en**.

(pas) assez de	*(not) enough of*
beaucoup de	*a lot of*
combien de	*how much/many*
ne... plus de	*not any more of*
peu de	*little of*
plus/moins de	*more/less of*
tant de	*so much/many of*
tellement de	*so much/many of*
trop de	*too much of*
un morceau de	*a piece of*
un peu de	*a little of*
un verre de	*a glass of*
une boîte de	*a box/a can of*
un paquet de	*a pack/a bag of*
un rouleau de	*a roll of*
un tube de	*a tube of*
un pot de	*a jar of*
une livre de	*one pound of*
un kilo de	*one kilo of*

Expressions of quantity with **de**

To replace a noun that is accompanied by an expression of quantity with **de**, use the pronoun **en**, whether referring to people or things. Don't forget that the quantity itself (**beaucoup**, **assez**, etc.) must be retained at the end of the sentence.

Ils ont **beaucoup d'enfants**.	*They have a lot of children.*
Ils **en** ont **beaucoup**.	*They have a lot (of them).*
Il ne gagne pas **assez d'argent**.	*He does not earn enough money.*
Il n'**en** gagne pas **assez**.	*He does not earn enough (of it).*
Ce gâteau est délicieux, j'**en** reprendrai **un morceau**.	*This cake is delicious; I will have another piece.*

Other expressions of quantity

Some expressions of quantity do not include **de**. They are: all the numbers, the indefinite and partitive articles: **un, une, des, de/d'** (in a negative sentence), **du, de la, de l'**, and also indefinite expressions such as **certains** (*some*), **quelques** (*a few*), **plusieurs** (*several*), and **aucun** (*none*). To replace such articles of quantity + noun, use the pronoun **en**:

—Tu as encore mangé **des** bonbons!	*"You ate some candies again!"*
—Non... je n'**en** ai pas mangé.	*"No, I did not eat any."*
—A-t-il **de la** chance?	*"Is he lucky? (Does he have luck?)"*
—Il doit **en** avoir: il gagne toujours!	*"He must be (He must have some): he always wins!"*
—Veux-tu **du** chocolat?	*"Would you like some chocolate?"*
—Non, merci, je n'**en** veux pas.	*"No thanks, I don't want any."*

To replace a number + noun, also use the pronoun **en** and keep the number at the end of the sentence as you would when replacing an expression of quantity with **de**. Don't forget that **un/une** are considered numbers when it comes to choosing pronouns. **Un/une** therefore remains at the end of the sentence. Saying « **Prends-en** . » (*"Take some ."*) while presenting an open box of chocolates is not the same as saying « **Prends-en un.** » (*"Take one."*)!

Note that if the sentence is negative, **un/une** is dropped (example 3), unless you need to emphasize the lack of something (example 4).

—Veux-tu **une glace?**	*"Would you like an ice cream?"*
—Oui, j'**en** veux bien **une**, merci.	*"Yes, I'd like one, thanks."*
—Combien **d'enfants** ont-ils?	*"How many children do they have?"*
—Ils **en** ont **un**.	*"They have one."*
—As-tu **une** tablette?	*"Do you have a tablet"*
—Je n'**en** ai pas.	*"I don't have one."*
Des cheveux? Il n'**en** a pas **un** (**seul**)!	*Hair? He doesn't have (even) one!*

The same thing happens to **certains, plusieurs**, and **aucun**: they remain at the end of the sentence (examples 1 and 2). **Quelques** follows that rule as well, but it changes to **quelques-uns** for masculine nouns and **quelques-unes** for feminine nouns (example 3).

As-tu **des idées** pour la composition?	*Do you have (some) ideas for the essay?*
Je n'**en** ai **aucune**.	*I don't have any.*
Y a-t-il **des voitures** qui consomment moins?	*Are there cars that use less (gasoline)?*
Il y **en** a **certaines**.	*There are some.*
J'ai **quelques livres** de Proust.	*I have a few books by Proust.*
J'**en** ai **quelques-uns**.	*I have a few (of them).*

One exception: tout

Even though **tout** and **toute** (*all of it*), **tous** and **toutes** (*all of them*) express a quantity, the direct object pronoun **les** is used instead of **en** to replace the noun. In the **passé composé**, don't forget to make the past participle agree with the direct object.

Tu as lu **un tome de *Harry Potter***?	*Have you read a volume of* Harry Potter?
Je **les** ai **tous** lus.	*I've read them all.*
A-t-il fait **ses exercices de math**?	*Has he done his math problems?*
Il **les** a **tous** faits.	*He has done them all.*
Tu as fini **ta soupe**?	*Did you finish your soup?*
Oui, je l'ai **toute** finie.	*Yes, I finished it all.*

EXERCICE

13·1

Put the following sentences into French. Be sure to determine if the object of each verb or verb + preposition is human or inanimate.

1. There was water on the floor, and he stepped in it.

   _____

2. This hat is ridiculous. You can't go out with it (on).

   _____

3. A dog stole my sandwich and ran away with it.

   _____

4. The ice was thin, and he fell through it.

   _____

5. There were two squirrels, and she wanted to play with them.

   _____

6. It's cold out; take your gloves. Don't go out without them. (**tu**)

   _____

7. She has a son, and she takes care of him alone.

   _____

8. Friends! Always love them and trust them. (**vous**)

_____

9. There is too much noise. I will never get used to it.

_____

10. He saw a good opportunity, and he jumped on it.

_____

11. If they (*f.*) don't want to come, we'll have to leave without them!

_____

12. It is a difficult situation but we will talk about it.

_____

13. The sugar bowl was open and bees were flying around it.

_____

14. He doesn't want to use them. (*them* = **ses lunettes**)

_____

15. I will tell you about it later. (*it* = **mon voyage aux Antilles**)

_____

16. Do you (**tu**) remember it? (*it* = **la chanson**)

_____

17. Did you remember to do it? (*it* = *learn the lesson*)

_____

18. Use it! (*use the verb* **se servir**) (*it* = *the pencil*)

_____

Answer the following questions using a pronoun.

1. Est-ce qu'il t'a demandé de <u>faire son travail à sa place</u>?

   _____

2. Tu te souviens que <u>tu m'as promis de rentrer tôt</u>?

   _____

3. Combien de <u>frères</u> as-tu?

   _____

4. Tu te rends compte de <u>ce que tu as fait</u>?

   _____

5. Aimez-vous <u>voyager</u>?

   _____

6. As-tu envie de <u>manger une grosse glace au chocolat</u>?

   _____

7. Est-ce que je t'ai dit que <u>j'avais adopté un petit chat</u>?

   _____

8. Irez-vous <u>à la plage</u> en juillet?

   _____

9. As-tu peur <u>qu'il pleuve</u>?

   _____

10. Est-ce que tu as dit <u>à tes parents où tu allais</u>? (**deux pronoms**)

   _____

11. Est-ce que tu peux compter sur <u>tes amis</u>?

   _____

12. Est-ce qu'il s'est excusé de t'avoir fait attendre?

_____

13. Est-ce que je peux compter sur votre discrétion?

_____

14. Tu penses que ça va marcher?

_____

15. Pourrais-tu t'occuper de mon chat pendant les vacances?

_____

16. Est-ce que tu as oublié de faire tes devoirs?

_____

17. Est-ce que tu t'es souvenu de faire tes devoirs?

_____

18. Avez-vous vraiment vu tous les films de Truffaut?

_____

19. Est-ce que leur spectacle a eu beaucoup de succès?

Non, _____

20. Est-ce que tu as un chien?

Non, _____

21. As-tu envie de faire un grand voyage? (*2 options*)

_____

_____

22. Concentre-toi sur tes études.

_____

Rewrite the sentences by replacing the underlined clauses with one or two pronouns. Be sure to identify the correct construction of the verb.

1. Sa mère tient toujours à <u>fêter son anniversaire</u>.

   _____

2. Sais-tu <u>qu'ils ont eu un accident</u>?

   _____

3. Nous serons surpris <u>s'il échoue</u>.

   _____

4. Nous avons décidé <u>de partir en vacances en mai</u>.

   _____

5. Vous savez <u>comment ils ont fait ça</u>?

   _____

6. Elle ne s'est jamais intéressée à <u>la politique</u>. Je suis incapable de <u>jongler</u>.

   _____

7. Les élèves n'aiment pas <u>faire leurs devoirs</u>.

   _____

8. Je me demande <u>si c'est vrai</u>...

   _____

9. Ils sont trop égoïstes pour <u>se soucier des problèmes des autres</u>.

   _____

10. Il a été triste de <u>ne pas vous voir hier soir</u>.

    _____

11. Une règle n'est pas faite pour <u>jouer de la musique</u>!

    _____

12. J'ai l'impression qu'<u>on se moque de moi.</u>

_____

13. Il oublie toujours de <u>fermer la porte à clé en partant.</u>

_____

14. Es-tu satisfait <u>des progrès que tu as faits?</u>

_____

15. Ils ne nous ont pas permis de <u>sortir un soir de semaine.</u>

_____

16. En plus de <u>le soigner et de l'héberger</u>, ils ont donné <u>de l'argent à l'étranger.</u>

_____

EXERCICE

13·4

Rewrite the sentences by replacing the underlined nouns and expressions with one or two pronouns.

1. Elle fait toujours <u>des cadeaux à ses amis.</u>

_____

2. Éloignez-vous <u>du quai.</u>

_____

3. Elle ne s'est jamais intéressée <u>à la politique.</u>

_____

4. La peinture est fraiche. Ne t'appuie pas contre <u>le mur.</u>

_____

5. Ce danseur manque <u>d'énergie.</u>

_____

6. N'utilise pas <u>de ciseaux</u> contre ton frère!

   _____

7. N'utilise pas <u>mes ciseaux</u> contre ton frère!

   _____

8. Il n'a eu <u>aucune réponse.</u>

   _____

9. Nous ne nous sommes pas méfiés <u>des courants marins.</u>

   _____

10. Elle s'est approchée de <u>son père</u> sans faire de bruit.

    _____

11. Elle s'est approchée de <u>l'oiseau</u> sans faire de bruit.

    _____

12. Si tu ne tiens pas compte <u>des mesures,</u> tu risques de rater <u>ton gâteau.</u>

    _____

13. Il veut finir <u>sa vie</u> avec <u>cette femme.</u>

    _____

14. Je voudrais m'asseoir à côté de <u>mes amies.</u>

    _____

15. Cette fille parle toujours de <u>son copain;</u> c'est agaçant.

    _____

16. Donne-moi <u>tes clés.</u>

    _____

17. Il a couru après <u>les voleurs</u> pour reprendre <u>le sac aux voleurs.</u>

    _____

18. J'achète peu de <u>bonbons.</u>

    _____

19. Alice avait peur des chiens, mais maintenant elle adore les chiens.

    _____

20. Qu'est-ce que tu penses de Jacques?

    _____

21. Les étudiants s'intéressent à l'histoire du Texas.

    _____

22. Je n'ai jamais rencontré tes amies.

    _____

Position of object pronouns

An object pronoun precedes the verb of which it is the object, whether that verb is conjugated or in the infinitive. This is also true in the case of negative commands.

Je mange **ce gâteau**. Je **le** mange.	*I eat it.*
Je vais manger **ce gâteau**. Je vais **le** manger.	*I am going to eat it.*
J'ai mangé **ce gâteau**. Je **l'**ai mangé.	*I ate it.*
Ne mange pas **ce gâteau**. Ne **le** mange pas.	*Don't eat it.*

The main exception to this rule is in the affirmative imperative when the pronoun follows the verb instead of preceding it, as well as several verbs which demand a different position. (See "Exceptions," later.)

Mange-**le**!	*Eat it!*
Regardez-**les**!	*Watch them!*

With a conjugated verb

Once you know the main rule that says that the pronoun precedes "its own" verb, there are still a few details to learn. First, be sure to recognize that verb when there are several in a sentence. In example 1, **conseils** is the object of which verb? Does she *prefer* advice or does she *ask* for advice? Clearly, **conseils** is the object of **demander**, not of **préfère**.

Elle préfère **demander des conseils**.	*She prefers to ask for advice.*
Elle préfère **en demander**.	*She prefers to ask for some.*
Tu vas **rentrer chez toi** après le cours.	*You are going to go home after class.*
Tu vas **y rentrer** après le cours.	*You are going to go there after class.*

Also, you need to make sure that you understand what the object in the sentence covers. In the following examples, it would not make sense to leave **d'histoire** and **du Texas** in the new sentence with the pronoun. She remembers her first *history* teacher, not any other teacher. And the professor is interested in *Texas* history as opposed to other parts of history.

Elle se souvient bien **de son premier prof d'histoire**.	*She remembers her first history teacher well.*
Elle se souvient bien **de lui**.	*She remembers him well.*
Ce prof s'intéresse **à l'histoire du Texas**.	*That professor is interested in Texas history.*
Ce prof s'**y** intéresse.	*That professor is interested in it.*

Verb is negative

In general, the two negative particles (**ne... pas**) surround a conjugated verb (**je n'aime pas la pizza**). When the verb is preceded by a pronoun, however, the **ne** moves to the left slightly to make room for the pronoun + verb (**je ne l'aime pas**). When the pronoun is the object of an infinitive, it usually has no bearing on the position of the negative words (examples 3 and 4), except if the infinitive itself is negated (example 5). In that scenario, the pronoun stays closest to the infinitive, preceded by **ne pas**. For details on the negative, see Unit 18.

On **ne le** voit **pas** souvent.	*We don't see him very often.*
Ils **n'en** veulent **pas**.	*They don't want any.*
Nous n'allons pas y aller.	*We are not going to go there.*
Tu **ne** veux **pas leur** parler.	*You don't want to talk to them.*
Ne pas y toucher!	*Do not touch (it)!*

The rules explained previously also apply to negative commands, but not affirmative commands:

N'en demande **plus**.	*Don't ask for any more.*
N'y retournez **pas**.	*Don't go back there.*
Ne les perdez **jamais**.	*Never lose them.*

Compound tenses

When the conjugated verb is **être** or **avoir** (the auxiliary of a compound tense), the rules do not change. The object pronoun precedes **être** or **avoir**, *not* the past participle.

L'as-tu vu?	*Did you see it?*
Nous **y** sommes allés.	*We went there.*
Je **l'**ai déjà lu.	*I have already read it.*

In the negative, **ne** precedes the pronoun + auxiliary and **pas** follows the auxiliary.

Je **ne l'**ai **pas** vu.	*I did not see it.*
Nous **ne leur** avons **pas** parlé.	*We did not talk to them.*
Tu **n'y** es **pas** allé.	*You did not go (there).*

With the pronoun **en** in a negative sentence, you will hear two **n** sounds: only one is the negative **ne** (the first one), the other **n** sound is the **liaison** with the **n** of the pronoun preceding the auxiliary **avoir**.

Je **n'en** ai **pas** pris.	*I did not take any.*
Nous **n'en** avons **plus**.	*We don't have any more of it.*

With the direct object pronouns **la/l'** and **les**, **nous**, and **vous**, placed before **avoir**, the past participle should agree with the noun replaced. There is no agreement with the pronoun when the auxiliary is **être**.

J'ai mangé **cette tarte**. Je l'ai mang**ée**.	*I ate this pie. I ate it.*
Il **nous** a regardés. (**nous** = *m. pl.*)	*He looked at us.*
Je **les** ai vu**es**. (**les** = *f. pl.*)	*I saw them.*

Pronominal verbs

Like any other pronoun, the reflexive pronoun precedes the verb of which it is the object. If this verb happens to be in the infinitive, be sure to match the reflexive pronoun with its subject (example 2).

Elle ne **s'intéresse** pas à la politique.	*She is not interested in politics.*
Tu veux **te promener**.	*You want to take a walk.*

A difficulty may appear when two pronouns precede the verb, a scenario quite common with reflexive verbs. Just remember this: of the two pronouns, the reflexive pronoun is the one farthest from the verb (to the left).

Elle ne **s'y** intéresse pas. (à la politique)	*She is not interested in it.*
Tu **t'en** moques. (des problèmes de pollution)	*You don't care about them.*
Il **se les** brosse. (les dents)	*He brushes them.*

Exceptions

With certain verbs, the placement does not follow the normal rules mentioned earlier.

With **faire faire** (*to have something done*), **laisser faire** (*to let someone do*), **envoyer chercher** (*to send for*), **falloir** (*must*), and the verbs of perception, the pronoun precedes the conjugated verb, *not* the infinitive.

Il a laissé sortir **les enfants**.	*He let the children go out.*
Il **les** a laissé sortir.	*He let them go out.*
Elle a envoyé chercher **le docteur**.	*She sent for the doctor.*
Elle **l'**a envoyé chercher.	*She sent for him.*
Il **te** faut finir avant ce soir.	*You must be done by tonight.*
Elle regarde **la pluie** tomber.	*She watches the rain fall.*
Elle **la** regarde tomber.	*She watches it fall.*

This rule is important because some of the verbs affected by it are very common, in particular, the verbs of perception and the constructions with **faire faire** and **falloir**.

faire faire and laisser faire

Things can be tricky here, as both the object and the subject of the infinitive (**faire**) can be replaced by a direct object pronoun! Both constructions (**faire** and **laisser** + infinitive) follow the same rules. We will focus on **faire faire**, which is the most common of the two.

We need to distinguish two scenarios: only the subject or only the object of the infinitive is named (in this case, there is no problem), or they are both named (now you have a problem).

When only the subject of the infinitive (see following highlighted examples) is named (**mon fils** in example 1), the pronoun that replaces it is the direct object pronoun (**le/la/l'/les**).

Je fais **travailler** *mon fils*.	*I make my son work.*
Je *le* fais **travailler**.	*I make him work.*
La chaleur a fait **souffrir** *les plantes*.	*The heat makes the plants suffer.*
La chaleur *les* a fait **souffrir**.	*The heat makes them suffer.*

When only the object of the infinitive is named (**ma voiture** in example 1), the pronoun that replaces it is also the direct object pronoun (**le/la/l'/les**). Remember that there is no agreement with the past participle in the **faire faire** construction.

J'ai fait **réparer** *ma voiture*.	*I had my car repaired.*
Je *l'*ai fait **réparer**.	*I had it repaired.*
Je fais **arroser** *mes plantes*.	*I have my plants watered.*
Je les fais **arroser**.	*I have them watered.*

If both the object and the subject of the infinitive are named in the sentence, the subject is replaced by the indirect object pronoun (**lui/leur**), and the object is replaced by the direct object pronoun. The order of object pronouns is always direct-indirect (even in the imperative). There is never agreement between the past participle and the direct object pronoun.

Il fait écrire **son mot d'excuse par sa mère**.	*He makes his mother write his excuse.*
Il **le lui** fait écrire.	*He makes her write it.*
Je fais réparer **ma voiture par le mécanicien**.	*I am having my car repaired by the mechanic.*
Je **la lui** fait réparer.	*I am having it repaired by him.*

With an imperative

When the verb is in the affirmative command (*Do it!*), the pronoun follows the verb form instead of preceding it. (See Unit 1 for details on the imperative.) Here are a few important points to remember:

◆ For -**er** verbs including **aller**, the -**s** of the **tu** form of the present tense (normally dropped in the imperative) is put back on before the pronouns **y** and **en**.

Vas-**y**!	*Go!*
Parles-**en**.	*Talk about it.*
Offres-**en** aux enfants.	*Offer some to the kids.*

◆ The pronouns **me** and **te** become **moi** and **toi** *after* the verb, whether the pronoun is direct (**regarder** in example 1), indirect (**parler à** in example 2) or reflexive (**se reposer** in example 3).

Regarde-**moi** dans les yeux.	*Look me in the eyes.*
Parle-**moi** de tes problèmes.	*Talk to me about your problems.*
Repose-**toi** ce soir.	*Rest up tonight.*

Multiple pronouns

When there are two pronouns in a sentence, you need to follow a very specific order, depending on which pronouns are combined. The following table details the possible sequences, and the order in which the pronouns are placed in these sequences.

In the table, note that "verb" means the verb of which the pronouns are the object. This can mean that the verb is conjugated, including the auxiliary of a compound tense, or is in the infinitive. Remember that when the direct object precedes the verb in a compound tense with **avoir**, the past participle agrees with it, even when there is another pronoun in the sentence. Combinations not listed are not possible in French.

There are several combinations within the following categories: the direct object pronouns **le, la, l'**, or **les** with another pronoun, or the pronouns **y** or **en** with another pronoun.

For all tenses except imperative

With **le, la, l'**, or **les**

me, m' (*indirect* or *reflexive*)		
te, t' (*indirect* or *reflexive*)	le, l'	
se, s' (*reflexive*)	la, l'	+ *verb*
nous (*indirect* or *reflexive*)	les	
vous (*indirect* or *reflexive*)		
le, l'		
la, l'	lui/leur/y/en	+ *verb*
les		

Tu veux **me les** donner.	*You want to give them to me.*
Elle **nous l'**a dit.	*She told us about it.*
Vous **vous le** demandez.	*You are wondering about it.*
Je vais **le lui** demander.	*I am going to ask him about it.*
Il **les leur** a donnés.	*He gave them to them.*
Ne **le lui** suggérez pas.	*Don't suggest it to him.*
Te l'a-t-il donné?	*Did he give it to you?*

With **y** or **en**

m'		
t'		
s'		
l' (la *or* le)		
nous		
vous	y/en	+ *verb*
les		
lui		
leur		
y		

Il **m'y** a invitée.	*He invited me (f.) there.*
Nous **les y** retrouverons.	*We will meet them there.*
Tu **m'en** as déjà parlé.	*You already told me about it.*
Tu **t'y** habitues.	*You are getting used to it.*
Il **y en** a beaucoup.	*There are a lot of them.*

For imperative

With **le**, **la**, or **les**

le
verb + *hyphen* +   la   -moi /-toi/-lui /-nous /-vous/-leur
les

With **y** or **en**

verb + *hyphen* +   m'
t'
lui   -en/-y
l' (**la** or **le**)
nous
vous
leur

Dis-**le-lui**.	*Tell it to him.*
Parlez-**leur-en**.	*Tell them about it.*
Donne-**le-moi**.	*Give it to me.*
Parle-**m'en**.	*Talk to me about it.*
Méfie-**t'en**.	*Beware of it.*
Servez-**vous-y**.	*Serve yourself there.*
Mets-**l'y**.	*Put it there.*

EXERCICE

14·1

Place the pronoun(s) given in the following incomplete sentences. You may have to change the past participle in some cases.

1. Tu donnes. (me, les)

_____

2. Le professeur a fait lire. (leur, les)

_____

3. A-t-il envoyé? (les [*m*.], lui)

_____

4. Nous avons mis. (la, y)

_____

5. Je vais donner. (en, leur)

   _____

6. Vous n'économisez pas. (en)

   _____

7. Il a regardé tomber. (la)

   _____

8. J'ai préparé. (la, leur)

   _____

9. Avez-vous retrouvé? (y, les [*m.*])

   _____

10. Le président a expliqué. (la, leur)

    _____

11. Ne pas entrer. (y)

    _____

12. Ils veulent acheter. (la, leur)

    _____

13. Il faut dire. (le, me)

    _____

14. Nous ne voulons pas mettre. (les, y)

    _____

15. Elle va préparer. (se, les)

    _____

16. Je vais réparer. (la, lui)

    _____

17. Il va écrire. (en, leur)

_____

18. Nous pouvons apporter. (la, vous)

_____

Insert the pronoun(s) in the following command forms, first in the affirmative, then in the negative.

1. Donne. (me, les)

_____

2. Faites lire. (les, leur)

_____

3. Envoyez. (la, lui)

_____

4. Mettons. (la, y)

_____

5. Donnez. (leur, en)

_____

6. Regarde tomber. (la)

_____

7. Préparons. (la, leur)

_____

8. Retrouve. (les, y)

_____

9. Expliquez. (me, la)

_____

10. Dis. (me, le)

_____

11. Va. (y)

_____

12. Occupe. (te, en)

_____

13. Parle. (en)

_____

14. Parle. (en, leur)

_____

*Speed test 1. As fast as you can, give the French equivalent of the following short sentences. Remember that with singular indirect object pronouns, the gender becomes irrelevant. Note that all instances of "you" are informal **tu**, unless otherwise noted.*

1. I give it to you.   _____

2. I don't give it to you.   _____

3. You give them to me.   _____

4. Give it (f.) to me.   _____

5. Don't give any to them. (*formal*)   _____

6. She gives it (f.) to them.   _____

7. Give me some.   _____

8. Don't give me any.   _____

Position of object pronouns   **187**

9. He gave it to them. (*f.*)   _____

10. I saw them there.   _____

11. Did you see her?   _____

12. I am not going to see him.   _____

13. They did not see her there.   _____

14. I know her.   _____

15. Do you know them?   _____

16. She took it (*f.*).   _____

17. He took three.   _____

18. Take some.   _____

19. Take one (*f.*).   _____

20. You have a lot (of them).   _____

21. How many do you have?   _____

22. We don't have one.   _____

23. Do you want any?   _____

24. I don't like it.   _____

25. He writes to her.   _____

26. You (*formal*) don't write to us.   _____

27. Send it (*m.*) to me.   _____

28. I call them.   _____

29. Lend it (*f.*) to her.   _____

30. Show them to them.   _____

31. I showed it (*f.*) to you.   _____

32. They answered her.   _____

33. Is she going to answer them?   _____

*Speed test 2. As fast as you can, give the French equivalent of the following short sentences. Remember that with singular indirect object pronouns, the gender becomes irrelevant. Note that all instances of "you" are informal **tu**, unless otherwise noted.*

1. She didn't answer them. _____

2. They are going to ask for them from me. _____

3. You didn't ask it (*f.*) to me. _____

4. We come from there. _____

5. Do you want to meet me there? _____

6. Enter (there). _____

7. Don't enter (there). _____

8. Don't go there. (*formal*) _____

9. Go away. (*formal*) _____

10. I want to tell it to you. _____

11. Talk about it! _____

12. You are not going to talk about it to them. _____

13. I am going to tell it to them. _____

14. He told it (*m.*) to us. _____

15. Tell it to me. _____

16. You didn't tell it to me. _____

17. Tell it (*m.*) to her. _____

18. Talk to her about it. _____

19. I'm going to talk to them there. _____

20. He didn't tell it (*f.*) to you. (*formal*) _____

21. We have not talked to them about it. _____

22. He didn't sleep there. _____

23. We did not eat it. (f.) _____

24. We are going to drink some. _____

25. Did you drink any? _____

26. She needs it. _____

27. Put them there. _____

28. I put it there. _____

29. He remembers it. _____

30. Hurry up. _____

31. You are getting used to it. _____

32. He takes care of it. _____

33. Let's take care of it. _____

Expressing *this is* and *that is*: ce, ça, and il

·15·

There are three pronouns that can be used as equivalents of *this* or *it* in sentences such as, in English, *it is good, that's fine*. In French, they are: **ce**, **ça**, and **il** in a neutral sense. This unit explains the differences in usage of these three neutral subject pronouns. Some exceptions and literary forms will not be mentioned here.

The "neutral" pronoun ce

c'est/ce sont + noun

Ce/c' is a third person (singular and plural) subject pronoun used before **être** + noun to introduce or present a thing (examples 1 and 2) or a person (example 3). In French using a "neutral" pronoun to describe a person is perfectly correct, and, in fact, using **il** in example 3 would be incorrect.

—Qu'est-ce que **c'est?**	*"What is it?"*
—**C'est** un vieux chapeau.	*"It is an old hat."*
J'ai aimé ce film parce que **c'était** une histoire d'amour.	*I liked that movie because it was a love story.*
Je te présente Pierre. **C'est** mon frère.	*Let me introduce Pierre. He is my brother.*

C'est + singular noun and **ce sont** + plural noun often serves to put the emphasis on that noun. This usage is normally followed by a relative clause:

Ce sont les enfants **qui** ont fait ton gâteau.	*(It is) the kids who made your cake.*
Ce sont eux **qui** ont gagné.	*They are the ones who won.*
Ce sont les artistes **dont** on a parlé à la télé.	*These are the artists that were mentioned on TV.*

When a preposition precedes the noun emphasized, use **c'est** only, even before a plural noun.

C'est à toi que je parle.	*I am talking to you.*
C'est avec Pierre et Jean que je m'entends le mieux.	*It's Pierre and Jean with whom I get along best.*
C'est à eux qu'elle pensait en disant sa prière.	*They are (the ones) whom she was thinking of while saying her prayers.*

In the spoken language, it is common to use **c'est** + question word, without any other verb.

C'est qui?	*Who is it?*
C'est à quelle heure?	*What time is it at?*
C'est à quel sujet?	*What is it about?*

c'est or il est + adjective

An adjective describes a noun, and its form varies with that noun. You typically need to know the gender and number of the noun in order to match the adjective correctly.

When the noun follows **être**, it has been introduced either by **il** or **elle**, even for things (a situation where English would use *it*).

J'ai un ordinateur, **il** m'est très utile.	*I have a computer; it is very useful to me.*
Regarde ce chat: **il** est adorable.	*Look at this cat: it is adorable.*

However, **il** can sometimes be used as a neutral subject pronoun, without reference to any particular noun. The impersonal **il** alternates with **ce/c'** as the subject of **être** + adjective, either in a trigger expression for the subjunctive after **que**, or with the infinitive. **C'est** + adjective is more informal.

Il est dommage **que tu partes** tôt. **C'est** dommage **que tu partes** tôt.	*It is too bad that you are leaving early.*
Il est agréable **de lire** au jardin. **C'est** agréable **de lire** au jardin.	*It is pleasant to read in the garden.*

c'est instead of il est + adjective

You may, however, find **c'est** before an invariable adjective, instead of **il/elle est**, in two cases: before the names of professions, religions, and nationalities, and when making a comment about something.

Comments

When making a comment about a thing or an event (but not about a person), as opposed to describing it, use the neutral **c'est**. Using **il est** instead of **c'est** in example 1 would mean that the dog himself is sad, as opposed to the situation.

Ils ont perdu leur chien. Comme **c'est** triste!	*They lost their dog. It's so sad!*
Regardez la lumière dans ce tableau. **C'est** remarquable.	*Look at the light in this painting. It is remarkable.*
On est punis ce soir. **C'est** nul!	*We are grounded tonight. That stinks!*
Je n'ai jamais vu la mer. Est-ce que **c'est** beau?	*I have never seen the sea. Is it beautiful?*

Professions, religions, and nationalities

Words describing nationalities, professions, or religions can be nouns or adjectives. This distinction matters because **c'est/ce sont** introduces a noun (with an article) whereas **il est/ils sont** precedes an adjective (no article). This distinction does not exist in English as you will see in the examples.

    If you use **c'est** or **ce sont**, what follows must be a noun and include an article, but if you use **il est/ils sont** (or any other subject) + **être**, an adjective must follow. For nationalities, note that the noun is capitalized but the adjective of nationality is not.

Il est catholique ou juif?	*Is he Catholic or Jewish?*
C'est un juif.	*He is Jewish./He's a Jew.*
Son père est dentiste.	*His father is a dentist.*
C'est un chirurgien célèbre.	*He is a famous surgeon.*
Ils sont italiens?	*Are they Italian?*
Ce ne sont pas des Italiens.	*They are not Italian.*
—**Est-il** avocat? (*adjectival use*)	*"Is he a lawyer?"*
—Oui, **c'est** un avocat. (*noun use*)	*"Yes, he is a lawyer."*

The subject pronoun ça

Ça is a singular neutral pronoun describing things and concepts. It can act as a subject pronoun and also as an object pronoun. (See also Unit 13 on object pronouns.) As a subject pronoun, **ça** can be used concurrently with or replace **ce** before **être**. It is the only neutral subject equivalent to *it*.

Before être

In informal language, **ça** can (but doesn't have to) be used instead of **ce** before singular forms of **être** in all simple tenses, both affirmative and negative. It's not used, however, to replace the following forms: **c'est** (present affirmative), **c'était** (**imparfait** affirmative), **ce fut** (**passé simple**), and **ce fût** (imperfect subjunctive).

C'est bon.	*It's good.*
Ce n'est pas bon. (*or:* Ça n'est pas bon.)	*It's not good.*
Ce sera facile pour toi. (*or:* Ça sera facile pour toi.)	*It will be easy for you.*
C'était mieux avant.	*It was better before.*
Ce n'était pas pire. (*or:* Ça n'était pas pire.)	*It was not worse.*
Ce serait bien si tu venais. (*or:* Ça serait bien si tu venais.)	*It would be great if you came.*
Ce n'est pas la peine. (*or:* Ça n'est pas la peine.)	*It is not worth the trouble.*

Note that **ça** must replace **ce** before object pronoun + **être**.

Ça m'est égal.	*I don't care.*
Ça s'est passé quand?	*When did it happen?*
Ça lui est arrivé comment?	*How did it happen to him?*
Ça te fait plaisir?	*Does it make you happy?*

Before verbs other than être

Ça can be used as a subject of any verb other than **être** to express *it* or *that*. **Ce** can only be used with **être**.

Ça va faire mal?	*Is it going to hurt?*
Ça devrait plaire aux enfants.	*The kids should like that.*
Ça n'intéresse personne.	*It is of no interest to anyone.*
Qu'est-ce que ça veut dire?	*What does it mean?*

Expressions with ça

Ça y est!	*Done!*
Ça ne fait rien.	*It does not matter.*
Ça ira.	*It'll be fine.*
Ça fait (*price*).	*It will be (price).*
Ça fait mal!	*It hurts!*

Ça alors!	*I can't believe it!* (surprise or indignation)
Ça va pas!	*Are you nuts!*
Ça sera tout?	*Will that be all?*

In compound tenses

The difference between **ce** and **ça** to translate *it* depends on the auxiliary verb used to form the **passé composé**.

If the auxiliary verb is **être**, use **c'**.

C'est tombé tout seul.	*It fell on its own.*
C'est arrivé hier.	*It happened yesterday.*

If the auxiliary is **avoir**, use **ça**. Note that **être** takes the auxiliary **avoir** (examples 3 and 4).

Ça a dû se passer hier.	*It must have happened yesterday.*
Ça a pris plus de temps que prévu.	*It took longer than expected.*
Ça a été une catastrophe.	*It was a catastrophe.*
Ça a été formidable.	*It was great.*

EXERCICE

15·1

*Fill in the blank with **ça** or **ce/c'**. If both are possible, indicate with an asterisk (*).*

1. _____ ne s'explique pas. Il faut accepter, _____ est tout!

2. Qu'est-ce que _____ veut dire?

3. _____ leur est égal.

4. Tu as vu un Martien? _____ est difficile à croire.

5. _____ a été une journée bien remplie.

6. _____ ne sont pas des haricots... _____ sont des fèves.

7. _____ va mieux?

8. Ils sont allés en Corse et _____ leur a plu.

9. Je sais que _____ n'est pas idéal comme situation, mais _____ ira.

10. _____ n'est pas la peine de courir, le bus est déjà parti.

11. Pierre a eu des mauvaises notes. _____ ne va pas plaire à sa mère.

12. Si tu as acheté un kilo de tomates, _____ suffira largement pour la salade.

13. _____ était sympa que tu viennes.

14. _____ est dommage que vous vous dérangiez pour rien.

15. Tu verras, _____ sera vraiment bien.

16. Il faut que _____ soit ou vrai ou faux. Il n'y a pas d'alternative!

17. Elle a oublié d'arrêter le four, mais _____ n'est pas une catastrophe parce qu'il était vide.

18. Arrête de manger du chocolat. _____ fait grossir.

19. _____ serait bien si on pouvait avoir un jour de congé supplémentaire.

20. Tu te souviens de cette photo? _____ était le jour de mon anniversaire.

EXERCICE
15·2

*Fill in the blank with **il/ils** or **ce/c'**.*

1. —Ce film était nul. _____ était une horreur!

   —Oui _____ était un vrai navet.

2. J'aime ce livre parce que _____ est très bien écrit. En plus, _____ est une histoire vraie.

3. Faire l'Everest sans sherpa! Mais _____ est complètement fou! Cet alpiniste? _____ est fou de vouloir faire ça!

4. Leurs enfants sont obéissants et _____ sont toujours très polis. _____ sont des enfants parfaits.

5. Il a eu une petite faiblesse. _____ sont des choses qui arrivent.

6. _____ est pour toi que j'ai préparé ce dîner.

7. _____ n'est pas bien de dire des mensonges.

8. Medor? _____ n'est pas méchant du tout. _____ est le chien le plus gentil qui soit!

9. Je vous présente Anne et Paul. _____ sont les parents de Louis.

10. Tu connais Louis? _____ est assez grand et il a les cheveux longs. _____ est un garçon charmant.

11. Le bus est déjà parti. _____ est bête!

12. _____ est pour vous que j'ai écrit ce poème.

13. J'ai raté le bus: _____ était en avance sur l'horaire.

14. Je ne sais pas si _____ sont des Italiens ou des Espagnols.

Questions

This unit focuses on a few specific difficulties that can arise when asking a question: how to ask *who* and *what*, how to avoid mistranslations with **qui** and how to choose between **quel** and **qu'est-ce que** or **qu'est-ce qui**, as well as how to do the inversion when the subject is a noun or a name.

Reminders

Before we begin, it will help to remember certain essential facts about asking questions in French.

There is no *do you/does he*, and so on, in French. A question is asked using the verb directly, without an auxiliary.

Voulez-vous du café?	*Do you want some coffee?*
Est-ce que tu penses que c'est trop tard?	*Do you think it is too late?*
Comprend-elle la question?	*Does she understand the question?*
Est-ce qu'ils veulent venir avec nous?	*Do they want to come with us?*

If the verb has a preposition, the question must begin with that preposition. Never put the preposition at the end of a question in French. (There are some exceptions but they do not occur frequently enough to be worth mentioning.) Also remember that **que** changes to **quoi** after a preposition (example 3).

À qui parlez-vous?	*Who(m) are you talking to?*
Pour quelle société travailles-tu?	*What company do you work for?*
À quoi penses-tu?	*What are you thinking about?*

Use a construction with **est-ce que** or one with inversion to form a written question.

Quand partez-vous? *or* Quand est-ce que vous partez?
Que voulez-vous? *or* Qu'est-ce que vous voulez?

When forming a question using inversion, if the verb ends with a vowel and the subject pronoun is **il**, **elle**, or **on**, insert a -**t**-, in both written and spoken language, to "fill in" the pronunciation.

Parle-**t**-il chinois?	*Does he speak Chinese?*
Julie ira-**t**-elle à Paris cet été?	*Will Julie go to Paris this summer?*
Comment va-**t**-on à la gare d'ici?	*How does one go to the station from here?*
Quand arrive-**t**-il?	*When does he arrive?*
Pourquoi a-**t**-elle fait ça?	*Why did she do that?*

Asking *who* and *what*

When choosing the French equivalent of *who* and *what,* you have a choice between two constructions: **qui** and **que** can be used alone in most cases (short form), or they can be followed by **est-ce qui** or **est-ce que** (long form). Confusion may happen when dealing with the long forms of **que**: **qu'est-ce que** and **qu'est-ce qui** (*what*) and of **qui**: **qui est-ce que** and **qui est-ce qui** (*who*). This is what we will focus on here. To sort out the long forms, once and for all, there are two essential things to remember:

- The first **qu-** word in the long form marks the distinction between a person and a thing. When the question is about a person (*who, whom*), **qui** is the question word, and it can *never* be elided to **qu'**. When the question is about a thing (*what*), **que/qu'** is the question word.
- The second **qu-** word in the long form marks the grammatical distinction between two possible functions of the question word: subject or object of the verb. **Qui** as the second **qu-** word denotes the subject of the verb, whereas **que/qu'** as the second **qu-** word denotes the object of the verb.

Who/whom

When the question is about a person: ask **qui**, **qui est-ce que**, or **qui est-ce qui**. To choose the correct form, follow these guidelines:

- When the verb has its own subject, *who/whom* is the object of that verb. Use **qui** or **qui est-ce que**. Remember that, in English, *who* is the subject (or the informal object); *whom* is always an object.
- When the verb has no subject, *who* is the subject of that verb. Use **qui** or **qui est-ce qui** + verb in the singular.

LONG FORM	SHORT FORM
QUI EST-CE QUI + VERB	**QUI** + VERB
Qui est-ce qui a commencé? *Who started?*	Qui a commencé? *Who started?*
Qui est-ce qui va venir? *Who will come?*	Qui va venir? *Who will come?*
QUI EST-CE QUE + VERB	**QUI** + VERB SUBJECT (INVERSION)
Qui est-ce que tu as invité? *Who(m) did you invite?*	Qui as-tu invité? *Who(m) did you invite?*
Qui est-ce que vous préférez? *Who(m) do you prefer?*	Qui préférez-vous? *Who(m) do you prefer?*
PREPOSITION + **QUI EST-CE QUE**	PREPOSITION + **QUI** + VERB SUBJECT
À qui est-ce que tu parles? *Who(m) are you talking to?*	À qui parles-tu? *Who(m) are you talking to?*
Pour qui est-ce qu'elle travaille? *Who(m) does she work for?*	Pour qui travaille-t-elle? *Who(m) does she work for?*

Avoiding a common error with qui

In information questions, it is better style to invert the noun (or name) subject and the verb, instead of using a longer construction with **est-ce que**. (See "Inversion" for details.)

Quand part Pierre?
instead of: Quand est-ce que Pierre part?

When does Pierre leave?

Où va ce train?
instead of: Où est-ce que ce train va?

Where does this train go?

However, with the question word **qui**, this type of question can become completely ambiguous: it may be hard to tell if **qui** is the subject (*Who loves Bernard?*) or object (*Whom does Bernard love?*). How can we avoid the ambiguity in French?

French usage takes questions such as **Qui invite Marie?** as *Who invites Marie?*, with **qui** as the subject of the verb. As a result, in order to say *Whom does Mary invite?* in French, you need to use the inversion with a double subject: **qui** + noun subject + verb-subject pronoun: **Qui Marie invite-t-elle?** The **est-ce que** construction may be used although it is rather awkward and should probably be avoided.

Ambiguous

Qui aime Bernard?

Who loves Bernard?
or *Whom does Bernard love?*

Clear

Qui Bernard aime-t-il?   *Whom does Bernard love?*

Ambiguous

Qui invite Marie?   *Who invites Mary?*
                                          or *Whom does Mary invite?*

Clear

Qui Marie invite-t-elle?   *Whom does Mary invite?*
(Qui est-ce que Marie invite?)

What

When the question is about a thing, ask: **que/qu'**, **qu'est-ce que**, or **qu'est-ce qui**. To choose the correct form, follow these guidelines:

- When the verb has its own subject, *what* is the object of that verb. Use **que/qu'** or **qu'est-ce que/qu'**. (There are some exceptions with **que/qu**. See "The case of **que**," later in this unit.)
- When the verb does not have a subject, *what* is the subject of that verb. Use **qu'est-ce qui**.

LONG FORM	SHORT FORM
QU'EST-CE QUI	——
Qu'est-ce qui a causé l'accident? *What caused the accident?*	——
Qu'est-ce qui est meilleur? *What is better?*	——
QU'EST-CE QUE	**QUE** + VERB SUBJECT (INVERSION)
Qu'est-ce que tu veux? *What do you want?*	Que veux-tu? *What do you want?*
Qu'est-ce que le docteur a dit? *What did the doctor say?*	Qu'a dit le docteur? *What did the doctor say?*
PREPOSITION + **QUOI EST-CE QUE**	PREPOSITION + **QUOI** + VERB SUBJECT (INVERSION)
Avec quoi est-ce qu'il a fait ça? *What did he do this with?*	Avec quoi a-t-il fait ça? *What did he do this with?*
Dans quoi est-ce qu'on met les fruits? *What do we put the fruit in?*	Dans quoi met-on les fruits? *What do we put the fruit in?*

Preposition + *what or who/whom*

With a preposition in the question, things change. The distinction between the possible functions of *what* (object or subject of the verb) no longer matters, since a question word can only be the *object* of a preposition. All that remains therefore is the distinction thing-versus-person. **Qui** remains the equivalent of *who/whom* in preposition + *who(m)*, and **que** changes to **quoi** as the equivalent of *what* in preposition + *what*.

À qui est-ce que tu as parlé? À qui as-tu parlé?	*Whom did you speak to?*
Avec qui est-ce que tu travailles? Avec qui travailles-tu?	*Who(m) do you work with?*
Dans quoi est-ce qu'il est tombé? Dans quoi est-il tombé?	*What did he fall into?*
À quoi est-ce que tu joues? À quoi joues-tu?	*What are you playing (at)?*

qu'est-ce que or quel?

Both **quel** and its forms and **qu'est-ce qui/qu'est-ce que** translate as *what*, and to some extent *who/whom*.

quel

The interrogative adjective **quel** and its forms literally asks *what thing* or *what person*. It cannot be used without naming the thing or person. Since **quel** is an adjective, it must match the gender and number of the noun it asks about.

As a rule of thumb always look for a noun either directly after **quel** (**quel *jour* sommes-nous?**) or following **quel** + **être** (**quelle est *la date*?**), with **être** in the singular or plural, according to the subject.

The noun is directly after **quel**

Either the inversion (example 3) or the construction with **est-ce que** can follow **quel** + noun. No article is used with the noun.

Quelle couleur est-ce que tu préfères?	*What color do you prefer?*
Quel livre est-ce que tu as lu?	*What book did you read?*
Quels cours suis-tu ce semestre?	*Which classes are you taking this semester?*

After a preposition you must use the construction preposition + **quel** + noun:

De quel instrument jouez-vous?	*What instrument do you play?*
À quelle école vont vos enfants?	*What school do your kids go to?*

The noun is after quel + être

When **quel** is followed by **être** + noun, that noun must have a determiner such as **le, la, l',** **les** (*the*), **ce/cet/cette/ces** (*this*), or **mon/ma/mes**, and so on (*my, etc.*).

Quelle est **la** date?	*What is the date?*
Quelle est **ton** adresse?	*What is your address?*
Quels sont **les** meilleurs restaurants ici?	*Which are the best restaurants here?*
Quel est **ce** bruit?	*What is that noise?*

A relative clause (in parentheses in the following examples) may also follow the noun in this construction. Here we give a literal English translation that shows the article and will help you remember to use it in French:

Quel est le livre (que tu préfères)?	*What is the book that you prefer?*
Quels sont les fromages (que tu n'aimes pas)?	*What are the cheeses that you do not like?*
Quelle est la chose (dont tu as le plus envie)?	*What is the thing that you want the most?*

qu'est-ce que/qu'

Qu'est-ce que, as opposed to **quel**, introduces a clause instead of a noun, and there is never an inversion after it.

Qu'est-ce que tu vas faire?	*What are you going to do?*
Qu'est-ce que le prof a dit?	*What did the teacher say?*

However, when asking for the definition of a noun (*What is X?*), use **qu'est-ce que** + that noun, not a clause. (See the section in this unit on "Asking *who* and *what*.")

Qu'est-ce qu'un masque?	*What is a mask?*

Inversion

Using inversion to form a question is not a problem when the subject of the verb is a subject pronoun such as **tu, il, elle, on, nous, vous, ils,** or **elles** (**Allez-vous en ville?**). However, forming the inversion becomes more complicated when the subject is a noun (**les enfants**) or a name (**Pierre**). First, we will consider *yes/no* questions with a noun subject, and then information questions.

Yes/no questions

Yes/no questions can, of course, always be posed with intonation or with **est-ce que**—spoken language actually emphasizes these forms—but written language prefers inversion.

Inversion with a noun subject

It isn't possible just to switch a noun subject and the verb to form the inversion. To make the inversion work, the subject must be repeated with the equivalent subject pronoun (**il**, **ils**, and **elle** in the following examples). The noun subject remains before the verb, and the subject pronoun is attached behind it with a hyphen.

Pierre est-**il** parti?	*Did Pierre leave?*
Les enfants ont-**ils** de bonnes notes?	*Do the kids have good grades?*
Ta mère viendra-t-**elle** pour les fêtes?	*Will your mother come for the holidays?*

With the subject pronouns je, ce, and ça

When the subject pronoun is **ça**, you can't do a simple inversion. There are three possible forms for questions. Each belongs to a different level of language. Note that **ça** changes to **cela** for the "literary" level.

Spoken language

Ça va? (*with rising intonation*)	*How is it going?*
Ça ne vous dérange pas?	*It doesn't bother you?*

Written style

Est-ce que ça va?	*How are you doing?*
Est-ce que ça ne vous dérange pas?	*Does it bother you?*

Literary

Cela va-t-il?	*How are you feeling?*
Cela ne vous dérange-t-il pas?	*Does this not bother you?*

Using inversion with **ce** creates a very formal question, in both *yes/no* questions and in information questions, except for the everyday question **qui est-ce?** (*Who is it?*), which never changes. To avoid the formal inversion with **ce**, use **est-ce que**, or **c'est** with the correct intonation, depending on the type of question.*

Spoken language

C'est bon? (*with rising intonation*)	*It's good?*
C'est quand? (*with descending intonation*)	*It's when?*
C'est quoi?	*What's that?*

Written style

Est-ce que c'est bon?	*Is it good?*
Quand est-ce que c'est?	*When is it?*
Qu'est-ce que c'est?	*What is it?*

Literary

Est-ce bon?	*Is this good?*
Quand est-ce?	*When is it?*
Qu'est-ce ?	*What is this?*

*Remember that spoken intonation goes down at the end of an information question and up at the end of *yes/no* questions.

Always use **est-ce que** before **je** + verb in a question. In literary style, five verbs can take the inversion with **je**: **être** (including as the auxiliary of a compound tense); **avoir** (including as the auxiliary of a compound tense); **devoir** (*must*); **pouvoir**, with **peux** changing to **puis** (*can*); and **aller** (*go*).

Literary

Puis-je vous aider?	*May I help you?*
Où suis-je?	*Where am I?*
Ai-je rêvé?	*Did I dream?*
Vais-je le faire?	*Shall I do it?*
Que dois-je dire?	*What must I say?*

Nonliterary, spoken

Est-ce que je peux vous aider?	*Can I help you?*
Où est-ce que je suis?	*Where am I?*
Est-ce que j'ai rêvé?	*Did I dream?*
Est-ce que je vais le faire?	*Will I do it?*
Qu'est-ce que je dois dire?	*What do I have to say?*

Normal French usage avoids the inversion with **je**. The only one of the five examples you may hear is **Puis-je vous aider?** (*May I help you?*), when someone very politely offers to help you. The other four are strictly literary or satirical.

Information questions with a noun subject

In information questions, when the subject is a noun or a name, do not use the double subject inversion that you just learned for *yes/no* questions. In fact, the double subject inversion is quite formal in information questions. French prefers simply to invert the noun subject and the verb whenever possible. (See exceptions noted later.) In some cases such a simple inversion is even required.

Informal

Quand partent vos amis? *When do your friends leave?*

Formal

Quand vos amis partent-ils? *When do your friends leave?*

Informal

Combien de temps dure l'opération? *How long does the surgery last?*

Formal

Combien de temps l'opération dure-t-elle? *How long does the surgery last?*

Informal

Comment vont tes parents? *How are your parents doing?*

Formal

Comment tes parents vont-ils? *How are your parents doing?*

Mandatory inversion

These question words + verb are always followed by the subject:

quel + être

Quel est le meilleur restaurant?	*What is the best restaurant?*
Quelles sont les nouvelles?	*What is the news?*

comment + être

Comment est le nouveau restaurant?	*What is the new restaurant like?*
Comment sont vos nouvelles lunettes?	*What are your new glasses like?*

où + être

Où sont tes affaires?	*Where are your belongings?*
Où est la bibliothèque?	*Where's the library?*

quel âge + avoir

Quel âge ont vos enfants?	*How old are your children?*
Quel âge a cette femme?	*How old is that woman?*

The case of que

After **que** (short form) as the object of a verb (as in *What do you want?*), the simple inversion noun subject/verb is mandatory and you may not use the double subject inversion. Note that you can still use the **qu'est-ce que** form, although it should be avoided after **faire** (examples 4 and 5).

Que porteront les demoiselles d'honneur?	*What will the bridesmaids wear?*
Que vont dire tes parents?	*What are your parents going to say?*
Qu'a pris le voleur?	*What did the thief take?*
Que fait votre mari?	*What does your husband do?*
Que font les enfants après le dîner?	*What do the kids do after dinner?*

However, when the same type of question has a complement of place (see also later discussion) such as **derrière le rideau** and **dans sa bouche** in the examples, **qu'est-ce que/qu'** is the only way to ask *what* when it is object of the verb. The short form **que** is not possible.

Qu'est-ce que le magicien a trouvé derrière le rideau?	*What did the magician find behind the curtain?*
Qu'est-ce que le bébé a mis dans sa bouche?	*What did the baby put in his mouth?*

Exceptions

However, the common inversion with a noun (**Que fait Jacqueline?**) is not always possible. There are three cases when you must use the **est-ce que** construction or a double subject inversion:

First, when the verb has a complement that is essential to its meaning and without which the sentence would be incomplete, you cannot use the simple noun subject–verb inversion. Instead, use either **est-ce que** or the double subject inversion, except after **que**. (See earlier discussion.) In the following examples the complements are highlighted:

No complement

Quand partent vos amis?	*When do your friends leave?*

With complement

Quand vos amis partent-ils **au Pérou**?	*When do your friends leave for Peru?*
Quand est-ce que vos amis partent **au Pérou**?	*When do your friends leave for Peru?*

No Complement

Avec qui sort ta fille?	*Who(m) is your daughter going out with?*

With complement

Avec qui ta fille va-t-elle **à cette soirée**?	*Who(m) is your daughter going to this party with?*
Avec qui est-ce que ta fille va **à cette soirée**?	*Who(m) is your daughter going to this party with?*

Second, when the verb is transitive and its object is expressed (highlighted in the following examples), use either **est-ce que** or the double subject inversion. The exception is after **que** (see earlier discussion).

No direct object

Comment travaille le cuisinier?	*How does the cook work?*

With direct object

Comment le cuisinier a-t-il fait **ce délice**?	*How did the cook make this delicacy?*
Comment est-ce que le cuisinier a fait **ce délice**?	

No direct object

Sur quoi portent les questions?	*What are the questions about?*

With direct object

Sur quoi le prof a-t-il posé **des questions**?	*What did the prof ask questions about?*
Sur quoi est-ce que le prof a posé **des questions**?	

No direct object

Quand passera le facteur?	*When will the mailman stop by?*

With direct object

Quand le facteur apportera-t-il **le paquet**?	*When will the mailman bring the package?*
Quand est-ce que le facteur apportera **le paquet**?	

Third, after the question word **pourquoi**, use either **est-ce que** or the double subject inversion.

Pourquoi **Agnès pleure-t-elle**?	*Why is Agnes crying?*
Pourquoi **est-ce qu'**Agnès pleure?	
Pourquoi **les chats aiment-ils** le lait?	*Why do cats like milk?*
Pourquoi **est-ce que** les chats aiment le lait?	

Inversion in information questions: recap

To ask an information question, plan for the noun subject–verb inversion, then check for three things:

- Is the question word **pourquoi**?
- Does the verb have a direct object expressed?
- Does the verb have another essential complement?

If you answered yes to one of the three questions, then you can't use this type of inversion. Instead, use the double subject inversion or the **est-ce que** construction.

The following table illustrates the difference between the double subject inversion (more formal style) and its "lighter" equivalent with the simple inversion, in information questions with a noun subject.

PREFERRED FORM	FORMAL INVERSION FORM	
Où vont les enfants cet été?	Où les enfants vont-ils cet été?	*Where are the children going this summer?*
À qui parle le facteur?	À qui le facteur parle-t-il?	*Who(m) is the mailman talking to?*
Combien coûtent ces fleurs?	Combien ces fleurs coûtent-elles?	*How much are those flowers?*
Comment va ta grand-mère?	Comment ta grand-mère va-t-elle?	*How is your grandmother doing?*
Quand reviennent vos voisins?	Quand vos voisins reviennent-ils?	*When are your neighbors coming back?*

EXERCICE
16·1

*Using both the long form and the short form (when possible), ask the following who and what questions in French. Some questions with **quel** are included in this exercise.*

1. What happened last night? (*use **arriver***)

_____

2. Who arrived first?

_____

3. What do you write with?

_____

4. What time is it?

_____

5. Whom do they prefer?

_____

6. What do cats think about?

_____

7. What is this man watching?

_____

8. Which professor gives more *As*?

_____

9. What would help you?

_____

10. What did he catch the dog with?

_____

11. What's a name?

_____

12. Who(m) did your parents meet?

_____

13. Who(m) did the journalist talk about?

_____

14. Who(m) do you call every day?

_____

15. What classes is Julie going to take?

_____

16. Who talked to Anne?

_____

17. Which students did not write the essay?

_____

18. What is orange and round and edible?

_____

19. What did Julie take these pictures with?

_____

20. Why doesn't the rain stop?

_____

EXERCICE

16·2

*Using inversion whenever possible, ask the questions that correspond to the underlined section of each sentence. There is no **quel** in this exercise. Use **tu** for* you.

1. Je pense aux vacances.

_____

2. Mon livre est dans mon sac.

_____

3. Pierre travaille. (*yes/no question*)

_____

4. Marianne aime Paul.

_____

5. Les invités arriveront à huit heures.

_____

6. Julie va à la plage.

_____

7. Julie va à la plage <u>parce qu'elle est en vacances</u>.

   _____

8. Le facteur apportera le paquet <u>demain</u>.

   _____

9. Le facteur passera <u>demain</u>.

   _____

10. Elle a mis <u>les clés</u> dans le tiroir.

    _____

11. Maman a mis <u>les clés</u> dans le tiroir.

    _____

12. Maman a mis les clés <u>dans le tiroir</u>.

    _____

13. Nos voisins rentrent <u>le 12 mars</u>.

    _____

14. Nos voisins rentrent de vacances <u>le 12 mars</u>.

    _____

15. La pluie ne s'arrête pas <u>parce que c'est la saison de la mousson</u>.

    _____

16. Pierre conduit <u>une voiture de sport</u>.

    _____

Translating *for, since,* and a few other expressions of time

Translating a sentence with the time expressions *for* or *since* is tricky, because French and English do not look at the situation in the same way. This unit will help you understand two key concepts. The first difference is that both *for* and *since* are translated by **depuis** in French.

Tu es au téléphone **depuis** quarante-cinq minutes. Ça suffit!	*You have been on the phone **for** forty-five minutes. That's enough!*
Tu es au téléphone **depuis** huit heures du soir. Ça suffit!	*You have been on the phone **since** eight P.M. That's enough!*

The second difference is in the use of verb tenses. In French, the verb outside the **depuis** clause (or to the left of **depuis**) can either be in the present or in the past. In English, the present perfect (a past tense) is always used. Why the difference? In French, in this context, the present tense indicates that the action that began in the past is still taking place at the moment you are talking. In the first example, they "*still* live in Austin"; in the second one, they met during summer vacation, and they "*still* know each other." To indicate the same circumstances, English uses the present perfect (*have lived, have known*).

Ils habitent à Austin **depuis 1997**.	*They have lived in Austin since 1997 (and they still live there).*
Ils se connaissent **depuis les vacances**.	*They have known each other since summer vacation.*

213

Translating *since*

The French equivalent of *since* is **depuis** + noun *or* **depuis que/qu'** + conjugated verb. The verb of a clause introduced by **depuis que** (that is, to the right of **depuis que**) can be in any tense, depending of the context of the sentence. In example 1, "they took a French class together" in the past, so **suivre** is in the **passé composé**. On the other hand, in examples 2 and 3, the verb that follows **depuis que** is in the present because they denote actions that are still true at the moment you speak: "the children are *still* playing soccer together," and the "weather is *still* cool."

Ils se connaissent **depuis qu'ils ont suivi** le même cours de français.	*They have known each other since they took the same French class.*
Ils se connaissent **depuis que leurs enfants jouent** au foot ensemble.	*They have known each other since their kids have been playing soccer together.*
Nous dormons mieux **depuis qu'il fait** moins chaud.	*We have been sleeping better since the weather cooled down.*

depuis: *since* in a negative sentence

In a *negative* sentence with any negative except **ne... plus** (*no longer*), the main verb (outside the **depuis** clause) can be in any past tense: **passé composé, imparfait**, or pluperfect.

Elle **n'a rien mangé** depuis ce matin.	*She has not eaten anything since this morning.*
Elle **n'avait rien mangé** depuis la veille.	*She had not eaten anything since the previous day.*

Following **depuis que**, the verb tense is based on the context: the verb is in the present, usually translated by a progressive form in English (example 1), to indicate that the starting point (since when the action has *not* been happening) is an ongoing situation; in the past it indicates strictly the starting point.

Je n'ai pas vu mon père **depuis qu'il habite** dans les Alpes.	*I have not seen my father since he has been living in the Alps.*
Elle n'a rien mangé **depuis qu'elle a quitté** la maison.	*She has not eaten anything since she left the house.*

In a negative sentence with **ne... plus** (*no longer*), the main verb (outside the **depuis** clause) stays in the present.

Elle **ne travaille plus** depuis sa grossesse.	*She has not worked since her pregnancy.*
Il **n'y a plus** de fleurs depuis qu'il fait froid.	*There are no flowers anymore since the weather has been/is cold.*
Ils **n'ont plus** d'amis depuis qu'ils ont changé d'école.	*They don't have friends anymore since they changed schools.*

If the context is past, the **imparfait** is used for the main verb (never the **passé composé**), and the verb in the **depuis que** clause is in the *pluperfect*.

Nous **ne nous parlions plus** depuis qu'elle m'**avait menti**.	We were not talking to each other anymore ever since she (had) lied to me.

Expressions of age, such as *since he was ten years old*, occur frequently after *since*. In French, use the present tense after **depuis que** (examples 1 and 2), unless you are expressing *since he **turned** ten* in which case you must use the **passé composé** in French (example 3).

Nous sommes amies depuis que nous **avons** dix ans.	We have been friends since we were ten years old.
Il joue du violon depuis qu'il **est** tout petit.	He has played the violin since he was very little.
Il ne fume plus depuis qu'il **a eu** trente ans.	He has not smoked since he turned thirty.

Translating it's *been a while since . . .*

Since "a while" represents a length of time (duration) rather than a date, you can use either **depuis** + duration at the end of the sentence, or its alternatives **il y a** + duration + **que** or **ça fait** + duration + **que** at the beginning of the sentence. One major difference between English and French is the verb form: while both languages use a verb in the past tense, the English sentence is in the affirmative, but its French equivalent must be in the negative.

Nous **n'avons pas dîné** ensemble **depuis** longtemps.	
Ça fait longtemps **que** nous **n'avons pas dîné** ensemble.	It's been a while since we had dinner together.
Il y a longtemps **que** nous **n'avons pas dîné** ensemble.	
Je **n'ai pas vu** Paul **depuis** longtemps.	
Ça fait longtemps **que** je **n'ai pas vu** Paul.	It's been a while since I saw Paul.
Il y a longtemps **que** je **n'ai pas vu** Paul.	
Nous **ne sommes pas allés** au ciné **depuis** des mois.	
Ça fait des mois **que** nous ne **sommes pas allés** au ciné.	It's been months since we went to the movies.
Il y a des mois **que** nous **ne sommes pas allés** au ciné.	

Translating *for*

The word **depuis** + duration is the equivalent of *for*. **Depuis** can be replaced by two other expressions with the same meaning. Note, however, the change in word order (in the following first three examples). Again, the verb tense depends on the context: in examples 1, 2, and 3, **attendre** is in the present because "we are still waiting."

> **depuis** + duration
> **il y a** + duration + **que**
> **ça fait** + duration + **que**

Nous attendons **depuis** vingt minutes.	*We have been waiting for twenty minutes.*
Il y a vingt minutes **que** nous attendons.	*We have been waiting for twenty minutes.*
Ça fait vingt minutes **que** nous attendons.	*We have been waiting for twenty minutes.*
Nous **habitons** à Paris **depuis** dix ans.	*We have been living in Paris for ten years.*
Nous **habitions** à Paris **depuis** dix ans.	*We had lived in Paris for ten years.*

These alternative expressions are particularly useful to clarify possible ambiguities caused by the double meaning of **depuis** (*since* and *for*) as illustrated by the following:

Ambiguous

J'attends **depuis deux heures**.	*I have been waiting for two hours.* or: *I have been waiting since two o'clock.*

Clear

Ça fait deux heures que j'attends.	*I have been waiting for two hours.*
Il y a deux heures que j'attends.	*I have been waiting for two hours.*

For expressing a duration

When you are considering only the duration of a completed action, use **pendant** instead of **depuis**. **Pendant** is not necessarily attached to a past context; it can also be used with a verb in the present or future (examples 3 to 5). Note that **pendant** can be omitted in French (all examples).

Hier, j'**ai lu** (**pendant**) quarante-cinq minutes avant de m'endormir.	*Yesterday I read for forty-five minutes before going to sleep.*
Ils **sont restés** chez nous (**pendant**) trois jours.	*They stayed at our house for three days.*
Le dimanche il **reste** au lit (**pendant**) toute la matinée.	*On Sundays he stays in bed (for) the whole morning.*

Cet été nous **resterons** chez ma mère
(**pendant**) une semaine.

*Next summer we will stay at my mother's
for a week.*

Je **travaillerai** (**pendant**) deux heures et
puis je partirai.

*I will work for two hours and then I
will leave.*

For expressing a future date

When *for* sets a date by which something will be accomplished, its French equivalent is
avant in a sentence that uses the future perfect in the negative (but the simple future is also
acceptable, as in example 3).

Les meubles **ne seront pas livrés avant** six
semaines.

*The furniture won't be delivered for six
weeks.*

Je **ne serai pas rentré avant** quelques
heures.

I won't be back for a couple of hours.

Il **ne repartira pas avant** une semaine.

He won't be leaving again for a week.

Since and *for* in a past context

As in English, all of the previous rules can be expressed in a past context by "pushing" the
verb back one notch. As a general rule, change the verbs that are in the present to the
imparfait (**connaissaient** in the first example), and those in the **passé composé** to pluperfect (**avait menti**).

Present context

Ils **se connaissent** depuis les vacances.

*They have known each other since
summer vacation.*

Past context

Ils **se connaissaient** depuis les vacances.

*They had known each other since
summer vacation.*

Present context

Nous ne **nous parlons** plus depuis qu'elle
m'**a menti**.

*We don't talk to each other since she lied
to me.*

Past context

Nous ne **nous parlions** plus depuis qu'elle
m'**avait menti**.

*We weren't talking to each other since
she (had) lied to me.*

Present context

Elle **n'a pas vu** ses parents depuis
longtemps.

*It's been a while since she saw her
parents.*

Past context

Elle **n'avait pas vu** ses parents depuis longtemps.	*It had been a while since she saw her parents.*

The type of sentence in the **imparfait** often has a **quand** + **passé composé** clause that explains how the action in the **imparfait** was interrupted and ended.

Nous **attendions** depuis vingt minutes quand le docteur **est** enfin **arrivé**.	*We had been waiting for twenty minutes when the doctor finally showed up.*
Ils **se connaissaient** depuis plusieurs mois quand ils **ont décidé** de se marier.	*They had known each other for several months when they decided to get married.*

Translating *in* as an expression of time

When *in* is used to express time as opposed to place, it can have three different equivalents in French:

In = **depuis**

If *in* can be replaced by *for*, it indicates that an action has *not* happened during that time. Use **depuis** in French, with a negative verb. (See "Translating *it's been a while since . . .*")

Nous **ne t'avons pas vu depuis** longtemps.	*We have not seen you in (for) a while.*
Ils **ne sont pas rentrés** en France **depuis** deux ans.	*They have not been back to France in two years.*

In = **en**

If *in* indicates a simple duration (the time it takes to accomplish something), use **en** in French, with the main verb in the present, past, or future.

Je peux finir mes devoirs **en une heure**.	*I can finish my homework in one hour.*
Vous devrez finir cet examen **en moins d'une heure**.	*You will have to complete this exam in less than one hour.*

In = **dans**

If *in* indicates a duration that is a projection into the future (*"so much time" from now*), use **dans** in French, with a verb in the future, **futur antérieur**, or the imperative.

Dans cinq ans il pourra prendre sa retraite.	*In five years (five years from now), he will be able to retire.*
Rappelez-moi **dans deux jours**.	*Call me back in two days (two days from today).*
J'aurai fini mes devoirs **dans une heure**.	*I will be done with my homework in one hour (one hour from now).*

Ago

A sentence with *ago* emphasizes how far back in the past (how long ago) an action occurred and ended, no matter how long it lasted. Its French equivalent is **il y a** + duration, which must be placed at the end of the sentence. Based on context, the main verb can be in the **passé composé** or **imparfait**. Unlike **pendant**, **il y a** must always be associated with a past context.

Il est arrivé **il y a trois mois**.	*He arrived three months ago.*
J'ai fait des compétitions de natation **il y a vingt-cinq ans**.	*I competed in swimming twenty-five years ago.*
Elle dansait bien **il y a quarante ans**.	*She was a good dancer forty years ago.*
Ils se sont rencontrés **il y a vingt ans**.	*They met twenty years ago.*

EXERCICE

17·1

Fill in the blanks with **depuis**, **depuis que** (or its equivalents **ça fait... que**, and **il y a... que**) or **pendant**.

1. Je ne l'ai pas revu _____ il a déménagé.

2. L'été dernier, elle est restée chez ses parents _____ trois semaines.

3. L'enfant dort _____ l'avion a décollé.

4. Tu es en retard! _____ vingt minutes que je t'attends.

5. Elle ne mange plus de viande _____ elle a été malade.

6. Vous avez étudié le français _____ trois ans et puis vous avez arrêté.

7. Tu as regardé la télé _____ quatre heures ce matin! Tu ne crois pas que ça suffit?

8. Je travaille _____ sept heures du matin, mais je ne peux pas m'arrêter.

9. _____ combien de temps que tu n'as pas vu tes parents?

10. Le livreur a sonné à deux heures. Il est 2 h 10; il a sonné _____ dix minutes. Donc _____ dix minutes qu'il attend!

EXERCICE

17·2

Put the verb in parenthesis in the correct tense.

1. Pendant les vacances nous _____ (rencontrer) des gens agréables.

2. Elle _____ (ne pas manger) de chocolat depuis qu'elle a commencé un régime.

3. Nous _____ (jouer) au tennis ensemble depuis six mois.

4. Elle _____ (acheter) une nouvelle voiture il y a six mois.

5. Je _____ (ne pas lire) le journal depuis plusieurs jours.

6. Vous êtes en retard; le train _____ (partir) il y a dix minutes.

7. Depuis qu'il _____ (sortir) avec Julie, Marc ne regarde plus les autres filles.

8. Depuis combien de temps _____-vous (connaître) les Martin?

9. Je connais la mère de Pierre depuis que je _____ (être) enfant.

10. Il y a très longtemps, je _____ (savoir) parler espagnol. Maintenant j'ai tout oublié.

11. Ça fait une demi-heure que je te _____ (attendre). Qu'est-ce que tu faisais?

12. Elle _____ (ne pas dormir) depuis que son chat a disparu.

13. Nous _____ (ne pas se voir) depuis janvier.

14. Je _____ (décider) d'apprendre le français il y a quatre ans.

Put the following sentences into French.

1. Pierre has been very happy since he met Julie.

   _____

2. It's been four years since we had Christmas with our cousins.

   _____

3. We have not slept since the neighbors adopted a dog.

   _____

4. I had been writing for a few minutes when my pen quit working.

   _____

5. I have not eaten any candy since I started my diet.

   _____

6. She does not sleep anymore since her cat has disappeared.

   _____

7. The children had been watching TV since their parents left.

   _____

8. We have not talked to Alain since his birthday.

   _____

9. We have known him for ten years.

   _____

10. I have not seen Paul for a while.

    _____

11. I won't be back for a couple of hours.

    _____

12. I competed in swimming for ten years.

_____

13. I competed in swimming ten years ago.

_____

Indicate whether the equivalent English sentence would have since *or* for.

1. J'étudie le français depuis que je suis à la fac. _____

2. Ils sont mariés depuis trois ans. _____

3. Ils sont mariés depuis 2003. _____

4. Ils sont mariés depuis septembre dernier. _____

5. Il n'a pas plu depuis une semaine. _____

6. Il n'a pas plu depuis mercredi dernier. _____

7. Nous suivons ce cours depuis une semaine. _____

8. Nous suivons ce cours depuis le 29 mai. _____

9. Je joue du violon depuis que j'ai cinq ans. _____

10. Je joue du violon depuis cinq ans. _____

11. Je joue du violon depuis l'année dernière. _____

12. Je n'ai pas vu mes parents depuis Noël. _____

13. Je n'ai pas vu mes parents depuis six mois. _____

Negative sentences

An English negative rarely "matches" its French equivalent. In fact, a French negative looks like a double negative when compared to English as in **Personne n'est là**—literally *Nobody is not there.* So don't be tempted to go fast when you want to translate, and always focus on the rules.

In French, the basic negative is formed by two particles: **ne... pas**. These two negative words usually surround the conjugated verb. French has a number of alternative negative expressions that can replace **pas**:

ne... jamais   never

Le chameau n'a jamais soif.   *The camel is never thirsty.*

ne... pas encore   not yet

Il n'a pas encore fini son travail.   *He has not finished his work yet.*

ne... pas du tout   not at all

Le dimanche, on ne travaille   *On Sundays people don't work*
   pas du tout.   *at all.*

ne... pas/... non plus   neither/either

Je n'ai pas fini non plus.   *I am not done either.*

ne... pas assez   not enough

Il n'y a pas assez de sucre dans   *There is not enough sugar in my*
   mon café.   *coffee.*

ne... pas beaucoup   not much

Nous n'avons pas beaucoup de   *We don't have much time.*
   temps.

ne... pas grand-chose   not much

Elle n'a pas fait grand-chose   *She did not do much on Saturday.*
   samedi.

ne... personne   no one

Il n'y a personne au gymnase   *There is nobody at the gym on*
   le lundi.   *Mondays.*

223

ne... plus	*no more, no longer*
Il n'y a plus d'aspirine dans le tube.	*There is no more aspirin in the tube.*
Nous ne nous parlons plus.	*We don't talk to each other anymore.*

ne... rien	*nothing*
Il n'y a rien dans le frigo. J'ai faim!	*There is nothing in the fridge. I'm hungry!*

ne... ni... ni	*neither . . . nor*
Il n'aime ni les gens ni les animaux!	*He likes neither people nor animals!*

ne... aucun(e) (+ *noun*)	*not any*
Cet homme n'a aucun ami.	*That man has no friends.*

ne... nulle part	*nowhere*
Je ne peux trouver mes lunettes nulle part!	*I can't find my glasses anywhere!*

In spoken language, most of the expressions listed here (except for **plus** and **ni... ni**) can also be used alone, without the **ne**, when there is no verb in the sentence. In that case, they consist of either a single word answer, or they can be combined with a stressed pronoun.

Lui, perdre ses affaires? **Jamais!**	*Him, lose his belongings? Never!*
—Tu as fini?	*"Are you done?"*
—**Pas encore.**	*"Not yet."*
—Cet animal est féroce.	*"This animal is ferocious."*
—**Pas du tout.** Il est très affectueux.	*"Not at all. It is very affectionate."*
—Julie n'aime pas les escargots.	*"Julie does not like snails."*
—**Moi non plus.**	*"I don't either. (Me neither.)"*
—Qui a dit ça?	*"Who said that?"*
—**Personne!**	*"No one!"*
—De quoi as-tu envie?	*"What would you like?"*
—**De rien.**	*"Nothing."*
—Quel est le meilleur chanteur?	*"Which one is the best singer?"*
—**Aucun.** Ils sont tous assez mauvais.	*"None (of them). They're all quite bad."*
—Qu'est-ce que tu as fait ce weekend?	*"What did you do this weekend?"*
—**Pas grand-chose.**	*"Not much."*

When you are writing in French, however, the negative construction is part of a sentence with a conjugated verb, and the greatest challenge is certainly its placement. The second negative particle moves around in the sentence, depending on the verb tense, as we'll see.

Be aware of the English alternative forms of some negatives: *not anybody* and *nobody*, *not anything* and *nothing*, *nowhere* and *not anywhere*, *either* and *neither*, and so on. In French, such words as **quelqu'un**, **quelque chose**, and **quelque part**, never appear in negative sentences. Use instead: **personne**, **rien**, **nulle part**, and **non plus** as the second half of a negative.

Placement of negatives

When the verb is conjugated in a simple tense, including an imperative, the two negative particles surround that conjugated verb.

Il **ne** fera **plus** de natation.	*He will not swim again (anymore).*
Elle **ne** fait **aucun** effort.	*She makes no effort whatsoever.*
Ne dis **rien**!	*Don't say anything!*
N'allez **jamais** dans cette pièce.	*Never go in that room.*
Elle **ne** voit **personne**.	*She does not see anyone.*
Tu **n'**iras **nulle part**, tu resteras ici.	*You will go nowhere (won't go anywhere), you'll stay here.*
Nous **n'**avons **ni** chien **ni** chat.	*We have neither a cat nor a dog.*

For **ne... ni/ni**, the placement works a little differently when the negation bears directly on conjugated verbs as opposed to nouns. **Ne... ni** still surround the first verb, but the particle **ne** (not **ni**) is repeated in front of each subsequent verb.

Elle **ne** fume **ni ne** boit.	*She neither smokes nor drinks.*
Ma mère **n'**achète **ni ne** consomme de produits laitiers.	*My mother neither buys nor eats dairy products.*

This construction is rather formal; in spoken language people prefer two juxtaposed simple negative clauses.

Elle ne fume pas et elle ne boit pas.	*She does not smoke and she does not drink.*

With an infinitive

When an infinitive follows the conjugated verb, the negative particles are placed around the conjugated verb, except in the case of **personne**, **aucun(e)**, and **nulle part**, all three of which follow the infinitive (examples 4 to 6).

Je **ne** vais **pas** dire la vérité.	*I am not going to tell the truth.*
Je **ne** veux **rien** dire.	*I don't want to say anything.*
Elle **ne** sait **ni** coudre **ni** peindre.	*She doesn't know how to sew or how to paint.*

But:

Elle **ne** va voir **personne**.	*She won't see anyone.*
Il **ne** va aller **nulle part**.	*He is going to go nowhere.*
Nous **n'**allons avoir **aucun** problème.	*We won't have any problems.*

However, when the infinitive itself is being negated, both parts of the negative are grouped together and they both *precede* the infinitive, except in the case of **ne... personne**, **ne... aucun(e)**, and **ne... nulle part** all of which surround it.

Quand on a un rhume il vaut mieux **ne pas** fumer.	*When you have a cold, it is better not to smoke.*
Ne rien dire est la meilleure chose dans certains cas.	*To not say anything is best in some cases.*

But:

Quand on est malade il vaut mieux **ne** voir **personne**.	*When you're sick it is better not to see anyone.*
Quand on est malade il vaut mieux **n'**aller **nulle part**.	*When you're sick it is better not to go anywhere.*

With a past participle

In a compound tense (i.e., the sentence has a past participle), the conjugated verb is **avoir** or **être**, and the second negative particle must follow it. It is as if the past participle remains out of the (negative) picture.

Je **n'**ai **pas encore** dit la vérité.	*I have not yet said the truth.*
Elle **n'**a **rien** fait.	*She has not done anything.*
Il **n'**a **ni** écrit, **ni** téléphoné à son père.	*He neither wrote nor called his father.*

Once again, the three exceptions are **personne**, **aucun(e)**, and **nulle part**, all of which follow the past participle instead of the conjugated verb.

Il **n'**est allé **nulle part** pour les vacances.	*He went nowhere (didn't go anywhere) for his vacation.*
Nous **n'**avons eu **aucun** problème.	*We had no problem.*
Je **n'**ai vu **personne**.	*I saw no one.*

With prepositions

When a preposition is attached to the verb, only **rien** or **personne** can be used, and they must follow the preposition, no matter what tense the verb is in.

Tu **n'**iras **chez personne.**	*You will not go to anybody's house.*
Ne touche **à rien!**	*Don't touch anything!*
Ne va parler **à personne!**	*Don't go talk to anyone.*
Je **ne** me souviens **de rien.**	*I don't remember anything.*
Elle **ne** s'est occupée **de rien.**	*She did not take care of anything.*

With some verbs, the preposition does not follow the verb immediately. You'll need to be on the lookout for those:

entendre parler de	*to hear about*
faire la connaissance de	*to make the acquaintance of*

être + adjective + **de**

être amoureux/amoureuse de	*to be in love with*
être fier/fière de	*to be proud of*
être surpris(e) de	*to be surprised by*

avoir expressions + *de*

avoir besoin de	*to need*
avoir envie de	*to want*
avoir peur de	*to fear*

Ils **n'**ont peur **de personne.**	*They fear no one.*
Elle **n'**a été surprise **de rien.**	*She was not surprised by anything.*
Je **n'**ai besoin **de rien.**	*I need nothing/don't need anything.*
Nous **n'**avons entendu parler **de rien.**	*We did not hear about anything.*

rien and personne + adjective

Rien and **personne** can both be described by an adjective. In this case, **de/d'** + invariable adjective follows **rien** or **personne**. The placement of both **rien** and **personne** follow their regular rules. Remember that in this construction the adjective is always invariable in masculine singular.

Il **ne** fréquente personne **de plus vieux.**	*He does not see anyone older.*
Elle **n'**aime **rien d'exotique.**	*She does not like anything exotic.*

In a compound tense, **rien** precedes the past participle and is therefore separated from **de** + adjective by the past participle (first example). But **personne** and **de** + adjective are always grouped together, after the past participle.

Nous **n'avons rien** vu **d'intéressant**.	We did not see anything interesting.
Nous **n'avons** rencontré **personne de nouveau**.	We did not meet anybody new.

When an infinitive follows the conjugated verb, **rien** precedes it (and is separated from **de** + adjective), while **personne** follows it.

Il **ne** va **rien** faire **d'extraordinaire**.	He won't do anything extraordinary.
Je **ne** veux voir **personne de triste** aujourd'hui.	I don't want to see anyone (who's) sad today.

With object pronouns

When the sentence has one or more object pronouns (including a reflexive pronoun), the pronoun(s) follow(s) **ne**, unless there is an infinitive in the sentence.

If there is no infinitive in the sentence, the object pronoun follows **ne**:

Tu **ne lui** parles **pas**.	You don't talk to him.
Tu **ne lui** as **pas** parlé.	You did not talk to him.
Ne lui parle **pas**!	Don't talk to him.
Personne ne lui parle.	No one talks to him/her.
Je **ne m'ennuie jamais**.	I never get bored.
Tu **ne me l'as pas** donné.	You did not give it to me.

With an infinitive in the sentence, the negative words surround the conjugated verb, except for *personne, aucun/aucune* and *nulle part,* all of which must follow the infinitive (last two examples).

Tu **ne** peux **pas leur** dire non.	You can't tell them no.
Nous **n'allons pas nous** amuser.	We are not going to have fun.
Il **ne** veut **rien** me dire.	He does not want to tell me anything.
Elles **ne** peuvent **me** donner **aucun** indice.	They can't give me any clue.
Je **ne** peux l'emmener **nulle part**.	I can't take it anywhere.

With an adverb

Unless the adverb (**bien**, **mal**, **trop**) modifies the negative itself, such as in **vraiment pas** (*really not*), **sûrement pas** (*certainly not*), and **presque jamais** (*almost never*), and so on, it follows the negative word. Short adverbs generally precede the past participle.

Nous **n'avons pas bien** compris la leçon.	We did not understand the lesson very well.
Ne m'en donnez **pas trop**.	Don't give me too much (of it).
Tu **n'as pas mal** travaillé.	You did not work too badly (i.e., you worked well).

The negative as subject of the verb

Personne, **rien**, **aucun(e)** + noun, and **ni... ni** can be the subject of the verb. In that scenario, the order of the two negative words is reversed, and **ne**, which is usually the first one, follows **personne**, **rien**, **aucun(e)**, and **ni... ni**. Note that **ne** immediately precedes the conjugated verb, as it does for regular negatives.

The verb of such sentences is always singular after **personne**, **aucun(e)**, and **rien**, but usually plural after **ni... ni**. (Details on **ni... ni** follow.)

Personne ne viendra demain.	*Nobody will come tomorrow.*
Personne n'a rendu ses devoirs aujourd'hui.	*No one turned in their homework today.*
Rien ne lui plaît.	*Nothing pleases him/her.*
Rien ne va pouvoir l'aider.	*Nothing will help him/her.*
Ni le froid **ni** la neige **ne** le dérangent.	*Neither cold nor snow bothers him.*
Aucun son **n'**est sorti de sa bouche.	*No sound came out of his mouth.*

The verb that follows **ni** must agree in person and number with the nouns **ni** negates the same way it agrees with subject pronouns: it will be in the **nous** form when a first person (**moi**) is included in the subject (example 1), and it will be in the **vous** form when a second person (**toi**) is included in the subject (example 2).

Ni ma sœur ni **moi** n'**avons** envie de sortir ce soir.	*Neither my sister nor I feel like going out tonight.*
Ni tes amis ni **toi** n'**avez choisi** la bonne réponse.	*Neither your friends nor you have picked the right answer.*

Inversion with a negative

A sentence with an inversion and a negative is very formal, almost literary. When it occurs, the second negative word is placed after the subject pronoun. Spoken language would almost always use an intonation question.

N'êtes-vous jamais à l'heure?	*Aren't you ever on time?*
Isabelle **n'est-elle pas** la sœur de Caroline?	*Isn't Isabelle Caroline's sister?*
N'a-t-elle jamais visité le Mexique?	*Hasn't she ever visited Mexico?*

Additional considerations

Some negatives behave somewhat irregularly and deserve further consideration.

ni... ni

The use of articles with **ni... ni** varies quite a bit. Usually the partitive (**du**, **de l'**, **de la**, **des**) and indefinite articles (**un**, **une**, **des**) change to **de** in a negative sentence, whereas the definite articles (**le**, **la**, **les**) remain the same. (See Unit 8 on articles.) With the negative **ni... ni**, the rules change. One thing remains constant: words like **et** and **ou** are always dropped, and the first **ni** in **ni... ni** must follow a verb.

With indefinite and partitive articles

The indefinite and the partitive articles disappear unless the negative sentence insists on yet another choice (examples 3, 4, and 5), or when the verb is **être** (example 6).

—Tu veux de la glace ou du gâteau?	*"Would you like some ice cream or some cake?"*
—Je ne veux **ni glace ni gâteau**.	*"I want neither ice cream nor cake."*
—Tu as un chien ou un chat?	*"Do you have a cat or a dog?"*
—Je n'ai **ni chien ni chat**. Je n'ai pas d'animaux.	*"I have neither a cat nor a dog. I don't have any pets."*
Je ne regarde **ni un film ni un feuilleton**, je regarde **une émission culturelle**!	*I am not watching a movie or a serial; I am watching a cultural program!*
Si tu ne veux **ni des pâtes, ni du riz**, qu'est-ce que tu veux? **Du couscous**?	*If you want neither pasta nor rice, what do you want? Some couscous?*
Je n'ai vu **ni un chien ni un loup**. C'est **un coyote** que j'ai vu.	*I saw neither a dog nor a wolf. I saw a coyote.*
Ce n'**est ni de l'eau, ni de la vodka**.	*This is neither water, nor vodka.*

The negative construction with **ni** has an alternative in this type of sentence (with an indefinite or partitive article): **ne... pas de... ni de**. The article in its negative form (**de**) is maintained. The changed negative form is highlighted here:

—Tu veux de la glace ou du gâteau?	*"Would you like some ice cream or some cake?"*
—Je ne veux **pas de** glace **ni de** gâteau.	*"I don't want ice cream or cake."*
—Tu as un chien ou un chat?	*"Do you have a cat or a dog?"*
—Je n'ai **pas de** chien **ni de** chat.	*"I don't have a cat or a dog."*

With the definite article

If there is a definite article, it remains in the sentence. If the sentence has the verb **préférer**, it should be changed to **aimer** for the sake of logic in the negative.

—Tu as préféré le film de Chabrol ou le film de Rohmer?	*"Did you prefer the film by Chabrol or the film by Rohmer?"*
—Je n'ai aimé **ni le film** de Chabrol **ni le film** de Rohmer.	*"I liked neither the film by Chabrol nor the film by Rohmer."*

ni... ni and a preposition

When the verb is followed by a preposition, the preposition remains, and it must be repeated after each **ni**. The articles do not change and are maintained.

Ils n'habitent **ni à Lyon ni à Paris**.	*They don't live in Lyon nor in Paris.*
Je n'ai besoin **ni d'un couteau ni de ciseaux**.	*I need neither a knife nor a pair of scissors.*

ni... ni with a clause

When **ni** negates a whole clause, it must be repeated before each linking word that introduces the clause(s). The alternate construction with **ne... pas...ni...** may be used here.

Elle **n'a** besoin **ni que** tu l'**aides, ni que** tu la **plaignes**.	*She does not need you to help her or pity her.*
or: Elle **n'a pas** besoin **que** tu l'**aides, ni que** tu la **plaignes**.	
Tu **ne** te demandes **ni s'ils t'admirent, ni s'ils te craignent**.	*You don't wonder whether they admire you or whether they fear you.*
or: Tu **ne** te demandes **pas s'ils t'admirent, ni s'ils te craignent**.	

ne... plus

The word **plus** in a negative expression can refer to time (examples 1 and 2) as well as to a quantity. For quantities, **plus** is followed by **de** + noun, and the whole expression can be replaced by the pronoun **en** (example 3).

Time

Sa mère **n'a plus** vingt ans!	*Her mother is no longer in her twenties!*
Mes Lego? Je **n'y** joue **plus**.	*My Legos? I no longer play with them.*

Quantity

—Est-ce qu'il reste un peu de lait?	*"Is there a little milk left?"*
—Il **ne** reste **plus** de lait.	*"There is no milk left."*
or: —Il **n'en** reste **plus**.	*"There isn't any left."*

Answering **toujours, encore,** and **déjà**

In a question, the word **toujours** could be the equivalent of *always* or *still*. The negative answer to **toujours** (*always*) is **jamais**, and the negative answer to **toujours** (*still*) is **ne... plus**.

—Tu vois **toujours** Julie?	*"Do you still see Julie?"*
—Non, je **ne** la vois **plus**.	*"No, I don't see her anymore/any longer."*

—Tu crois **toujours** ce qu'on te dit?	*"Do you **always** believe what you are told?"*
—Non, je **ne** crois **jamais** ce qu'on me dit.	*"No, I **never** believe what I am told."*

In a question, the word **encore** could be the equivalent of *still* or simply of *again*. The negative answer to **encore** (*again*) is simply **ne... pas**, and the answer to **encore** (*still*) is **ne... plus**.

—Tu vois **encore** Julie?	*"Do you **still** see Julie?"*
—Non, je **ne** la vois **plus**.	*"No I don't see her **any longer**."*
—Tu as **encore** fait des bêtises à l'école?	*"Have you done **more** silly things at school?"*
—Non, je **n'**ai **pas** fait de bêtises.	*"No, I have not done silly things."*

In a question, the word **déjà** can be the equivalent of *yet/already* or of *ever*. The negative answer to **déjà** (*yet/already*) is **pas encore** (*not yet*).

—Tu as **déjà** fait tes devoirs?	*"Have you **already** done your homework?"*
—Je **n'**ai **pas encore** fait mes devoirs.	*"I have **not** done my homework **yet**."*

The answer to **déjà** (*ever*) could be **jamais** as well as **pas encore**. In fact, answering **Je ne suis pas encore allé en France** to the following question would have a different, more positive connotation: *I have not been to France **yet**.*

—Tu es **déjà** allé en France?	*"Have you **ever** been to France?"*
—Je **ne** suis **jamais** allé en France.	*"I have **never** been to France."*

Incomplete negatives in spoken French

In written French, **ne** is always part of the negative, whereas in spoken French, it is often dropped! On the other hand, you will always hear the second half of the negation.

The subject pronouns, too, are somewhat "shaved" in speech as the examples show:

WRITTEN	SPOKEN	
Tu **n'**as **pas encore** fini! (*or even*: T'as **pas encore** fini!)	Tu as **pas encore** fini!	*You're not done yet!*
Il **n'**y a **rien** à manger.	**Y'a rien** à manger.	*There's nothing to eat.*
Tu **ne** m'écoutes **jamais**.	Tu m'écoutes **jamais**.	*You never listen to me.*

Incomplete negatives in literary French

On the contrary, some verbs are hardly ever followed by the second negative words in a literary context, retaining only **ne/n'**. However, it's perfectly possible to use both negative particles with these verbs. They are:

cesser + infinitive	*to cease doing*
oser + infinitive	*to dare to*
pouvoir + infinitive	*to be able to*
savoir + infinitive	*to know to*

Cet enfant **ne cesse** de pleurer.	*This child does not stop crying.*
Je **n'ose** vous poser cette question.	*I do not dare ask you this question.*
Je **ne peux** m'y résoudre.	*I cannot bring myself to do it.*
Je **ne sais** comment il a réussi.	*I don't know how he managed.*

Multiple negative words

We have stressed the fact that in French you need two negative words in a negative sentence. Well, what about two or three? As in English, you may need to express more than one negative idea in the same sentence. To do so, you will always need **ne** and other negative words, placed according to the rules we have reviewed. The following examples give you an array of possible combinations, with the number of negations in parentheses.

Ils ne vont jamais nulle part. (2)	*They never go anywhere.*
Elle ne dit jamais rien à personne. (3)	*She never says anything to anyone.*
Il a promis qu'il ne le ferait jamais plus. (2)	*He promised he would not ever do it again.*
Elle ne veut jamais ni se coucher tôt, ni se lever tôt. (2)	*She never wants to go to bed early nor get up early.*
Personne n'a jamais vu ça! (2)	*Nobody has ever seen that!*
Il n'a jamais eu aucun problème. (2)	*He never had any trouble.*
Personne ne veut jamais être volontaire pour ce travail. (2)	*Nobody ever volunteers for that task.*
Rien n'est plus comme avant. (2)	*Nothing is as it was before anymore.*
Je n'ai plus rien à faire. (2)	*I have nothing left to do.*
Personne n'a plus rien à dire. (3)	*Nobody has anything left to say.*

Phony negatives

A number of expressions include a **ne/n'** but they don't have a second negative particle, and most importantly they don't express a negation!

ne... que

When **ne** is followed by **que** instead of a negative particle, it means *only* in the sense of a restriction. To reinforce the idea of a restriction, the adjective **seul** in the sense of *a single thing* may be used (example 2).

Je **n'**ai **que** cinq euros dans ma poche.	*I only have five euros in my pocket.*
Nous **n'**avons **qu'**une (seule) voiture pour nous deux.	*We only have one (single) car for the two of us.*
—Je croyais qu'ils avaient beaucoup d'enfants...	*"I thought they had a lot of kids . . ."*
— Ils **n'**en ont **qu'**un (seul).	*"They have only one."*

n'importe

The expression **n'importe** before a question word indicates *any* in a nearly derogatory sense, as in *just any old . . .* (examples 1, 2, and 5), or *any* in a far-reaching, all-encompassing sense (examples 3 and 4). In any case, the combination does not ask a question, nor does it make a negative statement, and it can't be followed by a verb. Note that **n'importe quel** must agree with the following noun; **n'importe lequel** must agree with its antecedent.

n'importe comment	*just anyhow/carelessly*
n'importe lequel	*just any one (of those)*
n'importe où	*anywhere*
n'importe quand	*any time*
n'importe quel + noun	*any + noun*
n'importe quoi	*(just) any old thing*
n'importe qui	*just anyone*

Tu dis **n'importe quoi** pour te rendre intéressant.	*You are saying anything/any old thing just to sound interesting.*
Il ne faut pas parler à **n'importe qui**!	*You can't talk to just anyone!*
Ce chien suivrait son maître **n'importe où**.	*That dog would follow his master anywhere.*
Vous pouvez venir **n'importe quel jour**, à **n'importe quelle heure**, ça ne me dérangera pas.	*You can come any day, at any time of the day, it won't bother me.*
Il a fait son travail **n'importe comment**. Il doit recommencer.	*He did his work carelessly. He has to start over.*

Note that **n'importe comment** is not the equivalent of *anyway* (previous example). To say *anyway*, use **quand même**.

Je ne voulais pas que tu le fasses, mais tu l'as fait **quand même**!

I did not want you to do it, but you did it anyway!

ne in literary style

With the conjunctions **avant que** (*before*), **de peur/crainte que** (*for fear that*), and **à moins que** (*unless*), as well as the verbs **avoir peur que** and **craindre** (*to fear*), **ne** is inserted before the dependent verb conjugated in subjunctive. In this rather formal usage, **ne** does not have an equivalent in English and you should not try to translate it. Still, there are numerous French speakers who use this "pleonastic" **ne** naturally in everyday speech. In less formal style, the subjunctive is still used (because of the trigger expressions), but the **ne** is dropped.

Dépêche-toi **de peur qu'il n'arrive** avant nous.

Hurry for fear (that) he might arrive before us.

Je parlerai à tes parents, **à moins que tu ne veuilles** le faire toi-même.

I will speak to your parents, unless you'd rather do it yourself.

Je crains **qu'il ne soit** trop tard.

I am afraid it may be too late.

EXERCICE 18·1

Answer the following questions with a negative sentence.

1. Aimez-vous tout le monde?

   _____

2. As-tu déjà visité la Chine?

   _____

3. Vous jouez encore à la poupée?

   _____

4. As-tu cherché partout?

   _____

5. Avez-vous beaucoup d'amis qui parlent français?

   _____

6. Avez-vous un chien ou un chat?

_____

7. As-tu déjà déjeuné aujourd'hui?

_____

8. Est-ce que tu as entendu quelqu'un?

_____

9. Est-ce qu'il a gagné quelque chose?

_____

10. Est-ce qu'il y a du beurre, des œufs et du lait dans ton frigidaire?

_____

11. Faites-vous souvent du sport?

_____

12. Irez-vous quelque part pour les vacances?

_____

13. Quelqu'un t'a parlé?

_____

14. Qu'est-ce qui est tombé?

_____

15. Vous avez peur de quelque chose?

_____

16. Est-ce que vous étudiez l'allemand et le chinois?

_____

17. Tu ressembles à quelqu'un dans ta famille?

_____

18. As-tu téléphoné à quelqu'un samedi soir?

_____

19. Qui pourra te remplacer?

_____

20. Est-ce que ton chien et ton chat sont tombés malades?

_____

21. Est-ce qu'il y a encore de la neige en juin?

_____

22. Qui t'a parlé?

_____

23. Où irez-vous: à Paris, à Rome ou à Berlin?

_____

24. Tu as besoin d'un petit cahier ou d'un grand cahier?

_____

25. De quoi as-tu besoin?

_____

26. Est-ce que l'avalanche a fait des victimes?

_____

27. Qu'est-ce qui s'est passé?

_____

28. Est-ce que votre fils joue du piano ou de la guitare?

_____

29. Est-ce que tous les députés ont voté?

_____

30. Est-ce que tu l'as déjà fini?

_____

31. Connaissez-vous des fées ou des magiciens?

_____

32. Qu'est-ce que vous allez faire le weekend prochain?

_____

33. Est-ce que le gouvernement surveille parfois les gens?

_____

34. Quel acteur apprécies-tu particulièrement?

_____

35. Qu'est-ce qu'on t'a offert pour ton anniversaire?

_____

36. As-tu rencontré des gens agréables pendant ton voyage?

_____

37. Est-ce que tu envoies souvent des textos?

_____

38. Est-ce que beaucoup de choses sont intéressantes ici?

_____

39. Qu'est-ce qui plaît aux enfants?

_____

40. Qui est-ce qui est tombé dans l'eau?

_____

EXERCICE

18·2

Put the following sentences into French. There are double and triple negatives included here!

1. He does not like to speak to anybody.

_____

2. There is nothing left anymore.

_____

3. Nobody wants anything anymore.

_____

4. Don't ever do this again!

_____

5. She neither drank nor danced at the party.

_____

6. He never wants anything for his birthday.

_____

7. They never listened to anyone.

_____

8. Nothing ever bothers me.

_____

9. I'd like a ten A.M. appointment, unless you can't.

_____

10. Take any book: they're all good.

_____

11. That boy calls at any odd hour, it's annoying.

_____

12. This job was done carelessly.

_____

13. It's better not to travel in the summer: it's more expensive.

_____

14. Neither you nor I can do this task.

_____

15. He is never surprised by anything.

_____

16. None of the cats ate the fish.

_____

17. He would follow her anywhere.

_____

18. We have neither the time nor the desire to finish now.

_____

19. Coffee? I haven't offered you any yet?

_____

20. I only have a few dollars left.

_____

21. Me neither!

_____

EXERCICE

18·3

Correct the following sentences by writing in the missing negative elements.

1. Personnellement, je pense que personne a tort.

_____

2. Quelle nouvelle ! J'en reviens pas.

_____

3. Aucun sport lui plaît vraiment.

_____

4. Il me restait plus qu'à attendre que le gâteau cuise.

_____

5. Ce bébé fait que pleurer. C'est agaçant.

_____

6. Dans la vie, on est jamais sûr de rien.

_____

7. J'ai pas fait attention; je suis désolé.

_____

8. Elle était pas trop sûre du chemin à suivre.

_____

9. « Bouge pas! »

_____

10. Nous avons cherché le chat partout mais il était nulle part.

_____

11. Aucun animal bizarre a surgi des bois.

_____

12. Personne a pris ton livre. C'est toi qui l'as pas rangé à sa place.

_____

13. Ils sont arrivés en retard parce qu'ils s'étaient pas dépêchés.

_____

14. La fête foraine? Je ne m'y suis amusée du tout.

_____

15. Elle a besoin d'aucune aide.

_____

Answer key

1 Understanding the verb

1-1   1. à   2. X. *In English to listen* **to***; but in French* **écouter** *is a transitive direct verb.*   3. à   4. à   5. à   6. X.   7. X. *Another case where the English verb is followed by a preposition (*for*), whereas the French verb is transitive direct.*   8. X   9. X   10. à   11. X   12. X

1-2   1. de   2. de   3. d'   4. de   5. à   6. de   7. à   8. à   9. à   10. à, de   11. à   12. à   13. d'   14. de   15. de   16. d'   17. de   18. de   19. à   20. de   21. à   22. à   23. À   24. à   25. de   26. de   27. de   28. de   29. de   30. de

1-3   1. Il leur a dit qu'il partait.   2. Le docteur m'a conseillé de manger moins. *In reported commands/advice use command verb +* **de** *+ infinitive.*   3. Ne reprochez jamais à vos parents de vous pousser à faire mieux. *Without context it could also be* **de vous avoir poussé.**   4. Demande à Julien de t'aider. *Indirect commands/requests are always followed by* **de** *+ infinitive.*   5. Qui a autorisé ce conducteur à ouvrir la grille? / Qui a permis à ce conducteur d'ouvrir la grille ? *You have a choice in how you translate "to authorize"; just be sure to use the correct preposition with each verb.*   6. Je te propose d'essayer une nouvelle approche.   7. Je vous remercie de nous avoir aidés hier soir. *The past infinitive is used because of* **hier soir.**   8. Connaître plusieurs langues permet aux enfants de comprendre d'autres cultures.   9. N'empêchez pas vos amis de vous aider.   10. Elle ne convaincra/persuadera jamais son mari de manger des escargots.   11. Ils ont obligé le marin malade à rentrer au port.   12. Essaie de penser à autre chose.   13. Il charge toujours ses employés de fermer.

1-4   1. Est-ce que tu seras arrivé à 7 heures? *"By 7" does not have a literal translation in French; using the* **futur antérieur** *+* **à 7 heures,** *a regular expression of time, is enough.*   2. Ils feraient un voyage autour du monde s'ils pouvaient.   3. Je t'avais prévenu!   4. Tu aurais été en retard si tu avais pris le bus. *The three-word past conditional form "would have been" in English has a two-word equivalent in French,* **aurais été.** *"Had taken," the two-word pluperfect in English, matches the French form,* **avais pris.**   5. Est-ce que tu pourras finir à temps? *In French the future is a simple tense, and the five-word "Will you be able to" is translated by* **tu pourras.**   6. Une solution facile a été acceptée. *In the passive, the past participle must agree with the subject* **une solution.**   7. Les résultats seront bientôt affichés.   8. On cherche des employés enthousiastes. **Chercher** *can't be put in the passive form.*   9. Un spécialiste m'a expliqué la raison. **Expliquer** *takes a double object construction; therefore a non passive form should be used in French.*   10. On a promis une gourmandise à Minette. **Promettre à** *takes an indirect object. Also, in the absence of an agent, use the "***on***" construction.*   11. On leur a permis d'aller au lit à minuit. *With* **permettre à,** *there is no passive form.*   12. On leur a donné deux options.   13. On aurait dû nous dire que c'était annulé. *Passive not possible with* **dire** *+ past conditional.*

1. Ça risque d'être difficile à faire.   2. As-tu appris à nager?   3. J'ai oublié de laisser sortir le chien. **Oublier** *is followed by* **de** + *infinitive; whereas* **laisser** *never takes a preposition when followed by an infinitive.*   4. Le président de la fédération a félicité les joueurs d'avoir gagné le match.   5. Je voudrais entendre les oiseaux chanter.   6. Veux-tu regarder le soleil se coucher? *Verbs of perception are never followed by a preposition.*   7. Nous avons failli rater le train.   8. Il a réussi à économiser assez d'argent pour sa retraite.   9. Tu auras du mal à faire ça seul.   10. Ne cherche pas à me suivre!   11. Il a choisi de venir seul.   12. Arrête de t'inquiéter! *Don't forget to match the reflexive pronoun to the actual subject:* **tu.**   13. Tu penses qu'ils risquent d'être en retard?   14. À quoi sert ce panier? *To be used for* = **servir à.**   15. Je me suis résigné à garder ma vieille voiture un peu plus longtemps.   16. Je tiens à faire ce travail seul.

1. préfère   2. sont   3. a réussi   4. passent   5. sors   6. a demandé   7. effaçons   8. ont, partent   9. a suffi   10. a abandonné, ont franchi   11. ont retenti   12. attends   13. apprécient   14. vous plaignez   15. n'a entendu   16. ont refusé, a voté   17. va   18. fait

2 Compound tenses and agreement of the past participle

1. recommandés. **Que** *is the direct object of* **recommandé.** *The past participle agrees with* **que**'s *antecedent:* **les articles.**   2. X. **Que** *is the object of* (**de**) **lire.** *No agreement.*   3. X. **Que** *is the object of* **inviter.** *No agreement.*   4. vue   5. élevés   6. mariés   7. X. (**De**) **quels chapitres** *is not the direct object. No agreement.*   8. X - eu   9. offerte   10. X - offert   11. attrapée   12. née   13. passée   14. choisie   15. X - brossé   16. cassée   17. X - laissé   18. mariés   19. servis   20. X - intéressé

1. posée   2. sentie   3. vu. **Les voleurs** *is not the subject of* **appréhender.**   4. brossés   5. entendu. **Leur chanson préférée** *is not the subject of* **siffler.**   6. vus   7. sentie   8. entendu. **La Marseillaise** *is not the subject of* **chanter.**

3 Use of the past tenses

Dimanche dernier, Paul et Virginie <u>sont partis</u> à la fête de la bière. Tous leurs amis y <u>étaient allés</u> l'année précédente et ils <u>voulaient</u> absolument voir ça à leur tour. Ils <u>pensaient</u> qu'ils s'amuseraient bien. Mais quand ils <u>sont arrivés</u>, ils <u>ont été</u> déçus. D'abord, il <u>faisait</u> froid. Ensuite, pour acheter de la bière ou des saucisses, il fallait attendre vingt ou trente minutes chaque fois. Puis, ils <u>ont voulu</u> danser, mais il <u>y avait</u> trop de gens sur la piste et pendant qu'ils <u>dansaient</u> quelqu'un a renversé sa bière sur Virginie qui <u>s'est mise</u> en colère! Alors, Pierre <u>a décidé</u> qu'il <u>était</u> l'heure de rentrer à la maison. Dans la voiture il <u>a demandé</u> à Virginie si elle <u>s'était amusée</u>... Virginie <u>n'a pas répondu</u> mais dans sa tête elle pensait: « Si <u>j'avais su</u>, je ne serais pas venue! »

1. a. passé composé b. imparfait   2. imparfait   3. imparfait   4. a. passé composé b. imparfait   5. a. passé composé b. imparfait c. passé composé   6. a. imparfait b. passé composé   7. a. passé composé b. passé composé   8. imparfait (*or* passé composé)   9. a. imparfait b. passé composé   10. a. imparfait b. can't tell   11. a. imparfait b. passé composé c. passé composé   12. a. passé composé b. passé composé

3-3 1. suis arrivé(e), n'étaient pas, étaient allés   2. a perdu, n'avait pas dit   3. était, allait, est partie, n'avait jamais vu   4. ne se sont pas parlé, s'étaient disputés   5. s'est réveillé, avait trop mangé   6. s'est levée, voulait   7. J'étais déjà arrivé(e), m'as téléphoné   8. nous sommes réveillés, était   9. faisait, avait neigé   10. n'avions pas encore fini, a dit   11. allais, te levais   12. n'ai pas voulu, l'avais déjà vu   13. marchaient, a commencé   14. se sont assis, s'étaient assis   15. nous sommes habillés, sommes partis, étions   16. n'avait jamais voté, a voté   17. installions, a commencé, s'est envolée   18. aviez étudié   19. avaient déjà ouvert, est enfin arrivé, avait eu   20. s'est arrêtée, a commencé   21. avons fait, n'avions jamais faite   22. a demandé, l'avaient déjà faite   23. s'était déjà couché, s'est souvenu, n'avait pas encore sorti

4 Translating the -ing form into French

4-1 1. Nous ne voulons pas que les enfants mangent sur le canapé. *The English gerund corresponds to a French subjunctive because* **voulons** *is a trigger verb, and each verb has its own subject.*   2. La fille portait une robe rouge.   3. Les clients ont quitté le bureau en riant. *If you wanted to make this sentence very formal you would use the present participle instead of the* **gérondif***: Riant, les clients ont quitté le bureau.*   4. Il l'a regardée partir. *Whether the sentence has one or two subjects, an infinitive follows a verb of perception.*   5. Je n'aime pas chanter en public. *In a sequence of verbs with a single subject, use the infinitive after the first conjugated verb.*   6. Écrire en français est difficile.   7. Je m'habituerai à dormir dans ce nouveau lit.   8. Arrête de m'embêter!   9. Je penserai à toi!   10. Elle a senti ses jambes qui faiblissaient. *or:* Elle a senti ses jambes faiblir.   11. Il s'est arrêté de fumer à Noël.   12. Ayant payé, il a quitté le magasin. *or:* Il a quitté le magasin après avoir payé. *The present participle is literary and you should try to avoid it as shown in the second version.*   13. Elle a pris ses clés sans qu'il s'en aperçoive.   14. L'auteur a pleuré en recevant son prix littéraire.   15. En entrant dans la cuisine, il a trouvé le chat qui buvait son lait.   16. Après avoir regardé les étoiles toute la nuit, ils se sont endormis à l'aube.   17. —Je peux entrer? —Non! Je suis en train de m'habiller. *Use* **en train de** *to emphasize that you're in the process of getting dressed.*   18. Elle a gâché sa jeunesse à l'attendre. *Waiting for him is equated with the waste of her youth.*

4-2 1. Elle a eu un accident de voiture en parlant sur son portable.   2. Je rencontre ma voisine en sortant la poubelle.   3. J'ai attrapé un rhume en embrassant ma fille qui était déjà enrhumée.   4. Je me suis cassé une dent en mangeant du poulet.   5. Elle a perdu dix kilos en ne mangeant que des légumes pendant un mois.   6. Tu as perdu ton portable en te promenant au parc. *Even though the* **gérondif** *is a non-conjugated form, the reflexive pronoun before it needs to match the subject.*   7. Il s'est fait mal en étant imprudent en roller.   8. Julia a fait beaucoup de progrès en s'entraînant beaucoup.   9. J'ai appris la vérité en téléphonant à mes amis.   10. Il a appris l'espagnol en allant en Espagne.   11. Elle a pu payer ses études en travaillant en même temps.   12. Nous sommes restés éveillés en buvant beaucoup de café.   13. Elle a glissé en prenant une douche.   14. Avez-vous fermé la porte en partant ?   15. Tu t'es perfectionné en écrivant beaucoup.

4-3 1. Charles est chanteur. Il gagne sa vie en chantant.   2. Virginie est prof. Elle gagne sa vie en enseignant.   3. Bernard est docteur. Il gagne sa vie en soignant des malades.   4. Conrad est écrivain. Il gagne sa vie en écrivant.   5. Wolfgang est pianiste. Il gagne sa vie en jouant du piano.   6. Josie est vendeuse. Elle gagne sa vie en vendant des choses.   7. Gérard est acteur. Il gagne sa vie en faisant des films.   8. Maxime est chauffeur de taxi. Il gagne sa vie en conduisant un taxi.   9. Martine est championne de tennis. Elle gagne sa vie en jouant au tennis/en gagnant des matchs.

10. Sylvie est pharmacienne. Elle gagne sa vie en vendant des médicaments/conseillant les clients/préparant des ordonnances.   11. Paul est cuisinier. Il gagne sa vie en faisant la cuisine. 12. Alain est pilote de course. Il gagne sa vie en conduisant des voitures de courses.   13. Pierre est plongeur. Il gagne sa vie en plongeant.   14. Guy est libraire. Il gagne sa vie en vendant des livres. 15. Francis est fermier. Il gagne sa vie en travaillant la terre/s'occupant de la ferme.

5   Relative tenses introduced by que

5-1   1. Le docteur a demandé ce qui n'allait pas. *Direct question* **qu'est-ce qui** *replaced by the neutral relative pronoun* **ce qui**.   2. Sa mère a dit à l'enfant que s'il mangeait trop il serait malade. 3. J'ai annoncé que j'allais me coucher. **Bonsoir**, *etc. belongs to spoken language and often disappears in indirect speech.*   4. Les enfants m'ont demandé ce que je ferais si je voyais un Martien.   5. J'ai promis que je n'arriverais plus en retard.   6. Mes parents m'ont demandé qui j'allais inviter à mon anniversaire.   7. Sa mère lui a demandé s'il s'était brossé les dents.   8. Le prof nous a conseillé de bien étudier avant l'examen. *or:* Le prof a conseillé que nous étudiions bien avant l'examen. *For reported commands, if the introductory verb can have an indirect object* (**nous**), *the infinitive construction is best, although the subjunctive construction may be used.* 9. Son amie lui a demandé si sa fille lui avait souhaité bon anniversaire. *After an introductory verb in the past, the verb tense needs to change from* **passé composé** *to pluperfect; the possessive needs to be in the third person; the* **est-ce que** *of the yes/no question becomes* **si**.   10. Julie demande toujours au facteur s'il a quelque chose pour elle.   11. Elle (Il) jure qu'elle (il) prendra une leçon de tango le jour de son anniversaire.   12. La serveuse nous a demandé si nous avions choisi.   13. Il m'a prévenu qu'il n'y arriverait pas seul et qu'il faudrait que je l'aide.   14. Sa mère lui a dit de faire ses devoirs. *An imperative becomes: indirect object pronoun* **lui** + **de** + *infinitive in reported speech.*   15. Il a demandé pourquoi il fallait qu'il fasse ses devoirs à l'instant et a ajouté qu'il venait d'arriver à la maison.   16. Les amis de Julie lui ont demandé si elle reviendrait les voir.

5-2   1. aurait   2. n'est pas. **Affirmer** *is never followed by the subjunctive.*   3. nous sommes rencontrés   4. avait commis   5. réussiras   6. de partir. *Sentences with* **dire**, *to tell someone to do require* **de** + *infinitive.*   7. sera   8. ont changé   9. avait gagné   10. de refaire   11. as mal fermé   12. viendrez   13. ne font jamais   14. était   15. se passe/se passait   16. ne dors pas

6   The subjunctive

6-1   1. Les parents ont permis aux enfants de regarder la télé jusqu'à minuit. **Les enfants** *is the indirect object of* **permettre** *and can serve as the subject for the following verb in the infinitive.*   2. La police ordonne aux citoyens de rester chez eux.   3. La petite fille demande aux autres de ne pas prendre ses jouets.   4. Le club interdit aux enfants de jouer sur le terrain de golf.   5. Il me faut finir ce travail aujourd'hui. *The subject of the subjunctive becomes the object of* **il faut**, *and the subjunctive is replaced by an infinitive.*   6. Les grévistes ont empêché le train de partir.   7. Il lui faut choisir le bon numéro.   8. Vous n'avez pas besoin de venir.   9. Je vous souhaite un rétablissement rapide.   10. Elle a dit aux enfants de dormir.   11. *Not possible.* Je sortirai sans que mes parents le sachent.   12. Il t'aidera malgré sa fatigue. *The conjunction is replaced by the equivalent preposition, and the verb in the subjunctive* **être fatigué** *by a noun, but the original sentence is also correct.*   13. *Not possible.* Je préfère que vous rentriez tôt. **Préférer** *is always followed by the subjunctive when the sentence has a second subject.*

6-2 1. fasse 2. viendras. **Espérer** *is followed by the indicative. Use the future because of* **samedi prochain** *in the sentence.* 3. es rentré 4. suis 5. soient 6. ne puisses pas 7. te souviennes 8. n'a pas dit 9. suis. **Croire** *is never followed by the subjunctive when the sentence is affirmative.* 10. prennes 11. va 12. n'a pas 13. ait. **Penser** *used in a negative sentence is usually followed by the subjunctive.* 14. trouvez 15. trouviez 16. aura. *Needed because of* **dimanche prochain**, *and there is no future subjunctive.* 17. est, donnions 18. faites 19. ayons 20. vous mariiez, fera 21. dois 22. a *or* avait 23. veuille 24. finissiez 25. servent 26. ne prennes pas 27. fasse 28. preniez 29. comprendra / a compris. *Without any context, it could be "that he understood," or "that he will understand."* 30. sortes

6-3 1. J'attendrai jusqu'à ce que tu finisses ton travail. 2. Il est temps que tu partes. 3. Il restera ici jusqu'à ce que tu lui dises la vérité. 4. J'ai demandé à Julie de se dépêcher. *An infinitive construction is preferred for reported commands or requests.* 5. Qu'est-ce que vous voulez que je fasse? 6. Je le ferai bien que je n'en aie pas envie. *Even though the subject is the same for both verbs, the conjunction* **bien que** *requires the subjunctive.* 7. Pensez-vous qu'il pleuve demain? *If you used the inversion, the subjunctive is used after* **penser**, *even though the English verb is in the future. If you asked the question with* **est-ce que**, *however, there is no subjunctive; use the future because of* tomorrow. 8. J'aurais peur de quelqu'un qui puisse lire dans les pensées des gens. *Such a person does not exist; that's what the subjunctive denotes.* 9. C'est l'histoire la plus surprenante que j'aie jamais entendue! 10. Je suis désolé que vous n'ayez pas pu venir. *The verb* **venir** *took place in the past, before the trigger verb, as could not indicates.* 11. C'est dommage que tu ne veuilles pas faire leur connaissance. 12. Nous sommes contents que tu sois là. 13. Nous voulons que tu viennes avec nous. 14. Je voudrais te donner ce livre avant que tu (ne) partes. **Voudrais** *and* **donner** *have the same subject, so no subjunctive; but* **avant que** *is a conjunction that triggers the subjunctive after a second subject* **tu**. **Ne** *here is not a negative and it may be omitted in less formal language. See Unit 18 on negatives for details on this "phony negative."*

6-4 1. aies prévenus 2. ayez été, n'ayez pas bu 3. ayez écrit 4. ne soit pas sortie 5. reprenne. *Trigger verb is in the past, but* **reprendre** *is simultaneous.* 6. ne soient pas venues 7. ne viennent pas 8. n'aies pas attendu 9. soit

7 Relative tenses *not* introduced by que

7-1 1. avaient eu. **Savoir** *is followed by an indicative. Use the pluperfect because the dependent action happened before the main action—***le mois dernier***—which is already past.* 2. ferait. *The conditional expresses the future in a past context, as in English.* 3. seraient 4. n'auras 5. n'aurions pas raté 6. boirait 7. ne serait pas sortie 8. avait pris 9. m'aiderais 10. pourrait 11. s'était trompée. **Admettre** *is not a trigger verb. Use the pluperfect because* **se tromper** *happened before the main verb which is already in the past tense.* 12. ne portait plus 13. n'oublierai pas. *The main verb is not a trigger verb and the dependent verb must be in the future to match the context of* **prochain rendez-vous**. 14. c'est 15. j'aurais apporté

7-2 1. S'ils avaient su, ils n'auraient jamais fait ça. 2. Je prendrai mes lunettes la prochaine fois que je vais au cinéma. 3. Dès que tu ouvriras la porte, tu verras ta surprise. 4. J'ai dit au vendeur que je voulais rendre cet objet. 5. J'ai dit au vendeur de m'aider. 6. Ils espéraient que le film serait intéressant. 7. Elle voulait que tu viennes la voir. 8. Ce matin-là, il nous a dit qu'il partait. 9. Mes grands-parents iront en Floride quand ils auront vendu leur maison ici. 10. Mon amie m'a dit qu'elle avait couru après un voleur. **M'a dit** *indicates reported speech: the* *dependent verb is conjugated in the indicative.* 11. Mon amie m'a dit de courir après le voleur. *Here* **m'a dit** *indicates a command, and the indirect object* **me** *is the subject of the infinitive* **courir**. 12. Parfois mon chat me regarde comme s'il ne me connaissait pas!

8 Articles

8-1 1. des, X. **Enfants** *is determined: they are the children of my best friend.* 2. de, X 3. du 4. X, X 5. d'. **Manquer de** *cannot be followed by a* **d-** *article. De replaces any* **d-** *article.* 6. de. *Description when the plural noun is preceded by a plural adjective.* 7. de l' 8. Le, de 9. X 10. le, le 11. X 12. de 13. du 14. un d'un 15. des. *Personal assessment with* **comme un ange**. 16. des 17. les 18. du 19. un 20. le 21. mes 22. X 23. X, X 24. X , les 25. une, des

8-2 1. des. *Combination of preposition* **de** + *article* **les**. 2. X 3. les, des, la 4. les. **Beaucoup** *refers to how much he likes sugary drinks, not how many there are.* 5. l' 6. les 7. X, X 8. du 9. le, X 10. de. *Indefinite* **des** *becomes* **de** *when followed by an adjective.* 11. les, la 12. de, le, un. *Negative after the verb* **être**. 13. X 14. X 15. de, de 16. X 17. X 18. le, un 19. X 20. une, des 21. la 22. les 23. X, le, la 24. une 25. de l' 26. le, d'un 27. de 28. du. **De + le**, *so get rid of* **de**. 29. le, les, les 30. X, la

8-3 1. de. *Negation of the partitive;* **de** *replaces the partitive.* 2. des. **Se servir de** + *definite article* **les** *contract to* **des**. *The negative is therefore irrelevant.* 3. de, le 4. un. *Negation of the indefinite article, after* **être**. *It is a contrast; the indefinite article remains.* 5. l'. *Negation of the definite article; definite article remains.* 6. de 7. un 8. de 9. les 10. un 11. des 12. de, un 13. les 14. d' 15. X 16. X 17. un. *Negative after the verb être.*

8-4 1. Il m'a tourné le dos. 2. La plupart des élèves ont eu une bonne note. 3. Je n'ai pas besoin des stylos qui sont sur la table. **Des** *is the contracted form of* **de** + **les**. **Les** *is used because the pens are specific—those on the table.* 4. Je n'aime ni les escargots, ni les crevettes. 5. Ils ont de jeunes enfants. 6. J'ai besoin d'œufs et de farine. 7. M. Esslin est un médecin célèbre. Son père aussi était médecin. 8. Prenez-vous le café avec ou sans sucre? 9. J'ai envie de chocolat. 10. Il ne mange ni viande ni poisson. *The article would be partitive in an affirmative version of this sentence. After* **ni** *the partitives are dropped. Compare with the definite articles in number 4.* 11. Il y a de l'eau sur la route. Fais attention. 12. Les enfants ont eu de beaux cadeaux. *Before an adjective* **des** *becomes* **de**. 13. Ce n'est pas une histoire gaie. 14. Pour la Toussaint, nous irons au vieux cimetière. 15. Le Cardinal Wolsey a eu une mort terrible. 16. Qui sera élu président? 17. Ils habitent dans le Michigan. 18. Le dimanche ils aiment se reposer. 19. Tu as besoin d'autres chaussettes! 20. J'ai rêvé du jour de notre mariage.

9 Other determiners

9-1 1. Son 2. mes 3. Nos 4. Ses, son 5. Mon. **Mon amie** *is feminine; use* **mon** *when the noun begins with a vowel.* 6. Leurs 7. notre 8. Ta 9. Leur 10. ses 11. Leurs. *In the plural there is no distinction between a masculine and a feminine noun.* 12. sa 13. leur. **Temps** *is a singular noun.* 14. ses 15. votre, vos

9-2 1. Cet 2. cette 3. cet 4. ce, -là/-ci 5. Ces 6. Cette 7. Cet 8. ce 9. Ces 10. Cet 11. cet, ce 12. Cette 13. Ces 14. ces 15. Cet 16. ces 17. ce. *The h in* héros *is h aspiré.* 18. Cet été-là 19. Ces 20. Cette 21. ces 22. ce temps-là 23. ce 24. Ce. H aspiré. 25. ces

10 Relative pronouns

10-1 1. Le journal parle de l'accident à cause duquel nous avons été en retard au cours.   2. Je ne connaissais pas l'homme à qui je t'ai vu dire bonjour.   3. Regarde ce vieux bureau sur lequel Balzac a écrit *Eugénie Grandet*.   4. Sur mon balcon il y a une plante dans laquelle un oiseau a fait son nid. *The verb already has a subject -**un oiseau** - and the relative pronoun for a feminine singular thing after a preposition is* **laquelle**. *Also:* Sur mon balcon il y a une plante où un oiseau a fait son nid. 5. Il y a un problème auquel je pense souvent.   6. Les allocations auxquelles elle a droit depuis qu'elle est au chômage l'aident beaucoup financièrement. *The verb is* **avoir droit à** -to be entitled to- *and* **allocations** *is a thing*.   7. La ville de la Ciotat est un endroit merveilleux dans lequel elle a passé les vacances. *Also:* La ville de la Ciotat est un endroit merveilleux où elle a passé les vacances.   8. Tu te souviens de ce match de foot à la fin duquel / où il y a eu une grosse bagarre? *You could also use* **où** *since* **match de foot** *indicates an event in time*.   9. Les passagers entre lesquels Julie se trouvait assise étaient bavards. *You can only use a form of* **lequel** *with* **entre**, *even when the antecedent is a person*.   10. Il n'y a personne à qui poser la question.   11. Les Martin sont des gens très gentils avec qui /avec lesquels nous avons dîné récemment.   12. La SPA (Société Protectrice des Animaux) a été choquée des conditions épouvantables dans lesquelles vivaient ces animaux.

10-2 1. Paul est une personne que nous connaissons bien. **Connaitre** *needs a direct object since it already has a subject –**nous**– and since it has no preposition attached to it, use* **que**.   2. C'est un petit bistro où on mange bien.   3. Quel est l'auteur du roman dont vous m'avez parlé? **Parler** *needs a direct object since it already has a subject –**vous**– and since it has a preposition attached to it –**parler de**–, use* **dont**.   4. Au moment où il s'est aperçu de son erreur, il a rougi.   5. Recyclez les journaux que vous avez lus.   6. Mes amis sont des gens que je vois souvent.   7. Je suis ravie des soldes dont j'ai puprofiter. *The verb in the relative clause is* **profiter de**.   8. Je vous présente l'ami dont je vous avais parlé. *The verb in the relative clause is* **parler de**.   9. Tu te souviens de la fois où le chat est tombé dans ton bain?   10. C'est une fille qui s'ennuie partout. 11. Il n'y a personne qui puisse te remplacer.   12. As-tu vu le film que je t'avais recommandé? 13. L'instrument dont il joue est une harpe.   14. L'enfant dont tu t'es moqué à la récréation veut se venger.   15. Le jour où j'arriverai à résoudre ce problème, nous boirons du champagne. 16. Lire le journal est une chose que je n'ai pas le temps de faire.   17. Un bikini n'est pas une chose dont tu auras besoin en Alaska.   18. C'est un sujet qui intéresse tout le monde.   19. C'est la deuxième fois qu'il reçoit une lettre d'elle.   20. Mon meilleur ami est une personne qui ne me critique jamais.   21. La manière dont il parle à ses parents est choquante.   22. Connais-tu l'endroit où il garde son trésor?   23. Grand-père nous a parlé des choses dont il a souffert pendant la guerre.   24. Elle a reçu des nouvelles d'une étudiante qui était dans sa classe il y a un an. 25. Il a un chien adorable dont il est fou.   26. Je viens de finir un livre dont j'ai oublié le titre! 27. Pour Noël, bébé a eu beaucoup de cadeaux qu'il ne méritait pas vraiment! 28. Nous avons fait connaissance d'une femme intéressante dont la fille est dans le même cours de danse que notre fille.

10-3 1. Les histoires qu'il m'a racontées sont amusantes. *The past participle* **racontées** *must agree with the antecedent* **les histoires** *which is feminine plural*.   2. Dans la carrière à laquelle il pense, il gagnera beaucoup d'argent.   3. Nomme la personne pour qui tu as le plus d'admiration.   4. Les enfants dont elle s'occupe sont très turbulents.   5. Le trophée dont il est si fier est sur sa table de nuit.   6. Comment s'appellent les gens dont nous avons fait (la) connaissance hier soir? *or:* les gens que nous avons rencontrés hier soir? *Depending on the verb you choose,* **faire connaissance de** *or* **rencontrer**, *the relative pronoun will be different*.   7. Il a une amie avec laquelle/ avec qui il ne s'entend plus. (*when a relative pronoun whose antecedent is a person is preceded by a preposition other than de, you can use either lequel or qui*)   8. Il n'y a personne en qui j'aie plus confiance.

(the verb of the relative clause is avoir confiance en; *with "personne" (no one) you can only use* **qui**, *not* **laquelle**) 9. Le lac à côté duquel nous avons campé l'été dernier est sec cette année. *The relative clause has a compound preposition that includes* **de**: **à côté de**, *but you can't use* **dont** *for a compound preposition.* 10. Sa femme est une personne avec laquelle/avec qui il partage tout. 11. Ce sont eux qui ont fait ça! 12. Les sports auxquels mon frère s'intéresse ne m'intéressent pas du tout. *or:* Les sports qui intéressent mon frère ne m'intéressent pas du tout. *The verb is either* **intéresser** + direct object *or* **s'intéresser à**. 13. La peinture est une chose pour laquelle il n'a aucun talent. *You can't end a sentence with a preposition in French.* 14. Les affaires dont cet avocat s'occupe sont intéressantes. 15. Ceux qui veulent rester à la maison devraient me le dire. 16. C'est moi qui t'ai dit ca. *The verb of the relative clause agrees with the relative pronoun's antecedent:* **moi**. 17. Une fois que vous aurez fini, rendez vos examens. [*With* **fois** + *number* (**une**) *you can only use the relative* **que**, *not* **où**.] 18. Il y a une personne ici à qui/à laquelle ils vont donner un prix. 19. J'aime le papier avec lequel tu as emballé mon cadeau. 20. La femme dont le mari a été licencié a dû reprendre le travail.

11 Neutral relative pronouns: translating a different kind of *what*

11-1 1. ce qui. **Arriver** *is one of the translations of* to happen. *In this sentence, we need a subject for the clause.* 2. ce que 3. ce que 4. ce qui. **Se passer** *is another translation of* to happen. *In this sentence we need a subject for the clause.* 5. ce 6. ce à quoi 7. ce que 8. ce qu' 9. ce qui 10. ce que 11. ce dont 12. ce dont. *The verb is* **parler de**. 13. ce que 14. ce dont 15. ce dont 16. ce qui 17. ce dont 18. ce à quoi 19. Ce dont 20. ce que 21. ce que 22. ce qui 23. de quoi

12 Determining a noun with prepositions

12-1 1. en, de 2. de 3. en, en, d' 4. à, de 5. à 6. de 7. de 8. de 9. en 10. de 11. d' 12. de 13. en 14. à, en, de 15. en 16. à, à, à 17. d' 18. en 19. aux, aux 20. en 21. de/en, de/en 22. de 23. à 24. à, de 25. en 26. au 27. aux 28. de 29. de, de 30. aux

13 Object pronouns

13-1 1. Il y avait de l'eau par terre et il a marché dedans. *After* **dans** + *thing, no pronoun can be used; placed at the end of a sentence it becomes* **dedans**. 2. Ce chapeau est ridicule. Tu ne peux pas sortir avec. 3. Un chien a volé mon sandwich et il est parti avec. 4. La glace était fine et il est tombé à travers. 5. Il y avait deux écureuils et elle voulait jouer avec. **Écureuils** *is not a person or a pet, and the stressed pronoun can't be used.* 6. Il fait froid; prends tes gants. Ne sors pas sans. 7. Elle a un fils et elle s'occupe de lui seule. *To replace the preposition* **de** + *human object, you need the stressed pronoun.* 8. Les amis! Aimez-les toujours et faites-leur confiance/ayez confiance en eux. **Faire confiance** *requires* **à**, *but* **avoir confiance** *requires* **en**. *For* **à** + *person use the indirect object pronoun, for* **en** + *person use the stressed pronoun.* 9. Il y a trop de bruit. Je ne m'y habituerai jamais. 10. Il a vu une bonne occasion et il a sauté dessus. 11. Si elles ne veulent pas venir, nous devrons partir sans elles! 12. C'est une situation difficile mais nous en parlerons.   13. Le sucrier était ouvert et des abeilles volaient autour.   14. Il ne veut pas s'en servir. *Using* **se servir de**. *Or* Il ne veut pas les utiliser. **Utiliser** *is not followed by a preposition.* 15. Je t'en parlerai plus tard. *Or* Je vous en parlerai plus tard.   16. Est-ce que tu t'en souviens?   17. Est-ce que tu t'es souvenu de le faire? *Replacing only "it." Or* Est-ce que tu t'en es souvenu? *Replacing the whole phrase "to do it."*   18. Sers-t'en! *In the imperative, pronouns follow the verb.*

13-2   1. Oui, il me l'a demandé. *The clause is replaced by the direct object pronoun* **le** *because* **demander** *is transitive direct.*   2. Oui, je m'en souviens. *This is the opposite of # 1:* **Se souvenir** *takes de before its object, so you need the pronoun* **en**.   3. J'en ai (trois). *or:* Je n'en ai pas.   4. Oui, je m'en rends compte.   5. J'adore ça!   6. J'en ai très envie.   7. Non, tu ne me l'as pas dit. *or:* Oui, tu me l'as dit.   8. Oui, nous irons. *Before verb forms beginning with an* **i**, *the pronoun* **y** *is dropped.*   9. Oui, j'en ai peur.   10. Oui, je le leur ai dit.   11. Oui, je peux compter sur eux.   12. Oui, il s'en est excusé.   13. Oui, vous pouvez compter dessus.   14. Oui, je le pense.   15. Oui, je peux m'en occuper. *or:* je peux m'occuper de lui. **Mon chat** *is a pet, almost a person, hence the choice between* **en** *and* **de lui**.   16. Oui, je l'ai oublié. **De** *was there to introduce an infinitive; without an infinitive* **oublier** *takes a direct object.*   17. Oui, je m'en suis souvenu. *Opposite of #16* **se souvenir de**.   18. Oui, je les ai tous vus. *Don't forget the agreement of the past participle with a preceding direct object.*   19. Non, il n'en a pas eu. *Better answer:* **Non, il n'en a eu aucun.**   20. Non, je n'en ai pas. **Un** *doesn't stay in a negative sentence.*   21. Oui, j'en ai envie. *Replacing* **de faire un grand voyage.** *or* Oui, j'ai envie d'en faire un. *Replacing only* **un grand voyage.**   22. Concentre-toi dessus.

13-3   1. Sa mère y tient toujours.   2. Le sais-tu?   3. Nous en serons surpris.   4. Nous l'avons décidé.   5. Vous le savez?   6. J'en suis incapable.   7. Les élèves n'aiment pas ça.   8. Je me le demande...   9. Ne t'y appuie pas. *or:* Ne t'appuie pas dessus.   10. Il en a été triste.   11. Une règle n'est pas faite pour ça!   12. J'en ai l'impression.   13. Il l'oublie toujours. *Another common and therefore acceptable answer would be* **Il oublie toujours de faire ça.**   14. En es-tu satisfait?   15. Ils ne nous l'ont pas permis.   16. En plus de ça, ils lui en ont donné.

13-4   1. Elle leur en fait toujours.   2. Éloignez-vous-en!   3. Elle ne s'y est jamais intéressée.   4. La peinture est fraiche. Ne t'appuie pas contre.   5. Ce danseur en manque.   6. N'en utilise pas contre ton frère!   7. Ne les utilise pas contre ton frère!   8. Il n'en a eu aucune.   9. Nous ne nous en sommes pas méfiés.   10. Elle s'est approchée de lui sans faire de bruit.   11. Elle s'en est approchée sans faire de bruit.   12. Si tu n'en tiens pas compte, tu risques de le rater.   13. Il veut la finir avec elle.   14. « Je voudrais m'asseoir à côté d'elles. »   15. Cette fille parle toujours de lui; c'est agaçant.   16. Donne-les-moi.   17. Il a couru après eux pour le leur reprendre.   18. J'en achète peu.   19. Alice en avait peur, mais maintenant elle les adore.   20. Qu'est-ce que tu penses de lui?   21. Les étudiants s'y intéressent.   22. Je ne les ai jamais rencontrées. *Don't forget the agreement of the past participle.*

14   Position of object pronouns

14-1   1. Tu me les donnes.   2. Le professeur les leur a fait lire. *With* **faire** + *infinitive, the pronoun(s) precede* **faire** *and there is no agreement of the past participle.*   3. Les lui a-t-il envoyés?   4. Nous l'y avons mise.   5. Je vais leur en donner.   6. Vous n'en économisez pas.   7. Il l'a regardée tomber.   8. Je la leur ai préparée.   9. Les y avez-vous retrouvés?   10. Le président la leur a expliquée. **Expliquée** *takes the agreement because* **la** *is placed before* **avoir**.   11. Ne pas y entrer. *The infinitive, here used as an impersonal imperative, is negated. The negative words are grouped together before pronoun + verb.*   12. Ils veulent la leur acheter.   13. Il faut me le dire.

14. Nous ne voulons pas les y mettre. *The negative surrounds the conjugated verb* **voulons** *and does not affect the position of the pronouns.* 15. Elle va se les préparer. 16. Je vais la lui réparer. 17. Il va leur en écrire. 18. Nous pouvons vous l'apporter.

14-2   1. Donne-les-moi. Ne me les donne pas. 2. Fais-les-leur lire. Ne les leur fais pas lire. 3. Envoyez-la-lui. Ne la lui envoyez pas. 4. Mettons-l'y. Ne l'y mettons pas. 5. Donnez-leur-en. Ne leur en donnez pas. 6. Regarde-la tomber. Ne la regarde pas tomber. 7. Préparons-la-leur. Ne la leur préparons pas. 8. Retrouve-les-y. Ne les y retrouve pas. 9. Expliquez-la-moi. Ne me l'expliquez pas. 10. Dis-le-moi. Ne me le dis pas. 11. Vas-y. N'y va pas. 12. Occupe-t'en. Ne t'en occupe pas. 13. Parles-en. N'en parle pas. 14. Parle-leur-en. Ne leur en parle pas.

14.3   1. Je te le donne. 2. Je ne te le donne pas. 3. Tu me les donnes. 4. Donne-la-moi. 5. Ne leur en donnez pas. 6. Elle la leur donne. 7. Donne-m'en. 8. Ne m'en donne pas. 9. Il la leur a donnée. *Agreement of the past participle with the direct object of* **donner**, *placed before* **avoir**. 10. Je les y ai vus. 11. Tu l'as vue? 12. Je ne vais pas le voir. 13. Ils ne l'y ont pas vue. 14. Je la connais. 15. Tu les connais? 16. Elle l'a prise. 17. Il en a pris trois. 18. Prends-en. 19. Prends-en une. 20. Tu en as beaucoup. 21. Tu en as combien? / Combien en as-tu? 22. Nous n'en avons pas. *Don't keep* **un** *in the negative.* 23. Tu en veux? 24. Je ne l'aime pas. 25. Il lui écrit. 26. Vous ne nous écrivez pas. 27. Envoie-le-moi. 28. Je les appelle. 29. Prête-la-lui. 30. Montre-les-leur. 31. Je te l'ai montrée. 32. Ils lui ont répondu. *No agreement of the past participle with indirect object pronouns.* 33. Est-ce qu'elle va leur répondre?

14-4   1. Elle ne leur a pas répondu. 2. Ils vont me les demander. 3. Tu ne me l'as pas demandée. 4. Nous en venons. 5. Tu veux m'y retrouver? 6. Entres-y. *Verbs like* **aller** *and* **entrer** *require a pronoun.* 7. N'y entre pas. 8. N'y allez pas. 9. Allez-vous-en. *The pronouns come strictly from the infinitive* **s'en aller**, *to go away.* 10. Je veux te le dire. 11. Parles-en ! 12. Tu ne vas pas leur en parler. 13. Je vais le leur dire. 14. Il nous l'a dit. 15. Dis-le-moi. 16. Tu ne me l'as pas dit. 17. Dis-le-lui. 18. Parle-lui-en. 19. Je vais leur y parler. 20. Il ne vous l'a pas dite. *Agreement of the past participle with the direct object of* **donner**, *placed before* **avoir**. 21. Nous ne leur en avons pas parlé. 22. Il n'y a pas dormi. 23. Nous ne l'avons pas mangée. 24. Nous allons en boire. 25. Tu en as bu? / En as-tu bu? 26. Elle en a besoin. 27. Mets-les-y. 28. Je l'y mets. *Gender of the pronoun doesn't matter because it gets elided either way.* 29. Il s'en souvient. 30. Dépêche-toi. 31. Tu t'y habitues. 32. Il s'en occupe. 33. Occupons-nous-en.

15   Expressing *this is* and *that is*: ce, ça, and il

15-1   1. Ça, c'. *Use* **ça** *before any verb other than* **être**, *and when a pronoun precedes the conjugated verb. Before* **est** *you can only use* **c'**. 2. ça 3. Ça. *Don't use* **c'** *before pronoun +* **être**. 4. C' 5. Ça 6. Ce, ce 7. Ça 8. ça 9. ce*, ça 10. Ce* 11. Ça 12. ça 13. C' 14. C' 15. ça* 16. ce* 17. ça*. *Before* **n'est pas** *you can often use* **ça** *or* **ce**. 18. Ça 19. Ce* 20. C'. *Before* **être** *in the* **imparfait** *use only* **ce**.

15-2   1. C', c'. *A noun follows* **être**, *and this is a comment more than a direct description of the film; therefore* **c'était**. 2. 'il, c' 3. c', Il. *The first sentence is a comment on climbing Everest without a sherpa.* **Il** *directly describes the mountaineer.* 4. ils, Ce 5. Ce 6. C' 7. Ce 8. Il, C' 9. Ce 10. Il, C' 11. C' 12. C' 13. il 14. ce. **Italiens** *and* **Espagnols** *are nouns: they are preceded by the article* **des** *and they are capitalized.*

16 Questions

1. Qu'est-ce qui est arrivé hier soir? *No short form for the "what" subject. If you used* **Qui est arrivé?** *you would be saying* Who arrived? 2. Qui est-ce qui est arrivé le premier? Qui est arrivé le premier? 3. Avec quoi est-ce que tu écris? Avec quoi écris-tu? 4. Quelle heure est-il? 5. Qui est-ce qu'ils préfèrent? Qui préfèrent-ils? 6. À quoi est-ce que les chats pensent? À quoi les chats pensent-ils? *The preposition always begins the question in French; and* **que** *becomes* **quoi** *after a preposition.* 7. Qu'est-ce que cet homme regarde? Que regarde cet homme? 8. Quel professeur donne plus de A? Quel est le professeur qui donne plus de A? *The second version with a relative clause is a little more formal. Don't forget the article* **le** *in the construction* **Quel est** + *noun.* 9. Qu'est-ce qui t'aiderait? *No short form.* 10. Avec quoi a-t-il attrapé le chien? Avec quoi est-ce qu'il a attrapé le chien? *After a preposition* **que** *becomes* **quoi.** 11. Qu'est-ce qu'un nom? *The questions asks for a definition. That's the only time that* **Qu'est-ce que** *is followed by a noun.* 12. Qui tes parents ont-ils rencontré? Qui est-ce que tes parents ont rencontré? **Tes parents** *is the subject of the verb. The question asks* whom did your parents meet? *Because the sentence has a noun subject, the simple inversion would be ambiguous.* 13. De qui a parlé le journaliste? De qui est-ce que le journaliste a parlé? *Inversion with a noun is the preferred form to ask this information question, but the form with* **est-ce que** *is grammatically correct.* 14. À qui téléphones-tu chaque jour? À qui est-ce que tu téléphones chaque jour? 15. Quels cours Julie va-t-elle prendre? Quels cours est-ce que Julie va prendre? 16. Qui a parlé à Anne? Qui est-ce qui a parlé à Anne? *No ambiguity here with a "who" subject. Don't forget that the verb is always in the singular after* **qui.** 17. Quels sont les étudiants qui n'ont pas écrit leur composition? Quels étudiants n'ont pas écrit leur composition? *With the question word* **quel** *you have two possible constructions to choose from. However, the relative clause* **qui n'ont pas écrit leur composition** *can only be used after the* **quel** + **être** *construction.* 18. Qu'est-ce qui est orange, rond et comestible? *No short form.* 19. Avec quoi Julie a-t-elle pris ces photos? Avec quoi est-ce que Julie a pris ces photos? *The verb of this information question has a direct object:* **ces photos,** *therefore you can't use the inversion noun subject–verb.* 20. Pourquoi la pluie ne s'arrête-t-elle pas? Pourquoi est-ce que la pluie ne s'arrête pas? *With the question word* **pourquoi,** *the "preferred" noun subject inversion can't be used.*

1. À quoi penses-tu? 2. Où est ton livre? *With a noun subject in the information question* **où** + **être,** *the use of the inversion is required.* 3. Pierre travaille-t-il? *With a noun subject, you can't use a simple inversion in yes/no questions. You need the double subject inversion.* 4. Qui Marianne aime-t-elle? *The question word* **qui** *is too ambiguous as it could be the object as well as the subject. It is therefore recommended to use the double subject inversion.* 5. À quelle heure arriveront les invités? 6. Où va Julie? 7. Pourquoi Julie va-t-elle à la plage? *After* **pourquoi,** *you cannot use the inversion noun subject–verb.* 8. Quand le facteur apportera-t-il le paquet? *When the verb has a direct object* (**le paquet**)*, you cannot use the inversion noun subject–verb. Compare with the next question (#9) that has no direct object.* 9. Quand passera le facteur? 10. Qu'a-t-elle mis dans le tiroir? *No noun subject here and the inversion subject pronoun* (**elle**) *and verb is correct.* 11. Qu'est-ce que Maman a mis dans le tiroir? *The question asks "what" with a noun subject, and it has a complement of place* (**dans le tiroir**)*, so the only option is* **qu'est-ce que.** 12. Où Maman a-t-elle mis les clés? *When the verb has a direct object* (**les clés**)*, the inversion noun subject* (**Maman**)*–verb cannot occur. You need the double subject inversion.* 13. Quand rentrent vos voisins? 14. Quand vos voisins rentrent-ils de vacances? *or:* Quand est-ce que vos voisins rentrent de vacances? *The sentence has an essential complement and the simple inversion is not possible.* 15. Pourquoi la pluie ne s'arrête-t-elle pas? *In an information*

question with **pourquoi** *you cannot use the inversion noun subject–verb.*   16. Que conduit Pierre? *If you use the inversion to form your question, the simple inversion noun subject–verb is mandatory after* **que**, *but you can always use the* **est-ce que** *form if the inversion is not required.* **Qu'est-ce que Pierre conduit?**

17 Translating *for, since,* and a few other expressions of time

17-1   1. depuis qu'   2. pendant. *The verb to the left of the blank is in the* **passé composé** *and* **trois semaines** *expresses a duration, not a starting point.*   3. depuis que   4. Ça fait *or:* Il y a vingt minutes—*clearly a duration—is followed by* **que**.   5. depuis qu'   6. pendant. **Avez étudié** *is a completed action and* **trois ans** *represents a duration, not a starting point.*   7. pendant. **Quatre heures** *itself could be ambiguous: four hours or four A.M.? But* **ce matin** *(not* **du matin***) makes it clear that it is a duration.*   8. depuis   9. Il y a *or:* Ça fait   10. il y a, ça fait

17-2   1. avons rencontré. *Here the verb (***rencontrer***) dictates the use of the* **passé composé**. **Rencontrer** *does not describe an action that could still be going on at the time you speak.*   2. n'a pas mangé   3. jouons. *And we still play together.* **Jouer ensemble** *is still true at the time you speak.*   4. a acheté   5. n'ai pas lu   6. est parti   7. sort   8. connaissez. *This is a negative sentence with* **ne... pas**.   9. suis   10. savais   11. t'attends   12. n'a pas dormi   13. ne nous sommes pas vus   14. J'ai décidé

17-3   1. Pierre est très heureux depuis qu'il a rencontré Julie. *He met Julie at some point in the past and he has been happy ever since. The verb* **est** *is in the present tense to indicate that he is still happy at the time we say this.*   2. Ça fait quatre ans que nous n'avons pas fêté Noël avec nos cousins. *Celebrating Christmas with our cousins has not happened in four years. In French, the negative form is preferred. In a regular negative sentence (with "not"), use the* **passé composé**.   3. Nous n'avons pas dormi depuis que les voisins ont adopté un chien.   4. J'écrivais depuis quelques minutes quand mon stylo a arrêté de fonctionner.   5. Je n'ai pas mangé de bonbons depuis que j'ai commencé mon régime.   6. Elle ne dort plus depuis que son chat a disparu.   7. Les enfants regardaient la télé depuis que leurs parents étaient partis.   8. Nous n'avons pas parlé à Alain depuis son anniversaire.   9. Nous le connaissons depuis dix ans.   10. Je n'ai pas vu Paul depuis longtemps.   11. Je ne rentrerai pas avant quelques heures.   12. J'ai fait des compétitions de natation pendant dix ans.   13. J'ai fait des compétitions de natation il y a dix ans.

17-4   1. since   2. for   3. since   4. since   5. for   6. since   7. for   8. since   9. since   10. for   11. since   12. since   13. for

18 Negative sentences

18-1   1. Non, je n'aime personne.   2. Non, je n'ai pas encore visité la Chine. *or:* Non, je n'ai jamais visité la Chine. **Déjà** *in the sense of ever has two possible answers; the one that includes* **pas encore** *is more open-ended.*   3. Non, nous ne jouons plus à la poupée.   4. Non, je n'ai cherché nulle part.   5. Non, nous n'avons aucun ami qui parle français. *With* **aucun**, *the quantity is zero and the noun and the verb must be singular, even if the question had a plural.*   6. Non, je n'ai ni chien, ni chat. *or:* Non, je n'ai pas de chien ni de chat. *In a regular negative with* **ni**, *the indefinite article is dropped or you can use the alternate construction with* **pas de... ni de**.   7. Non, je n'ai pas encore déjeuné aujourd'hui.   8. Non, je n'ai entendu personne.   9. Non, il n'a rien gagné.

10. Non, il n'y a ni beurre, ni œufs, ni lait dans mon frigidaire.   11. Non, nous ne faisons jamais de sport.   12. Non, nous n'irons nulle part pour les vacances.   13. Non, personne ne m'a parlé.   14. Rien n'est tombé.   15. Non, nous n'avons peur de rien! **Rien** *must follow the preposition, not the conjugated verb.*   16. Non, nous n'étudions ni l'allemand ni le chinois.   17. Non, je ne ressemble à personne dans ma famille.   18. Non, je n'ai téléphoné à personne samedi soir.   19. Personne ne pourra me remplacer.   20. Non, ni mon chien ni mon chat ne sont tombés malades.   21. Il n'y a plus de neige en juin.   22. Personne ne m'a parlé.   23. Nous n'irons nulle part. *or:* Nous n'irons ni à Paris, ni à Rome, ni à Berlin.   24. Je n'ai besoin ni d'un petit cahier ni d'un grand cahier!   25. Je n'ai besoin de rien. *Because of the preposition* **de**, *rien must go at the end of the sentence, after* **de**.   26. L'avalanche n'a fait aucune victime. *Victime is feminine so* **aucun** *must match it.*   27. Rien ne s'est passé.   28. Mon fils ne joue ni du piano, ni de la guitare.   29. Non, aucun député n'a voté. *Don't forget to change the verb to singular when the subject is* **aucun**.   30. Non je ne l'ai pas encore fini.   31. Non, nous ne connaissons ni fées ni magiciens. *The indefinite articles are dropped with* **ni... ni...**   32. Nous n'allons rien faire le weekend prochain.   33. Non, le gouvernement ne surveille jamais personne/jamais les gens.   34. Je n'apprécie aucun acteur particulièrement.   35. On ne m'a rien offert pour mon anniversaire.   36. Non je n'ai rencontré personne d'agréable pendant mon voyage. **Agréables** *is singular in the negative sentence.*   37. Non, je n'envoie jamais de texto.   38. Non rien n'est intéressant ici. *You can't use* **aucun** *with* **chose** *because* **rien** *pretty much means "no thing"!*   39. Rien ne plaît aux enfants.   40. Personne n'est tombé dans l'eau.

18-2   1. Il n'aime parler à personne.   2. Il ne reste plus rien.   3. Personne ne veut plus rien.   4. Ne fais plus jamais ça!   5. Elle n'a ni dansé ni bu à la soirée.   6. Il ne veut jamais rien pour son anniversaire. *Both* **jamais** *and* **rien** *normally follow the conjugated verb, and when combined, they are simply juxtaposed.*   7. Ils n'ont jamais écouté personne. *Regular placement:* **Ne** *and* **jamais** *surround the conjugated verb, and* **personne** *follows the past participle.*   8. Rien ne me dérange jamais.   9. Je voudrais un rendez-vous à dix heures, à moins que vous ne puissiez pas.   10. Prends n'importe quel livre; ils sont tous bons.   11. Ce garçon appelle à n'importe quelle heure; c'est embêtant.   12. Ce travail a été fait n'importe comment.   13. Il vaut mieux ne pas voyager en été: c'est plus cher.   14. Ni toi ni moi ne pouvons faire ce travail. *With a* **ni** *subject, the verb is always plural. And* **moi** + **toi** = **nous**.   15. Il n'est jamais surpris de rien.   16. Aucun chat n'a mangé le poisson. You could also say Aucun des chats n'a mangé le poisson.   17. Il la suivrait n'importe où.   18. Nous n'avons ni le temps ni l'envie de finir maintenant.   19. Du café? Je ne vous en ai pas encore offert?   20. Il ne me reste que quelques dollars.   21. Moi non plus!

18-3   1. Personnellement, je pense que personne **n'**a tort.   2. Quelle nouvelle ! Je **n'**en reviens pas.   3. Aucun sport **ne** lui plaît vraiment.   4. Il **ne** me restait plus qu'à attendre que le gâteau cuise.   5. Ce bébé **ne** fait que pleurer. C'est agaçant.   6. Dans la vie, on **n'**est jamais sûr de rien.   7. Je **n'**ai pas fait attention; je suis désolé.   8. Elle **n'**était pas trop sûre du chemin à suivre.   9. « **Ne** bouge pas! »   10. Nous avons cherché le chat partout mais il **n'**était nulle part.   11. Aucun animal bizarre **n'**a surgi des bois.   12. Personne **n'**a pris ton livre. C'est toi qui **ne** l'as pas rangé à sa place.   13. Ils sont arrivés en retard parce qu'ils **ne** s'étaient pas dépêchés.   14. La fête foraine? Je ne m'y suis **pas** amusée du tout.   15. Elle **n'**a besoin d'aucune aide.

Printed in the USA
CPSIA information can be obtained
at www.ICGtesting.com
CBHW081319030224
3996CB00002B/9